Stoney Armadillo
HEAVEN BOUND

Annie Wampler

Stoney Armadillo Heaven Bound
Copyright © 2006 by Annie Wampler

All rights reserved. No part of this book may be reproduced or transmitted in any form or by any means, electronically, including photocopying and recording, or by any information storage and retrieval system, without permission in writing from the publisher. Address inquiries to:

LifeBoat Ministries, Inc.
P.O. 306
Walters, OK 73572

ISBN: 978-0-6151-3652-3

All Scripture quotations, unless otherwise indicated are from the Holy Bible, New King James Version. Copyright © 1979, 1980, 1982 by Thomas Nelson, Inc. Used by permission of Thomas Nelson Inc. All rights reserved.

Citation on page 139 was taken from Nelson Study Bible, New King James Version, Copyright © 1997, Used by permission of Thomas Nelson, Inc. All rights reserved.

The Scripture quotations marked KJV on pages 73, 339, 365, 376 are from the King James Version of the Holy Bible.

I have sought to secure permission for all copyrighted material in this book. Where acknowledgment was inadvertently omitted, the publisher expresses regret.

Some names have been changed to protect the privacy of some individuals.

Cover photo by photographer Cheryl Nuss, Copyright © 1992 San Jose Mercury News. Used by permission of San Jose Mercury News. All rights reserved.

Copyediting by Jina Nickel
Cover design by Dixie Press

First Edition
Printed in the United States of America

Author's Notes

I believe that Christian hero, C. H. Spurgeon's book, *All of Grace,* was divinely placed in my hands at this particular time to be used of God for those who think they have no hope, as well as a confirmation to those who have that hope of forgiveness. Throughout this book, I have used paraphrases and quotes of Spurgeon to further emphasize these truths to its readers.

Much prayer and love has gone into the writing of this book so that all may know they are loved by God, no matter the circumstances. Like All of Grace, …this book does not come to make demands on you; it comes to bring you something. I am not talking about duty, law and punishment, but I am talking about the love, forgiveness, mercy and eternal life that Christ offers to all, no matter the offense.

Acknowledgments

*A*lthough this death row experience is not what I would have chosen for my life, I am deeply grateful to God for it. As I look back on the difficulties of the situation, I can see that God used it to draw me into a more intimate relationship with Jesus Christ than I have ever known. I thank God that He never allowed me to get rid of the urge to share the experience in writing.

I am deeply indebted to my former pastor, Dr. Tony Nickel, for his suggestions as he checked for biblical accuracy, while his wife, Jina, who is an English and Composition teacher, edited, polished, and labored to put it in the correct form.

I wish to thank my family, especially my husband, Dale; my daughters, Sandy and Beverly; my grandson, Cory; and my granddaughter, Cassie, who were my prayer partners and support team. They realized Donnie's desire for a close family relationship and became that family. I wish to thank my sister, Betty, for always being available to take a trip to Texas Death Row and for loving Donnie so much. I am deeply indebted to my niece and nephew, Sherry and Bobby Nance and their son, Nick, for their support and making Donnie an important part of their lives. I thank my sister, Bonnie, for being there during a situation that I hope none of us ever forget.

I wish to thank all who supplied me with information to aid in the writing of this book. Special thanks go to inmate friends who cared enough to write words of encouragement when they themselves were so discouraged. My heartfelt thanks to each one of you.

About the Author

*A*nnie Wampler loves the Lord, loves others more than herself, and has inspired so many with her words of wisdom and her spiritual integrity. As her pastor for almost five years, the Lord allowed me to witness a transformation within Annie as she began to work with the prisoners on death row, including her own cousin.

Annie inspired (and continues to inspire) so many of them, offering them hope and spiritual encouragement.

Annie developed LifeBoat Ministries, a ministry-based outreach to those in prison as well as their close family and friends. In addition, she has written a beautiful work, *Stoney Armadillo: Heaven Bound.*

Annie's book gives hope to prisoners and their families—this group of people who are an almost secret society on whom we turn our backs and look the other way. Annie's book gives others the gift of God—and for those outside the prison walls, this book gives them a very personal glimpse inside the walls of death row and a peek into the very heart of a man who eventually is executed—a changed man.

With great conviction and no hesitation, I recommend Annie Wampler to you as well as her work.

Dr. Tony D. Nickel
Senior Pastor
First Baptist Church of Harrah, Oklahoma

Contents

Prologue		9
Introduction		11
1.	**Donnie's First Letter**	19
	"I think God and I are through"	
2.	**Memories**	41
	"He was my friend, my brother"	
3.	**Mice for Pets**	51
	"It's just like watching cartoons…"	
4.	**Ready to Die**	69
	"I've had enough…"	
5.	**Watching Friends die**	85
	"It comes to me and I talk to God"	
6.	**Final Visits**	93
	"God's gonna make a way for us"	
7.	**Saying Good-bye to JC**	105
	"There will be no more appeals for JC"	
8.	**A Difficult Time**	117
	"These walls are closing in on me"	
9.	**A Struggle with Purpose**	127
	"…living in a closet"	
10.	**Giving God Control**	137
	"…I wish I had it to do over again"	
11.	**A Request from Donnie**	147
	"…would you be able to be there?"	
12.	**Family Visits**	161
	"…we don't belong to ourselves…"	
13.	**The Confession**	173
	"What hurts and pains me is the human side of me…"	
14.	**A Family's Love**	189
	"…I can honestly say it was an accident."	
15.	**Wanting to Be Free**	195
	"…and finally, finally have a life in heaven."	
16.	**Love Bears All things**	207
	"I would give anything to be there with you all."	
17.	**Family**	221
	"…I've wasted my life."	

18. **A Million Thoughts**	**237**
"I wanted to be that little boy again."	
19. **The Move**	**249**
"We were on our way, chains, cuffs...."	
20. **The Hearing is Over**	**263**
"For me to move on is a blessing for me."	
21. **Lockdown**	**275**
"...fear coming at me from all sides."	
22. **Freedom Rings Around Me**	**287**
"This place is growing heavy on me."	
23. **Prayer**	**299**
"God is all around me, in me, and over me"	
24. **For a Season**	**307**
"27 days..."	
25. **No Fences**	**321**
"...14 days..."	
26. **Nearing the Execution**	**329**
"...13 days..."	
27. **A Final Visit**	**339**
"Six days."	
28. **Going Home**	**353**
"Annie, you were a vessel for God"	
29. **No More Chains**	**363**
"I'm finally free of my chains!"	
30. **Home**	**371**
"Do not stand at my grave and cry; I am not there; I did not die"	
Notes on Sources	**385**

Accepted Just As I Am

Left home for Uncle Sam,
   Ended up in Nam.
Lost my way in that place.
   Came home I thought a disgrace.

Many years have gone by.
   I know soon I shall die.
Lonely days I have spent,
   Wondering where my life went.

God's been working for a while,
   So I write to say, "smile."
God's in my life every day.
   And has taught me how to pray.

My family has come for me.
   Their love not hard to see.
Will be here my last two days
   To help smooth the way.

Galatians 2:20 my last words
   Family said it with me you have heard.
Now I am free at last.
   I don't remember the bad past.

I pray to see you all again.
Stick together; try not to sin.
Love your family every day.
   See you when you come this way.

Poem by Bobby Nance
   May 20, 2000

Prologue

*H*e was known as Stoney Armadillo.

A neglected child, he was adopted at age two into a Christian family. He served his country in Vietnam, returned to find he was "lost" in society, and turned to drugs to take him away from his suffering. On April 5, 1984, Donnie Foster, high on drugs, robbed a Springtown, Texas, feed store for money—money he planned to use to buy another drug "fix." Gary Cox, the young owner of the feed store, was shot and killed in that robbery. On Veteran's Day, 1985, a Texas district court found Richard Donald Foster guilty of Gary Cox's death. For this crime, he was sentenced to die. He was sent to Texas' Death Row.

Meanwhile, Annie Wampler was living her life in a small, Mayberry-like community, blessed with three wonderful children, a loving husband, precious grandchildren living near-by, and a loving church family. Family and friends enjoyed her generous nature. Annie was the kind of person who gave all she had. For example, on July 1, 1990, Annie responding to the desperate need of a relative in Illinois, donated that relative a life-saving kidney.

In his book, *All of Grace*, the famous Christian writer, C. H. Spurgeon wrote, "It is worthy of consideration that when the Lord takes away the stony heart, that deed is done; and when that is once done, no known power can ever take away that new heart....

Man's reformations and cleanings up soon come to an end.... But when God puts a new heart in us, the new heart is there forever and it will never harden into stone again."

Such was the transformation of Stoney Armadillo.

This book shares the letters from Donnie Foster on Texas Death Row to Annie Wampler. Reading these letters, one can personally witness how God took the heart of stone belonging to a man known as Stoney Armadillo and turned it into a heart of flesh.

Introduction

"*I*'m doing the right thing, huh Lord?" Donnie asked as he read "Heaven Bound," the sign on an eighteen wheeler as it passed the prison van transporting him to the United States District Court in Fort Worth, Texas. He was being taken there to determine his mental competency after requesting that his appeals process be stopped—the process which had kept him alive for almost fifteen years. Donnie took that sign "Heaven Bound" literally as a message from his Lord and Savior. It was not surprising to us as we had watched him turn from a bitter, angry man to the radiant Christian we saw in Judge Terry Means Courtroom on March 9, 2000. Donnie felt he must stop his appeals process because he was guilty of this crime.

My husband, Dale; my daughter, Sandy; my sister, Betty; her husband, Hop; and my niece and nephew Sherry and Bobby Nance, and I arrived at the Federal Courthouse in Ft. Worth, Texas, at approximately 8 a.m. While the family waited outside, Judge Means' Courtroom, I went directly to the U. S. Marshal's Office to ask if we would be allowed to visit with Donnie, either before or after the hearing. We knew that this would be the only chance in a million of a possible hug before Donnie died.

The man I asked was quick to respond negatively. He told me that the Texas Department of Criminal Justice (TDCJ) did not have him there yet; I joined the family and waited for Donnie's arrival.

As we heard what sounded like chains, we all turned at the same time to see Donnie and the guards topping the stairs. He was walking in a stooped position as if in pain. We all sensed Donnie hated for us to see him this way, and we later learned that although he was shackled and chained, he'd had a rough trip over in the van.

After a short wait, we were allowed to enter the courtroom where only a small group of people was already seated. Donnie had been concerned that there would be people from the media there. He was worried that the family would be bothered with reporters. As I looked around the courtroom at the few that were there, I saw a small, dark haired lady wearing spike-heeled shoes; she was the only reporter there. It seemed another prayer was answered for Donnie. This reporter, seated to the right of my nephew, Bobby Nance, immediately began to question Bobby if we were relatives of the prisoner.

Already seated to the front of the courtroom were Donnie's three attorneys: Craig Budner, a handsome young man with hair and eyes as black as coal; Jim McCarthey, a very professional, middle aged man; and Cameron Gray, a tall, slender, young man that we had not met before the hearing. The firm's legal assistant, Alexa Parnell, whom Donnie had said reminded him of Princess Di, came back to see if we were as comfortable as the situation would allow. These attorneys and their legal assistant had become close friends of the family over the years. Seated opposite them in the courtroom was the Assistant Attorney General, Tommy Skaggs. Our family was not allowed to sit closer than the mid-section of the courtroom.

As we waited for Donnie to be escorted into the courtroom, I thought about the greenish street clothes the state had given him to wear to court. I had taken nice clothes for Donnie to wear the day of the hearing, but TDCJ did not get him there in time to change. Donnie had Craig tell me it was okay that he would wear the state-issued clothes, which were wrinkled, too big, and sagging on him.

He later told us that because he was cuffed, he had asked one of the guards to pull his pants up before he entered the courtroom but was refused the request. Donnie was a nice looking man and cared about his appearance.

Still cuffed, chained, and shackled, the prison guards brought Donnie into the courtroom. Upon entering, Donnie looked upset yet somewhat embarrassed, but he glanced over at us and smiled and lifted his head as to wave. After being seated with his lawyers, a guard removed his cuffs, and he looked back at me with a frown, then raised his hands as if to suggest pain. Realizing how the black box works, I nodded. (The black box is a device attached to the handcuffs between the prisoner's wrists holding them rigid for the purpose of preventing a prisoner from picking the lock.)

We were asked to rise as Judge Means entered the courtroom. He was a pleasant looking man with dark, slightly peppered hair and appeared to be about the age of Donnie. We were pleased he opened his court with prayer.

Judge Means explained that the Fifth Circuit had ordered the court to conduct a hearing to determine if Donnie was making an informed, knowing, and voluntary decision when he instructed his attorneys not to pursue any further appeals in his case for which he had received the death penalty. Judge Means asked that one of Donnie's attorneys read the meritorious issues that his attorneys believed could benefit him in the courts should he decide to go on with his appeals process. Jim McCarthey read the issues to the court. McCarthey stated to the court that there were issues to be pursued that they believed were in violation of Donnie's rights.

After McCarthey had finished reading the issues, Judge Means asked Donnie to come forward. At this moment all of the anger and frustration was completely gone from Donnie. He reminded me of the Apostle Paul standing before the court that day, and like Paul after his transformation, Donnie was speaking with a new spirit and a new heart of flesh. The following is a portion of the trial transcript of proceedings that began the crucial process of ending Richard "Donnie" Foster's life on earth.

PORTION OF TRIAL TRANSCRIPT OF PROCEEDINGS:

March 9, 2000

THE COURT: Mr. Foster, would you step to the lectern?

Mr. Foster, did you hear what your counsel said about the matters that he believes would justify a good faith assertion of an appellate—of an appeal in this case and a further pursuit of habeas corpus relief?

PETITIONER FOSTER: Yes Sir.

THE COURT: And do you feel that you fully understand the points that he would make on your behalf in the Fifth Circuit?

PETITIONER FOSTER: Yes I do. I fully comprehend everything he said.

THE COURT: Let me say this. Do you understand that if he's right and his position were accepted by the Fifth Circuit, there would likely be an order that a new trial be granted?

PETITIONER FOSTER: I understand.

THE COURT: So that if you were to proceed here and not pursue your appellate rights, you, in effect, would be saying, even though my attorney may be correct and that I am entitled to a new trial that could result in my exoneration, I, nevertheless, choose to drop all those proceedings and accept the judgment of the Court that I be put to death. Do you understand that that's what you would be saying?

PETITIONER FOSTER: Yes, sir, I do.

THE COURT: Before I finally ask you if you really want to persist in that decision, let me first make a few notations to you.

Withdrawal of your right to pursue further relief on appeal and habeas corpus would prevent the opportunity for those issues that your attorney has just set out for you to obtain a substantial review by the court of appeals, and I believe you just told me that you understand that?

PETITIONER FOSTER: I understand everything fully, Your Honor.

THE COURT: Okay. Because those issues would not then be presented to the Fifth Circuit Court of Appeals, you could not then seek review of those same existing claims to the Supreme Court of the United States through a petition for writ of certiorari. Do you understand that as well, sir?

PETITIONER FOSTER: I understand that, Your Honor.

THE COURT: And it is possible that even if the Fifth Circuit Court of Appeals did not agree with you and your counsel, that the supreme Court could agree with you and order your release or a new trial. Do you understand that could happen?

PETITIONER FOSTER: Yes, I understand that.

THE COURT: And, in fact, that if your attorney is correct in his assessment of the law and facts, that such a result from the Supreme Court would even, perhaps, be likely. Do you understand that, sir?

PETITIONER FOSTER: Yes, I do.

THE COURT: I understand, this is your first federal habeas corpus petition, and the existing claims that have already been made in this court that you have made as grounds for your appeal, withdrawal of those would bar you from raising these claims again in any successive federal habeas corpus petition. Do you understand what I have just said?

PETITIONER FOSTER: Yes, I do.

THE COURT: Okay. And any future petition that you might wish to present, these claims that you would be giving up here would be given up forever and could not be asserted in any future and successive application for writ of habeas corpus. Are you aware of that as well, sir?

PETITIONER FOSTER: I'm aware of that as well, Your Honor, and I understand.

THE COURT: Mr. Foster, let me speak to you personally just a minute.

As a judge that has been involved in your case---

PETITIONER FOSTER: Yes, sir.

THE COURT: ----we are never one hundred percent certain of what we're doing.

PETITIONER FOSTER: Right.

THE COURT: We reach our conclusions based on what we see in the record and what we see in the law, and we try to put the two together. And we take some comfort in knowing that whatever our decision is, especially when it's a decision to put a man to death, that there will be someone up the line to give another look at it.

Now, I'm not saying by that that I would change anything that I have decided. Those decisions were made to the best of my skill and ability. But it pains me some to know that you would at this point forego your right to challenge the decisions that other judges have made, including me, because there are close questions that might very well be decided differently by a court that looks at things differently, has a different perspective, than a trial court has. That's why we have appellate Courts.

And so my concern is that you not give up a valuable right that would result in your death without, not only thinking it through, but doing some very careful consideration that, perhaps, these points may very well fall on much more sympathetic ears than you have found so far because of the different perspective that an appellate court has versus a trial court. So I urge you to take more time; think this through and make your decision based, not only on what you've thought heretofore, but on what you've heard here today.

So in that regard I'm going to give you just a little while to visit with your counsel and to reflect on what I have said here and on what you have heard here about your potential chance for a different result on appeal, and then we'll reconvene here at 11:30.

The court recessed and the family remained seated in the courtroom while Donnie conferred with his lawyers about his decision.

"Did you think that salvation was for the good and that God's grace was for the pure and holy who are free from sin?"

C.H. Spurgeon

Chapter One

Donnie's First Letter

"I think God and I are through"

September 1995

*O*n a still, hot summer afternoon in Southwest Oklahoma, I had just returned home from a local hospital where my brother and his wife had lost their son to a massive heart attack; my nephew was only thirty-two. I felt such sadness when I reached into the mailbox on my front porch and took out a letter. I immediately noticed the return address: Richard D. Foster, #815, Ellis One, Huntsville, Texas 77343.

My cousin, Donnie, better known to his fellow inmates as Stoney Armadillo, had been residing on Texas Death Row for almost eleven years. I had to admit that I had forgotten about Donnie, but God was about to bring him to my attention in a profound way. It had been a difficult day at the hospital. After laying my purse on the arm of the couch, I took the letter and walked through the house to the patio in the backyard. Donnie's letter began:

> I hope this letter finds you doing well. I am sorry that I never wrote you before. But I mostly decided to just stay low and try not to disgrace the family anymore than I have already. I want to thank you for being there for Cliff [Donnie's adoptive father]. I am real sad about my Mom [dying]. No one from the family called or wrote.

Although Donnie was courteous in his letters, before long it became evident that he was quite angry. After corresponding with Donnie a while, it seemed that much of his anger stemmed back to his childhood. The feelings of not being wanted by his biological parents often came out in his letters. He seemed to feel if his parents could not love him that something must be terribly wrong with him. And as it often does, hurt turns to anger and frustration. Donnie would often express this anger towards the courts that had convicted him as well as his fellow inmates; however, I was privileged to observe as God replaced that anger with love and a spiritual concern towards his fellowman as well as a deep faith in Christ...but that was in the years to come. As I continued to read his first letter, Donnie wrote:

> I did get to see Mom before her illness got the best of her. She told me the same thing five times as if it were new. I cried. I was a rotten son. I would have gave anything if I could have said more to her and just said that I loved her. —Donnie

In the following years as Donnie wrote of his prison life, I became quite familiar with life on Texas Death Row. One of his first letters explained:

> I write my own [news] paper, *The Armadillo Times*. It keeps me busy. I also make Harleys by hand. I build the pieces myself out of junk. I just use my imagination. I am still a club member. I'm no longer a Bandido (motorcycle club member). Was glad to get out of it cause of the young generation coming in. I mean after 96 of them got busted in five different states and over 50 signed statements on others! Well, I'm an outlaw, a 1%er always (some say it means only 1% are good enough to wear the club patch). It's just me and I'm not ashamed of it. I am the president now of a growing club. I'll send you a flyer and you can see our patch. I'll be buried in this to. We have club by-laws and we live by them in here. I do believe in God and I was or thought that I was very close to Him for years. My morals and beliefs

are good. I can hide nothing in my heart from God. But lately I'm a little like Thomas. There has been so many things that have happened to me that I know it had to be God. But I'm not doing so good lately. Maybe if we can write we can talk about some things. I'd like that. But I do understand if you choose not to. I know that I am an embarrassment to the family. But if you do, I will send you some things that *you* can look at and maybe understand what happened to me. I just got lost, Annie.
—Donnie

October 1995

Donnie continued to write and reflect upon his life on Texas Death Row:

The last time I wrote you I wasn't in lockup. Nothing unusual for me though. We have real wars in here. I have sat and watched so many in line to die. I lost a couple of friends that I knew here for years. They just killed Joe Lane here and I knew him ever since I drove (arrived) up here. Such a good dude too. I got moved down here three days before they moved him to the last stop. And I believe that is why I'm down here. Things happen like that all the time to me. I hadn't seen Joe in about a year. But he was waiting on me when I got here in lockup. Smile. I spent a day with him in the yard. Three hours. His mom had died about a month before to. She was all Joe had left. I mentioned it and he broke down crying. I had to hold my brother there in the yard. I knew then that I was far away from God, that I should have been closer in my walk. But I prayed the right things for Joe. I pled the blood of Jesus over him and prayed angels all around him all the way to the table. But he was so ready to go. And it's not the first lesson that I've learned on that. I've seen many leave here happy. I've had friends make it all the way to the table and then it would get called off and they come back here. I can see the change to. My first date I had went down to eight hours. I wasn't sure about our system here, then either.

If you got no one out there, then life here can be a real hell. I don't even know why I'm still alive. I serve no purpose. And this God thing has me confused. Sometimes I'm not sure that I really believe. I was at the point where I wanted to holler out and throw my Bible out on the run. I hate to say this but I think God and I are through. —Donnie

As Donnie complained, I thought about how often we try to set up our own agenda with God. I assured Donnie that he and God were not through, but perhaps God may be waiting on him to do something. God wants the same from all of us, a personal relationship with Him through His Son, Jesus Christ. I told Donnie that God doesn't force Himself on us, and it seemed to me that it was Donnie's move towards God.

Regulations do not permit families to mail items to prisoners, but I began to have the bookstores in my area send Donnie books that I felt might help him in his situation and coping with life there in prison. I recalled telling Donnie that we are not our own. We are God's, bought and paid for with a high price. Jesus paid that price for our sins with His death on the Cross. I assured him that if he had ever asked God's forgiveness and asked Jesus into his life, Jesus was still there, and He would not disown him or adopt him away. God not only made this promise to Moses and Joshua in the Old Testament, but in the New Testament, Hebrews 13:5 tells us that "He Himself said 'I will never leave you nor forsake you.'"

January 12, 1996

As Donnie reflected back on two individuals that tried to bring God into his life, he wrote:

Glenda lives in the town where I fell out [was arrested]. And this jailer dude that was supposed to be a full-gospel preacher came in and gave me a letter and a book. Bible. Annie, Sonny Buckingham can tell you stories about me in that jail that would be hard to believe. I was a real animal. I couldn't rest. No one would come in there unless they asked me first. But I just couldn't stand it when he would come in there all happy and whistling away. He would come in there playing that guitar and singing hymns and preaching. I mean I went crazy. And then I would listen to all the stuff that he would tell the guys (other inmates) there while preaching. I had to laugh at all the lies he would tell them to get them to believe. He told them that he saw an angel once; then about his dad dying and saying that Jesus was there to get him before he died. I pulled him over alone one day and asked him about it and told him, 'Man, you should be ashamed to lie like you do to get these people to fall into this Christian thing and change.' He told me it wasn't a lie. Then I remember the night I was going to get out. A friend was going to break me out. I waited and waited and he never came. Someone may have got hurt that night too.

Donnie wrote that he found out later that his friend, Glenda, was on her knees praying for him at 2:30 a.m. that same night.

I told her to stop praying for me; she was goofing everything up. She would write and tell me about what the Lord was doing in her life. I would read the letters and then throw them in the trash and then I'd get them out and re-read them. I can remember the night (in 1985) I read the Bible and about Thomas. I crawled into the shower and cried out to God that I didn't know if He exists or not, but I told Him to show me that He is real; that I was just like Thomas and needed to hear His voice and see Him. I never have I guess. But I do know something is there, but I can't get a grip on it. I get at times where I have pain and cry and it's always for someone else. I do care about others, Annie. I hurt for other people, but lately I hurt for me. I guess I'm of self and always will be. I can't let go of things, you know like God wants. I never can do that. I looked around the other day and I figured it out, there is no God, and these simple minds that become so complex at times is just us. We do good or bad. We fall and lose, or we just get by and make it. I have a tape that was made by the guy that was a hostage over there in the bank. He did it for a friend of mine that did a documentary on me, then she slowly slipped away from me. Then there was this guy, Morrison [Texas writer] that was going to do a book on me. Two years and it was done, but he died before it was published. Then I watched a special on television one night and thought, they really do care about Vietnam Vets! But no one knows the pain of what that war did to so many.

Annie, I look around and I'm alone. I think in all my life, I have never been so alone. I want you to get to know a little about me before my time comes. Dad says I will be buried in Walters next to Mom. But who will come and get my body? Who will stand up and say something for me? I want the truth, no phony words.
I am what I am and I don't know how God can let this go on.
—Donnie

Donnie didn't realize it, but God was preparing him for a real transformation in time. It wasn't going to be easy. But the impossible is where God does His best work, and His timing is always perfect.

January 13, 1996

Donnie wrote asking if I would come visit him with his adoptive dad, [my uncle] Cliff. I remember the different thoughts I had. I recalled a Bible verse: "Thus faith by itself, if it does not have works is dead" (James 2:17). I believed this verse was saying to me that if I see someone in need and I say, "God bless you, I'll pray for you," yet I am unwilling to make an effort to help, my faith is of no good to them or me.

Then I dealt with the fear of what others might think and say; however, my poor excuses quickly diminished, and Donnie put me on his visitor list; with some reluctance, Cliff and I made plans to visit Texas Death Row. All these years I had sat in my comfort zone, enjoying all the blessings of God and pretty well protected from the horrors of the world. I had raised my children in a Christian home and taught Sunday school at my hometown church. I was blessed yet not often out of my comfortable Christian world. That is, until I was invited to Texas Death Row where God gave me the challenge of a lifetime. I had a lesson to learn on being useful for God.

In his book, *My Utmost For His Highest*, the great Christian hero, Oswald Chambers, writes, "If you are going to be used by God, he will take you through a multitude of experiences that are not meant for you at all, they are meant to make you useful in His hands, and to make you understand what transpires in other souls so that you will never be surprised at what you come across." Chambers continues, "We never realize at the time what God is putting us through; we go through it more or less misunderstandingly; then we come to a luminous place, and say— 'Why, God has girded me, though I did not know it'"[1] And so I found myself in the unspeakable world of Texas Death Row.

In the meantime, discouraged and angry, Donnie continued to write:

> I go days here without talking. People here drive me crazy! There is not an important conversation going on anywhere in this place. Talk about oppression and depression! Sure, this place and the rules here are all bull, but I wonder sometimes if I'm losing my mind or what, because of what people do at times. And never have I heard worse gossiping and people starting

trouble. No respect and that is something I demand in my walk here. I don't let anyone disrespect me and get away with it, but I see it happening to others and they just take it. And snitches, I never saw so many people telling on one another. That's why I don't get out of my circle. At least I know who my real brothers are. Even my cellie gets on my nerves and he's a Christian! Yet he runs his head and has more problems than I ever saw. Makes me wonder. I don't throw it in his face. I just watch him. He does exactly what he talks about others doing. Well, that was a depressing conversation. Hey, I just want to go home and get back to the country. If I can't do that, then I'm ready to die and go on wherever it is I'm going. That book you sent, <u>Within Heaven's Gates</u>, there has to be something to that, Annie.
—Donnie

January 14, 1996

Donnie wrote:

You remember I told you about my cellie getting on my nerves. Well, he got locked up, so I'm alone for a while. It's nice to not have someone in here with me for a change. But I have a friend that wants to move away from the guy that he is with, so maybe tomorrow I'll have a 50/50 in here. He is part Mexican and part white. He's a good dude. He works on the other lockdown wing and we workout together.

Donnie was writing about his friend, Martin Gurule, the man who would die three years later after escaping from Death Row and leading prison officials on one of the largest manhunts in Texas history. In the early hours of November 27, 1998, Gurule would go over the two, 12-foot tall fences topped with razor wire and become the first one to escape Texas Death Row in 64 years.

January 15, 1996

Donnie wrote:

    I was thinking about what my life is all about today. I guess we make our own beds in this life. We make the wrong decisions and we fall down. I have so many regrets on so many things. And I've wondered a thousand times why some of us have life like this? Did I really make it all like it is, or did something happen that could never get back on track? I think about loneliness. I have always been a loner to a degree. And in my travels across this land, I became accustomed to it. All the emotions that come with it are set deep within me. I think it goes all the way back to Duncan when I found out I was adopted. I always wondered why I was gave away. I think the key lies when I would stay at Lisa's [Donnie's sister who was adopted at the same time as Donnie by Cliff's brother, Frank and his wife, Martha]. Martha would get drunk and talk. She was a very mean woman inside. She once told me she knew where our real parents were. It affected me. Some people don't understand kids or what goes on inside them. But all through life before Nam I was always wondering. I would run away from home and look for them. I guess for a kid to run away means he's not a very good kid. I was a screw up from day one. And to this day I can remember the day that I was adopted when I was taken home with Cliff and Bertha. I remember Bertha putting me in the tub with her and I was so scared of water. I remember Bertha pulling that big old rubber stopper out of the plug and the water going down. I cried and thought I was going down that hole. Smile... People say you can't remember that far back. But that's not true. I can remember the house we lived in before being adopted. It's frightening at times to remember it all so clear. I awake at times and I am there in my dreams and it's all so real. I can remember the stairs.... And I heard hollering and screaming. I can remember being in the yard and I was crying, and the fear in me. —Donnie

January 26, 1996

Donnie began:

Annie, if I was as tough spiritually as I am physically I'd do okay. At one time I was stable, but now I'm lost. I am angry and it's worse than before. I have put up with nothing but preaching from Glenda for over ten years. It doesn't bother me, but I can't do all the things we are suppose to do. I have the knowledge and the wisdom, but I can't walk it at all. My world is so different. In here I'm still at war.

Donnie felt he had to keep a certain image on death row; therefore he was still not ready to trust God completely.

March 5, 1996

With much uneasiness, Cliff and I made my first trip to Texas Death Row. I found Donnie to be a handsome man in his early forties. He was only a few years older than my son, Steve. Donnie had a receding hairline, dimples, and a fairly nice tan. I mention tan because at that time, death row inmates were allowed group recreation, and they took more advantage of their time in the prison yard. Several inmates could play handball or basketball. But after Gulrule's escape in 1998, TDCJ discontinued group recreation for death row inmates. They discontinued many things after that escape.

After my first visit to Death Row, Donnie wrote:

I was very glad to see you today. I did ask God to see you home safely. I feel a need to get to know the people that have been a part of my life in the past. I don't really know why lately this has all come upon me like it has, but I think that maybe I'm just trying to get back to what I was before this long journey started. All I have is my memories and thoughts. But no one tells me anything about anyone anymore. It makes me feel unwanted in many ways. I don't think that Dad understands this, or there is nothing he can do about it. I think today I wanted to say that I know the rules of God, and I understand the Word. I have studied and read and I have done my homework. I just didn't pass the class. I used to walk so much better. I spent time with God and prayed about everything. But I can't explain what happened to me. It's like all the stuff that I thought was out of me has resurfaced again. I'm once again angry and I can feel hate in me at times. I guess you could say that I have lost touch with who I was or am. I am not close to God at all, but further away. I guess with my lifestyle and all, that I do belong here. I wasn't a very good kid. I have tried to pray today and get back on my feet some. But this place won't let me. I battle every day just to hang on. I forgot to tell you today that a couple of the motorcycle clubs that we got to sanction us are thinking about letting us wear their patch, and set this one that we have aside. There are only five outlaw MC clubs in the USA. We may be wearing Hells Angels patches before it's over. I bet God don't like that at all, huh? I need to think about it myself. —Donnie

After visiting Donnie, I became acquainted with his friend, Glenda by phone. She told me that Donnie had always had a girlfriend. I could see why they would be attracted to him, but Donnie didn't seem like the type to push himself on the ladies. Because of where he was, Donnie felt that most looked at him as nothing more than…a murderer on Death Row. I told Donnie that God loved him and me as much as He loves the best Christian in the world. In the years ahead, Donnie would see how much my family would come to love him, and he would experience God's Love which would be the ultimate climax of his life. Calvary Baptist Church, my hometown church in Walters, Oklahoma, put Donnie on their Wednesday night prayer list and began sending him prayer slips every week. (A prayer slip is a small piece of paper that tells someone, "I prayed for you." On these slips of paper, a church member writes the prayer recipient's name as well as his/her name…they are then mailed to the prayer recipient and are quite encouraging).

March 18, 1996

Donnie wrote:

I wondered what your reaction would be to the Hell's Angels comment? I already wear one patch on my back. I know inside that God wants me to lay it down. I can't do that just now it seems.

April 23, 1996

Donnie's letter began:

Annie, I have to admit something is different, something is changing in me. .. it must be all those prayers. I think with all those prayers going up God can't ignore me.

You told me to read Psalm 91. Glenda had sent me the same one earlier. I especially like the last three verses. 'Because, he has set his love upon me, therefore, I will deliver him. I will set him on high, because he has known My name. He shall call upon Me and I will answer him; I will be with him in trouble; I will deliver him and honor him, and show him my salvation. With long life I will satisfy him, and show him My salvation' (Psalm 91:14- 15).

Do you think He was talking about me, Annie? —Donnie

I explained to both Donnie and Glenda that God had not revealed to me that Donnie would be free on earth. Donnie hoped I would reassure him of this but later admitted he was tired of false hope; he realized that he needed to realize his imminent death and get serious with God.

May 5, 1996

I later realized that after each visit, Donnie would go back to his cell and write a letter. After this visit, Donnie wrote:

> I enjoyed our visit very much. I get a little anxious about things I know, but I want you to get to know me and how I am in this life. I need you to understand me, and what is going on inside me and why I am the way I am. Maybe I seem a little unstable at times, but believe me I'm trying to get a grasp on things. Maybe I'm just scared of what is headed my way. Maybe you are right about once God's always God's. I know that it has been preached that way but still we have doubts in things. I think we have to be responsible and account for our actions. I think we can drift away from God and get out there all-alone at times; but yes He is still with us waiting on us to call upon Him I know. But I have written stories on the warfare that goes on around us. I did my homework there, Cous. But then as the years went by I just fell down bad. I see in the time I grew up the things that were wrong then are okay now. You know what I mean, Annie?
> —Donnie

I assured Donnie that I did know what he meant, and it does seem that way at times. Although we are never alone, I knew from experiences of my own that there are consequences to bad choices. We do have to account for our actions. Bad choices equal bad consequences. We choose to believe. We choose not to believe. We choose to do what is right. We choose to do what is wrong.

Early in our relationship Donnie had hoped that my purpose for being in his life would be to help him to find a way out of Death Row. Because I did not believe he had received a fair trial, I wanted to be sure that everything had been done that could be done to help him.

It didn't take a professional to see that evidence had been allowed in his trial that violated Donnie's rights and I wanted to believe he was innocent of this terrible crime. In God's time, however, we both would see the purpose of being re-acquainted as we were.

Donnie had told me that he was afraid I would leave one day and never come back. During several of our visits, he would say something like, "People always get tired and stop coming," He needed to know he was loved and someone cared that he was going to die. He liked the word, "unconditional." I suppose we all do.

May 29, 1996

Donnie's letter began:

We learn from each other, Annie; I have read Hebrews 6: 1-6 and I agree with you on that. I know what is right and wrong and yet I do wrong most of the time. I'm pretty sure I'm not living the way God wants of me. I'm not singing songs and I'm not all joyful like those dudes in prison in the Bible. I reckon you noticed that about me though. I saw your pastor, Stacy, on Thursday. I was outside running when he got here and I was hot. Summers in Texas are so hot. We talked some and I felt comfortable with this guy. He bought me something to drink, too. I wanted him to know how I live here and what I believe in. I'm pretty sure he thought I was an idiot. There's a very high possibility that I am an idiot. Like Forrest Gump. Anyway, we had a good visit.

He asked me if I had truly asked Jesus into my life. I feel like I did at one time. I mean I know I'm not exactly on track right now. There is no way I could explain myself to this guy or anyone else. Stacy said he was going to come back, but I'm sure he thought I was a nut. I think he's a fine man and he helped me a lot in things. He said he is as human as I am. I thank you for caring so much and sending this guy down here for me. Do you really think he will come back? —Donnie

My pastor did visit Donnie two other times before moving to another pastorate in the Oklahoma panhandle area.

June 6, 1996

Donnie continued:

Deliverance is a big word, huh Annie? I often wonder if I'm not cursed. I remember one day asking God to allow me to be something one day. It worried me ya know, sins of generations and all that. Then I would get back in my defensive position again. I asked God to let me find my real family and I was allowed that, but it was a disaster. Mom never wanted to see me.

But I got you and dad and a few friends like Glenda. Anyway, deliverance is something that one day, if I ever walk from here, I'll have to go through. If the spiritual war is real then something is trying hard to destroy me or keep me like I am. It's been bugging me lately too. I can't explain it. At times the war intensifies. But I know I want to go to heaven to be with Jesus when I die. Like in the book, huh? Jesus was always with the children. I remember once seeing a picture of Jesus with a bunch of kids. And one was asking Him what was wrong with His hands? From what I know about Jesus and his ways, I'd give anything just to walk with Him and tell Him all that is on my mind and how I see things. And maybe even ask Him why things were the way they were for me here. Funny thing about this place or this world here, ways and all. I can adapt to it and know what is expected of me here. But there is a line and in here I've had it. I'm so tired of it all. But something is making me hang on, I can tell you that. I don't exactly portray the great citizen. Kinda like my body. I got tattoos all over me. Got one leg done up, and on my back I have a dragon in the middle. I have about 38 skulls on me in all. Some are small, but they do add up. Club signs on both arms. Spider webs and Harley wings on one arm and a cat with Vietnam on it. Got the word "Nomad" wrote across my stomach. So as you can see, I'm not exactly right in the head as the public would say on art. —Donnie

June, 1996

I later asked on a visit, "What's with all the skulls?" Donnie replied:

It represents death, Annie. Death has always been just outside my door. I'm pleased that people think about me and are praying for me. I think it is for a reason too. The war is great here on Death Row. I need the strength to stay right and not be an animal. I can be a real pain to anyone if I want to be and like I said; sometimes in here I have to do something that goes against what I believe.

The heat here really drives us. It was so hot I thought I was going to die. I poured water on me several times today and let it run on me, then got in front of the fan. It helps, but not for long. The heat index was 115 degrees in this building.

July 8, 1996

Donnie wrote:

Long day. No work today. Sometimes I just think all day about things and I tend to get lost. Some days are all war, and some days are just laid back. I got snitched on twice today by two guys in lock up that think they're real convicts. One thing you don't do is tell the man (bosses) on others. But it's becoming a new trend here, cooperation with the man to get things here and there. When the sergeants came in and asked me what was going on I just shrugged my shoulders. They just laughed. They know me that well. I mind my own business. A lot of the guys I know here say they will get them right in time. Smile. In other words, the guys that snitch get tied down (locked in) to a cell and behind screens for their protection. Just stupid people! I watch people that are smart and tough (or think they are) dig a hole for themselves and then just fall in it. Shame. —Donnie

August 9, 1996

Donnie's letter began:

I'm a little sad about a boss (guard) that got stabbed today for no reason. It was where I work in lockup. It was the same dude that snitched on me yesterday too. I got called out earlier and was asked if I was going to do anything stupid to this guy, cause of what he filed on me. It's a well-known fact about this guy; he's had a hit out on him for a year now. The Mexicans have got him twice, but it didn't kill him. Filled him full of holes but he lived and made it. Now he's just a coward. Carter is one of the best guys I know. He just went up to the guy's house [cell] to get him out for a shower and this dude had a bar tied on a broomstick and he shoved it through a hole and got him. My work partner was right there and saw it all. I was downstairs and heard him yell. He was trying to get the guy, but he was in the cell locked up. Anyway, I heard he is going to live. They got Martin and me out of there and made us leave. Racial stuff. And as always, I'm right in the middle of it all. They are probably going to call Martin and me out to make a statement. But I only heard it. Guy said he was going to do something. So he is a coward to start with for just saying that. He wouldn't come out of the yard cause I was on the floor. He was scared that I was the guy that was going to hit him. Wasn't me! I can't even mind my own business. But now the guy is facing attempted murder charges. Then the other idiot that told him to do it is a racist. He hates white people. Anyway, I'm glad the boss is going to be okay. Things are not lookin good for a lot of the guys here on their cases. The attorney general says that he is going to get 50 this year, cause of this new law. Can you believe that, Annie? I mean to come out in public and say that! It'll make him a big man on campus I guess. But I have a few friends that are in trouble and will die soon because of this law. —Donnie

July 17, 1996

Donnie wrote:

Well, I just got up and watched a friend of mine that weighs about 260 climb up the windows and get a bag of coffee that he was trying to throw up to three row. It went in the window. I didn't think he was going to make it, and the worst was getting down. Smile! All I could do was squirt him with a bottle of water. It was funny. He's gained too much weight.

July 18, 1996

Donnie wrote:

We were outside talking about this lady and her two kids that was killed in that plane crash today. She was a very strong advocate of the death penalty. Everyone was out in the yard whooping and hollering about it, but I just sat here and thought about it.

August 1996

Donnie began:

I really hate my life, Annie. I'm stuck in a bad way here on a few things, wars and battles of all kinds. I wonder how I can just turn away from this. This world is so different from the one out there. Many times I lay down at night and I never want to wake up again. I would like to talk to Dad about some things if I could. I just feel that he can't relate to me and the things I need to talk about at times. I love dad, but it's so hard to talk to him about the things I need to say. Since you get to visit four hours and Dad only gets to visit two, I would like for him to visit with my cellie for the other two hours. His mom and sister live in Colorado and he never gets to see them. He is just a youngster and he needs a visit. —Donnie

When I first began corresponding with Donnie, I thought it would be a temporary correspondence. It was likely that we would write a few times then it would gradually stop, but as he shared his thoughts of life on Death Row with me, I began to think more about Donnie being executed. I believed that he had committed other drug-related crimes, but in this case it looked to me as if his previous record played a large role in his conviction, and this caused me to doubt his guilt. Realizing Donnie's life experiences helped me to understand why he was so angry, but I knew God was in control. If He hadn't been, I am pretty sure I would not have stuck it out to the end. But like the Christian author, Stormie Omartian wrote in her book, *Just Enough Light for the Step I'm On*, "He constantly calls me to stretch beyond what's comfortable."[2] God gives *Just Enough Light for the Step I'm on* at the time.

Again in early September 1996, Donnie asked:

Do you think you can ever feel what's inside me, Annie? I don't expect you can. I just need you to be there for me, Friend. Someone to see me to my rightful spot in the ground there in Walters. I want no lies said, or good words said that are wrong. I am just different. But I have never, ever disrespected kids, the ladies or animals. These are the things I have always loved. I haven't lost my morals and I still believe in the things I was taught. But I just should never have went to town. Annie. Don't be scared for me…Just listen to me when I talk to you. If it is hard on you, then maybe at last I have found someone to feel what I feel at times, and will understand why I have to do what

I will have to in time here. I know you probably see me as Glenda does, and so many others that have come my way. That I'm just lost and don't know what I'm talking about. It's not like that at all. In no way do I want you holding on to your seat or worrying or anything, but just be there and listen.

There are things that happened in my life that follow me everyday and I have to live with them. The only hope I have at this point in my life is death. And if a person is in their right mind, then you know that is where life begins, right? I know that there are some that hang onto this life. Myself? I still dream of riding, and rivers, and trees, and mountains, forests and fields full of all kinds of creatures that roam through them. That's me, Annie. It was all I knew when I came home from Nam. No one knew that though. I had to be what they wanted me to be, work and be responsible. Believe me I tried too. I mean after a while, seems someone would have asked, 'Hey man, what's up?' No one did. And I'm not sure I could have told them anyway. I could be at work at that Oil Company and just walk out to my car and leave and not come back for a month. I even went to the VA Hospital to get help cause everyone said I was screwed up. And funny thing, it was from there that I was sneaking out at night. I would leave and steal guns and ammo to supply the others there on the eighth floor of the hospital. We just needed guns to sleep. But no one knew why. We were just nuts. But I got caught one night and I never saw that hospital again. I went to jail. Then nine months later I saw this lawyer in court and that day I got eighteen years in prison.

I didn't know anything about the law then. But I was supposed to be returned to the VA Hospital and no one did anything about it. No one knew that I lived there. Smile. I didn't want anyone to know, cause I would be a nut or whatever people call them? And no one ever asked me what happened there, or what they did to treat us. Anyway, I did over six years in prison before I got to go home again. I'm just not your average dude, Annie. After Nam I only wanted to live on the river and not see anyone ever again, just my kind. Like biker folks that travel and see things and sleep out in the woods and also have loved ones and kids and families and all that you have. I just blew that. Maybe you don't understand it all, but I need someone to talk to in what we call my last days. Many times I have sat here and tried to talk about things in my life, but it only worsens my position here. I have a hard enough time sleeping at night as it is. I'm a hyper dude and very active. I'm 44, but I can tear the wing up here and it's just exercise to me. I know I'm not a good Christian.

I know that lately I've had a hard time believing. And yes, I must be selfish in many ways. I can't give up some things in this life like we should. But something is there and it's spiritual and I know to get there I've got to die. And don't think I'm not scared. But if I'm livin at all here it's through your letters and pictures of the family. I have told my story to strangers that come here and pretend to care, and they are awestruck and can't believe the life I've lived, but they go away. So the way I see it is, maybe this God we got is closing doors to my life and sealing them up and preparing me for the journey that I have to take to get home. I asked God to send me someone to listen and care about me and be there all the way to the end, no matter what end it might be.

Thank you Annie, for helping me to get through the days here. I want you to just save these letters. You may need them to look back on. —Donnie

September 10, 1996

Donnie wrote:

> Long day here. I worked and came in and can't get a decent thought in my head. I'm just not in a good mood at all. Looks like trouble brewing again. Believe me Annie, I always look at the situation and try to do the right thing. Just at times the only thing you can do is not good at all. But they are never going to break me of my want for freedom. Revelations is a heavy book for sure; so much to it all. I have always loved prophecy and have done some studies on it. It's what brought so much attention to me about God. Sure, I know I'm not in all that good shape now in my walk, but I'm stuck here on a few things. So much going on here, wars and all.
>
> I did find out one thing; you can't drop your appeals while a judge is waiting to make a decision on you case. But I can tell you now I'm waiting on that day when the ball will be in my hands, then I can make the decision I want. —Donnie

Little did I know that this was the beginning of something that would forever change my life. As our letter writing continued, our relationship began to grow and strengthen. The Lord gave me a real mission to help him find his own spiritual journey within the walls of Texas Death Row. As time went by, our letters became more frequent instead of occasional. Donnie had a tremendous need to talk about his life. He didn't promise to change. He didn't expect that he could, but he began to sense that perhaps God cared after all.

Chapter Two

Memories

"He was my friend, my brother"

Untitled Short Story
By Donnie Foster

Sometimes I close my eyes and I see a boy running across a field of wheat that's been harvested and already turned under. Nothing but turned rows of dirt. But the boy runs fast and hard and jumps over the rows, sometimes two at a time. He reaches the fence and vaults over without touching the top of the barbed wire. He runs a little more and then slows. Behind him is his dog and she's still crawling under the fence. He waits for her to catch up and then he heads out again. In the distance there is a tree line. One more fence and this time he holds the fence for the dog. He walks and finds a stick to pick up and throw for the dog. He throws it and she races after it.

He runs the other way and when she snaps, she stops and looks at the stick and then takes off running for the boy. He reaches a tree where he has a tackle box hide up in the tree. He climbs and the dog comes up and barks and then just lays down at the base of the tree. The boy is now setting and talking to the dog while he goes through his stuff in the box.

In the box is an old catalog from Sears Roebuck. It's the Christmas Issue. The boy looks at all the toys. The bb and pellet guns, and bikes that he wished he had. He closes his eyes and dreams of a Stingray bike. Flamboyant gold it is, and it has the chrome fenders and a slick for a back tire. Banana seat and it has a leopard cover for it. Prettiest bike the boy ever saw. High rise handlebars, and a front hand brake. On the back fender it has a flare on the end of it. A big reflector on the seat post. The boy looks across the creek and just stares at nothing. He sleeps till the dog barks.

He wakes and the catalog falls to the ground. The dog smells of it and the boy climbs down and pets the dog and puts the catalog in his pocket. He takes off running again and runs all the way to the barn where he hides the catalog in between bails of hay. The dog is drinking water from the trough, and the boy does the same. He reaches down and trys to catch some of the little catfish he's put in there. The dog barks and wants to catch one too. The boy talks to her and she looks and is panting hard and barking, almost talking to him. The boy pets her and she licks his face and moans. She loves him and he loves her too. She's his best friend. His only friend. The boy walks to the house and pulls his shoes off. The dog is crawling under the porch.

After supper the boy goes out and takes bones and leftovers to the dog. She eats and knaws on the bones and crunches them. Her tail waggin hard as she eats. She always lets the boy pull the stickers out of her hair and cut the cuckaburrs out too. She trusts him and loves him. She knows the boy will never hurt her, and she depends on him always for everything. The love he gave her and the love she gave him was the only love that the boy knew or understood. It was real. She never changed on him. She was always there and ready to go. She loved no matter what and was loyal as could be. She didn't hit him, or bite him, or get mad at him. When he was sad, she was sad. When she hurt, he hurt.

She was my best friend then.

S. Armadillo 10/98

Author's Note:

Richard Donald Evatt was born in Lawton, Oklahoma. At the age of two years, Donnie was given up for adoption by his biological parents to Clifton and Bertha Foster. Donnie was raised 22 miles east of his birthplace in Duncan, a small city of 21,000; the hometown of actor/director, Ron Howard.

In 1969, when many young men were leaving the country to avoid the draft to keep from having to go fight a war in Vietnam, Donnie not only volunteered for the Army, but he also volunteered for duty in Vietnam. It was in Vietnam that an event took place on the sidelines that changed the course of Donnie's life.

On August 19, 1969, Donnie enlisted in the United States Army; he was just seventeen years and three days old. In February of 1971, he was sent to Vietnam to serve his country there. Shortly after arriving in Vietnam, he met another young man, Michael Bonds. They became best friends and were practically inseparable.

Donnie occasionally would talk of Vietnam and how hard it was. Still mere children themselves, Donnie and Michael felt totally on their own in a foreign country, in a war they didn't understand, and in a place where drugs and alcohol became an escape for many of the soldiers.

It was hard for Donnie to speak of Vietnam because on May 6, 1971, Donnie accidentally shot and killed his best friend, Michael. He later wrote a story he titled "Bad Dreams." Unfortunately, this was not a bad dream; it was a factual account of the incident that "ruined his life."

BAD DREAMS
By Donnie Foster

...I was setting here thinking of a time on the river where I lived. "Brazos River" I loved that land too. So pretty and rough. When I was on it I felt like there was no other place in the world, just this one place. There was no cities, towns, highways or roads. All one could hear was the wind in the trees and the animals and the river flowing so slow. I was all alone. It was like I was the only person left in the world. I loved it so much. I lost touch with the real world I guess. So they say anyway. They called me "The Brazos River Stoney Armadillo." Some called me Rambo. They might as well have called me Sambo for all I cared. All I knew was, after Nam I couldn't live in a place no more where people were. I had tried many times and failed. I just couldn't get it together. Not even the VA Hospitals could help me. There was no cure for one who was hooked on excitement, and adrenalin highs. It was addictive. And to produce the high, one usually did the most dangerous thing he could to produce the high. For a long time I didn't know this and the people that had known me didn't know this either, or understood. And with that and trying to lead a normal life, and the life that produced my highs. Just got way too much for me. I pushed as hard as I could and waited for death to come my way. Only then would it all go away. Maybe then the score with Michael would be settled.

May 5, 1971, I remember waking up from a hangover from the night before. Already it was 110 degrees outside and the heat was a killer. I could hear a Heuy fly over the hootch, and it sounded like it was right on top of me. You got use to it after awhile. After all, Phu Bai was just one long airstrip with nothing but choppers from one end to the other. Hueys, Cobras, Chinooks, and loaches, we called them Scout choppers. So one was bound to hear this noise all day. You got use to it.

I opened the door and I could see that the Babysaun was already there and gone. Clean clothes and all. I hadn't had a shower in a week it seemed. But the clothes felt good. Nothing like a flight suit in 110 degrees temperature. But they were better than reg. issue. Besides, when one was going to be flying to the beach in a ragged Huey that was long overdue to be retired, it was best to take all the chances one could.

A day off and nothing to do but find my Bro Michael and go to Red China Beach for a few brews and some surfing, smoke and women. Only a couple of hours flying time away. Yea, this was the life. I walked a few hootches down and found Michael setting there smokin a cigarette. We never had to talk. We always knew what the other was thinking anyway. We headed to the mess hall and ate some food and headed to the flight line. We stopped and went into a little shop that tailored clothes. Gave haircuts and shaves too. This was one of the only places to go in Phu Bai. Between a commissary and this place and a makeshift club to buy beer, that was it. After all this was the middle of nowhere. Mike and I set around and watched the Choppers come in and go out for a few minutes. We waved as some bros were leaving to fly all day in Charlie Co., Buddies of ours that we partied with every night. Then we took out for a chopper that was going to the beach, and away we went. I guess that Nam was the prettiest land that we had ever seen. We would set by the door gunners and hang our feet out and the pilot would fly close to the giant statues that were everywhere. This one was of Jesus and I remember the thought, "is Jesus really real?" Further on the pilot would fly so close to the ground and scare the South Vietnamese out of the rice paddies. After that we would crawl up in the bird and set on our helmets across this stretch of land. Bullets had a habit of going right through the floor of a Huey.

Eight hours later we came back the same way we had left. It was nearing dark, and we headed to my hootch for a beer or Jim Bean.

I remember it was movie night and we could go and set in the sand and watch some old rerun that we had seen a hundred times. What else could one do? All Phu Bai was is a spot with razor wire and mine fields around it. Wasn't like we could go to the city. Could sneak into the village. But guys got killed there all the time by the VC after dark.

Before we left I slipped the 38 Smith and Wesson in my boot and away we went. Never know what we'd run into there and there was always a fight. Besides, everyone carried a gun. Rules were loose and this place was as wild as any western town you see on TV, like in the old days when the cattlemen came to town. Same thing! Anyway, Mike and I was cruising along talking about the states and wishing. In the background a few 122s (rockets) landed and the sirens went off. We headed for a bunker and it was over in a minute. We walked to the club and drank a few brews and talked. Watched the Vietnamese girls dance while some chinks[sic] sang a Beatle song. Funniest thing that Mike and I ever saw. Sounded like chipmunks singing. After a couple of hours of this we would walk down to the flight line and watch more choppers come and go. Sometimes you could watch the Cobras release their load over the hill, and it looked like a ray gun being fired at a distance. It was a powerful sight. Again we walked down the flight line and one could hear Jimmy Hendrix playing or some Doors, and pot smoke in the air and a gunshot here and there. Had to keep the bunker rat population down somehow. We decided to crash at my hootch and listen to some tunes.

Now one thing about Nam that was rare was dogs and cats. After all, this was the meat that the Vietnamese like to eat. Mike and I had a pet cat that we had found and we kept it locked up in the hootch. Mike sat down as I tuned in the reel to reel with some country music. I sat on my bunk and unloaded my pistol. I got the gun cleaning kit out and was cleaning away. Mike was playing with the cat. Craziest cat I ever saw. He would bite on the barrel of the gun and we would laugh and holler. We were so drunk like anyone else in Nam, and the heat was a killer. Just a regular day in Nam. Two best friends about the same age and just trying to make it.

I remember putting the gun back together and loading it. I turned the cylinder a few times and then unloaded it. The cat was still trying to bite on the barrel and we was laughing away. I pulled the trigger a couple of times while it was in his mouth, and again we laughed and hollered. We were so stoned and anything was funny. Two old country boys and best friends having a ball to forget where we was. Again the cat stuck a paw out at the gun barrel and bit it and chewed on it. Mike was laughing so hard, and I pulled the trigger six times.

The flash and the recoil from the pistol was hard. The noise was deafening. I was in shock from it and what I saw. The cat's head slammed up against Mike's chest and fell to the floor. It slowly dragged itself outside the door. I looked at Mike and I saw the blood pour from his upper abdominal area. His eyes were wide and he clutched his chest. I couldn't speak. Mike whispered, "Why, what happened?" I remember saying "Brother, I'm sorry, I didn't know it was loaded. Hang on. I didn't mean to shoot you." I screamed as loud as I could for help. The Sarge and my other friends came, and I tried to tell them what happened. Mike was still setting in the chair and we put a poncho liner on the wound and around him. "No, no, please don't die on me!" I cried. And as I said that Mike shut his eyes. In shock I screamed and threw the gun as far as I could. It took days to find it. They carried Mike out and put him in a truck, and took him to a chopper to an Evacuation hospital. I thought he was dead already. I remember going to the hospital and setting out in the front of the tent waiting on anything to bring Mike back. At 0100 hours, May 6, 1971 a doctor came out and told me that he was dead. Two hours to pronounce him dead. I tried to get back to where Mike was in the tent. I struggled with the doctor and he slapped and grabbed me. He hollered, "you're a soldier, act like one." I just fell to the floor and cried. At 0100 hours, May 6 that Mike was pronounced dead. I had killed my best friend. And all of a sudden I was more alone than I had ever been. I cried out to God, but He never heard me.

That day I was charged for the murder of Michael D. Bonds. I was released in the custody of my Sergeant and my Company Commander. I was under a heavy drug that was to put me to sleep. When I awoke I looked to see if I could see Mike anywhere. I was taken to Phu Bai, and the Commander told me to go to my hootch and just stay. I walked passed guys I knew and they looked but said nothing. I walked to the hootch and just looked at the door. I couldn't go in. I sat and a small figure caught my eye. It was the cat. He was still alive. It looked me in the eye and ran into the wire and into the minefield.

I opened the door to my hootch and I could see the blood stains on the floor. I cried and all I could do for days was re-live the horror of it all. My babysaun tried to feed me and comfort me. A few friends came by and we talked and it was like I wasn't there anymore. I had hatred in me for the war and for the Vietnamese people. It was like it was their fault that all this happened. It changed everything for me. My life did a complete turn around that day. And when I found out I was being accused of murdering Mike, it doubled the pain and confusion I felt inside. It was an accident. I didn't kill him on purpose. He was my friend, my brother.

Days later I was given a lawyer by the name of Captain Stevenson in Camp Eagle, Vietnam. I was being accused of out right murdering Mike. I told the lawyer the whole story and an investigation and a statement of all I said was taken. I had everyone in my company came forward and tell them Mike and I was the best of friends. That they never saw one without the other, and that in no way could I have killed him on purpose. A few days later I was taken to Camp Eagle to see my lawyer. It was the first time that I had read any statements by anyone. This one was by Dwight T. Bennet of the 85th Evac Hosp. (Smbl) It read: The patient said repeatedly, "he didn't mean it." /////////Nothing follows////////

I then read the statement made later on by this man. It would be his testimony at my trial.

Statement: SFC Dwight T. Bennet, 85th Evac. Hosp.

SFC Bennet said that PFC Bonds kept saying that SP4 Foster did not mean to shoot me, it was an accident, he really did not mean it, he is my best friend. And at the end of this, Bonds was taken into the operating room where he died 90 minutes later.

I was then told the charges had been reduced to Culpable Negligence and that I would face a General Court-Martial and go to trial. I never said I wasn't guilty, and made a statement to all that had happened. I then went back to my unit and waited for the trial to start. And all the time the words of my brother, Mike rang in my ears. His last words had saved me, and he had told them I was his best friend.

June 3rd my trial started. I faced five high ranking officers that served as Judges. A large amount of character witnesses were called forward to tell their side of things. My *Uncle, Ted Foster had flown down from Thailand a week before, and had spent time with me before the trial. He helped me in a big way telling the courts what kind of kid I had been. I listened to all the peoples thoughts of me and then the doctor that last seen Mike that night. His story shook me, and the words of Mike in the end saddened me.

When it came my time to take the stand, I stood before the court and told them I was guilty. But that it was an accident and that I never meant to kill my best friend. I was asked a thousand questions and relived the night a hundred times. When it was over, I was to face punishment. They argued over kicking me out of the Army and receiving a Dishonorable Discharge. The witnesses were called again and they said it would in no way help me and would destroy me if I were kicked out of the Army. My age also had a lot to do with it, cause I was only 18, but already an E-4 in the Army. And that I had joined the Army and not been drafted, showed that I wanted to serve my country. I had also volunteered for Nam.

Two hours later, I was called back in and was given my sentence. I was given a Bad Conduct Discharge, Confinement to hard labor for six months (The bad conduct discharge and confinement, suspended for six months with a provision for automatic remission), and forfeiture of $50.00 pay per month for six months. What all this amounted to, was that I couldn't get into any trouble for six months (probation). I talked to my lawyer and friends after the trial and was comforted some. It was over and I could return to my unit to serve out the rest of my tour. I didn't feel that I deserved what I got. It should have been more. I felt I should be the one dead, and not Mike. It was an accident, but none of this added up to me, or felt right. My best friend was gone and I was still here. Alive!

I finished my tour in Nam and received the National Defense Service Medal and the Vietnam Service Medal. I regained my E-4 status and came home and took a six months early out, with an Honorable Discharge.

It is now twenty years later. I currently reside on Texas Death Row. I won't tell you my whole life story, but it has always been like Nam. I lived with this everyday since my return. Many events have taken place in my life, that I felt Nam caused me. And in my trial in 84, all this was thrown at me again. I was convicted of the crime cause I was capable of doing it. And I won't get into all that now. But during the time of 1984 when I was arrested for this crime, I have had to deal with all this again. Life has never been the same for me since Michael.

Chapter Three

Mice for Pets

"It's just like watching cartoons…"

On October 3, 1996, my husband, Dale, drove me to Huntsville to visit Donnie; we met up with his adopted father, Cliff, in Palestine. Since only two people are allowed to visit an inmate, Cliff and I visited for two hours; it was a pleasant one. When we left, Donnie wrote the following:

October 4, 1996

> I make my own paths in here and do my own time the best way that I can. I just wonder how some people look at me? Ya know being here and all, in one of the worse places one can be in, in life. I mean, end of the line Buddy! Hey, I reckon that's being normal to wonder that? I feel it is. —Donnie

Donnie often seemed concerned if all that he was thinking and feeling was normal. After Cliff and I had visited Donnie, he wrote:

> Glad we talked about life in here, Annie. Or I'm glad that you listened to me anyway. I felt a need to let you see how I live and the way that I am. Someone has to know me and what I was like. And any relationship that I have with anyone I'd like it to be honest and caring. In other words, real people! And you're like that to me. Just like Glenda is, too. I'd give anything to be out there and free and be in real people's lives.

You and Glenda are so alike. Both very good Christians and sincere in what I have come to believe to be the true way. Know what I mean, Annie? So I know there has to be more like that out there in the world and it means something to me. But I realize this world is not for me. I know the right way, but walking it is the hardest thing that I've ever attempted. And lately I realize that the 'I' part is what has held me back. I know that from where I am now, I'm very selfish. I got my own will in things here and there. None of us will ever be perfect. Righteous? Most important thing is just to know something is going on in this world, and that so many can't see it but God's people is sad. We know where we're going after death and that's when our life will really start, the New Jerusalem.

Now all we got to do is always remember that this war will get us down and kill us if we let it. Satan has this world for now and it's definitely run by a highly organized army of spiritual demons. They oppress with all the evil ways in this life. That's the real war and you got to be a warrior to survive that war.

In this life here, all those prayers that you and others have said for me? They hold me up here. We have to have that. I'd surely die without them. Warfare is fought with prayers to God. I believe that. Like my prayer slips, I save them and keep them together. I got a stack of them too! They're like coupons, Annie. Smile. This is the stress and hate factory here and they breed only the best. —Donnie

October 13, 1996

Donnie wrote:

I think the biggest worry I have at times is, am I really saved? You already know that. I guess I look at myself as a pretty good person, but here no one looks at you except for the bad. Oh some of the bosses over the years have seen that most of the people here could be set free today and would do great out there.

This play about heaven and hell that the church youth went to sounds like it might wake some people up. I thought about it for a while after I read all that you said about it. I wonder where I'll be on that day? I know me, yet I'm not sure God likes who I am. I pray and I believe there is a God, but is that enough? It's strange that you wrote all you did on that. It's still a question with me that I figure is stupid to keep bothering people about. Know what I mean, Annie? —Donnie

October 21, 1996

Donnie wrote:

Lots of gang stuff going on here and there. Tempers flaring on some things too. Some guys out in the factory caught a boss scratching some words about H wing. Also something like, kill all death row murderers. Then the building sergeant started harassing all the work program cause of it. I mean he was threatening us and when we go to the store [commissary] they were punishing us by not letting us go, saying we didn't shave, or have the right haircut. Tear our cages up then lie when he was asked about it. It was getting serious and I fear something is going to happen to someone soon. I hate that too. We just don't need the heat. Some coward signed a statement on me and said I was going to kill him. He did that to just get me moved. He stabs a boss just to get some attention. He's still in solitary cause some people are trying to get to him. As I said, we just don't need all that. Put some heat on some groups here and you know how that goes.

We're trying to get an investigation going on some second shift leaders. They pick on someone and get him all mad, and then wait till they say something back, then holler fight and beat the guy down bad. I never tell Dad about that stuff.

If a guy don't have anyone out in the world, then they don't worry about beating the guy real bad. These are the kinds of things that make me have to deal real hard with anger and hate in me. I can't get rid of it because I want to fight back. Well, enough of that. Football is on tonight. Raiders and San Diego. So we got a busy night, huh Cous?

I'm gone for now. —Donnie

October 27, 1996

Donnie wrote:

I love to read all the articles about Dale, Steve and Cody [author's husband, son and grandson]. It's almost like a TV show to me. I have wondered so much about my own brothers and sisters lately. I prayed for all of them to come to me and they come, and it was like falling off a cliff in what happened afterwards. So weird. Why? Is it just me? I mean Lynn and Rachel were so close to me, then they just dropped out of sight. —Donnie

November 4, 1996

Donnie wrote:

When I went to the Federal Hearing they knew who I was as for being a Bandido at one time, then now a Bandolero. Can't hide from big brother, huh? It's just common here that they keep up with that. Been on record for years. —Donnie

[Author's note: Some inmates are members of clubs and gangs; the justice system keeps track of those who appear to be involved in a club or organization in prison.]

November 14, 1996

Donnie wrote:

I cleaned my cage this morning and fed my mice. I got two little bitty ones. Not even a month old yet. They're coming in from the cold now as they do every year and they're hungry and nosey. I love them. They're so cute. Fast too! But I've got them a big cage and they just eat and sleep and play together. It's my duty, cause so many here just kill them and it bother's me. I whipped one guy over that before. I just don't understand why people do it. One thing I've learned about field mice is that they are as scared of you as most are of them. They eat nuts and grains and wheat stuff. I can take a full-grown one and he's not very big at all, but I have a way of tying a small string around one's neck and then back behind his front legs and it's the perfect collar. I just leave it on him and attach the string to him when I take him out for his walk. I just slip the string over my radio on the desk here and he just runs around and gets into things. I can ignore him and he crawls up my arm and gets on my shoulder and cleans himself. The female I have is so cute. She's a real lady. Always wanting to go with me everywhere I go. So I just let her get in my shirt and I take her everywhere. I'll bring one of these out on a visit and let you see her. I'll just put her in my pocket. Smile. We use mayonnaise, mustard and peanut butter jars for their cages. We just attach them all together. It's built where we can flush them out everyday and keep them clean. —Donnie

I recall my response to the mice:

I wrote Donnie about bringing his mouse out to visit. "I'm sorry to tell you this my friend, but unless you want a scene out in the visiting area you best not bring the mouse out to visit. There are two critters I can't tolerate: one is a snake and the other is a mouse."

November 26, 1996

Donnie wrote:

Sorry you don't like mice. Funny thing about creatures, we grow up seeing them as just pests and they truly are. But they are never looked at close. I can guarantee that when you see one up close and hold it in your hand and look into those eyes you see a little character there. Smile. So funny when you watch them for hours like I do. This one crawls upon the toilet paper roll that I saved. I put it in the end of their cage. They get in there and sleep all day. One lies on her back, right on top of it and puts her little paws on the plastic jars and chews on a hole. When I look down at her she just stares and then slides off the roll and goes inside. It's just like watching cartoons. These two really are a pair. You're right; it's all a mental thing. One day with these two and you would want to catch them all and hide them from all the dangers they get into. I protect them whether they know it or not. I named the female Jenni Lee.

Now that it's cold I watch the birds. There is this one that gets on the window right in front of me here and roosts about 6 p.m. It looks so cold and hunkers down and tries to keep warm. I know God takes care of them, but I still worry about them. Hey, I got nothing else to do. Smile. The bad thing in it all is that when I'm thinking, I see that I worry more about the birds and creatures than I do the men here. I guess maybe my priorities are messed up. Weird though, huh Annie?

After writing about his "pets," Donnie tells of his health. He continues the letter saying:

I can buy vinegar here from the commissary for about forty cents for eight ounces. I need to figure out what to do with it to help break up the calcium in my kidneys. I have passed seven kidney stones in the last nine years here. I never once had any medical help. They just say to drink water and it will pass. I almost died twice from it. I layed on my floor for two days and just threw up, couldn't walk to the hospital. After that I was able to drink a gallon of water and did that till I passed it a few days later. It was the most painful thing I ever had. I really do ask God to keep me well and look after me. I always tell God, 'Remember those prayers now Lord.' Seriously Annie, I take these prayers serious. This is how God protects me. Do you see how I think in all this? It's so hard to explain. But I feel a need to write the church and tell all these that hold me up in prayer all the time how they handle spiritual warfare in a realm that we can't see with the eyes. It's a very real thing, Annie.

Well, my hands are freezing. It's a gray day too. I may just go outside and get totally frozen and when I come back in it will seem warm in here. Smile. I live in eight-cell. There are only eleven cells, so I am close to the end and the heat doesn't get back this far and as always, we're missing a few windows and the others don't shut right.

Annie, I hope you don't mind my ramblin thoughts at times.
—Donnie

Thanksgiving Day 1996:

Donnie wrote:

I got up and showered and listened to some Pearl Jam a bit. Waited for the dinner. We had ham & turkey, two potatoes, sweet and regular type (mashed), giblet gravy, corn, two rolls and butter.

Then I had coleslaw, fruit salad, pumpkin pie, peach pie, and pecan pie.

Then about eight onion rings, cut, nine slices of pickle, a piece of cheese and six celery sticks, six jalapenos and some cranberry sauce. That's about it. I ate all day.

Now, I'm watching the Cowboys and picking my teeth with a corvette radiator hose.

Model size. Smile.

Cowboys won. I kicked back and listen to some rock stuff. Now some country. I miss my family a bunch.

Look out the window. Rain and cold.

Wish I was in Walters, Okla.

I know Steve and Cody don't know me, but do you think they would take some before and after pictures of the 'vette'[Corvette] for me. I've been thinkin of that 'vette' everyday.

I wonder why I talk to you on paper? Smile.

I have a chance to talk.

I want my life back.

Bandoleros got together and ate some turkey. Famlia!

Clubs, gangs, rain and cold.

Watched a movie "Misery." Just what I needed.

Well Annie, I guess I'll close this Thanksgivin out. I kinda spent my Thanksgivin Holiday with ya. Lots of dumb thoughts and starin at the paper.

Most Memorable Thanksgiving? ...Argggg?

Ahhaag! Smell of jet fuel and cordite. The sound of a Huey and Cobra. They pass ten feet over and away they go. Power in different forms.

Hot sun and all the food, beer, music and drugs and somehow make it through a day of flyin.

Always remembering Michael.

Use up a couple of tins of ammo through a 60 and watch the barrel glow. Tracer every 5th round'll do it every time.

Look at people in the village (Phu Bia) and see where my babysaun lives and let her know it's me flyin over.

I hid the day I left Nam. Funny I still miss her....

Save food and silverware and steal turkey for Babysaun. Take home to Mamasaun.

Lonely night that night. Babysaun and others had to leave compound....

Think of home and wonder if I'll make it.

I didn't say it was the best Thanksgiving...just one I remember. —Donnie

December 1996

Donnie wrote:

I'm sorry I haven't wrote. I have, but just thoughts on paper. I don't mail them all. I write them and after a day or so, then it was all stupid anyway. Doesn't matter then. Feelings have a way of coming and going here. They may go, but they never die in me. I just bury them somewhere inside me. —Donnie

December 8, 1996

Donnie wrote:

I got the church's prayer slips and I noticed Sandy [author's daughter] changed her smilie face from one side to the other. Funny how we notice things like that. I was going to write the church there. But I don't feel worthy. If I said something nice and that I'm doing great, it would be a lie, Annie. I'm not sure who I am anymore, or where my life is headed. I'm strong but in all the wrong ways.

Jenni Lee is getting fat. I'm going to have to cut her on her oatmeal and peanut butter. She's cold today. I have her here beside me. It was in the twenties last night. I keep my coffeepot by her bed. It helps some.

You know I can't tell you all that goes on here in letters. They read our mail. I don't mean to worry you, Annie, but I need to talk about some things here, the wars and clashes and all.

Guess it will have to be on our next visit. Maybe more will fall on this. It doesn't look good. They took our sticks, so now we can't do presses until I get another. Bummer!

I was setting here thinking about all you was saying about the youth there in the church. I don't know if I ever told you, but for a while they used to bring these young people through here. They would always let me know, and believe me before they got out the door they wanted out of here. Mostly bosses sons that were having trouble. This one particular boy I remember well. I knew his kind because of the way he walked. I saw him coming down the hall and I knew I had one that thought he was everything. Well, it was yes sir and no sir before he left. He even cried. I told his mom later that I hoped that somehow I made a difference. She assured me that I did. So hopefully he'll make it out there. I wrote this story up for the youth there [Walters].

Following is a portion of Donnie's story he wrote in 1997:

Don't Come This Way

By Donnie Foster

I got up today and I sat here looking out the window. The sun is out, so I dress. I put my tennys on and lace them up real tight. I put my colors on and stretch out. I check my cage over and get things in order. I check on my friend and see if she ate last night. She's only a couple of months old and very shy. She loves to crawl on me and get in my shirt and feel my heart beat. She's really a pretty good mouse.

I go out as the door opens, and eat. Slop! But after that I get ready for a workout. We don't have weights here, cause they don't trust us. And someone always gets killed or beat real bad with them. So for weights we use each other. The workout is barbaric, but it works. I'm 44 years old and I'm in real good shape. When I was in population [general prison] I could power lift. But now it's all about the endurance. I weigh 228 pounds and I'm about 5'10" I guess. I'm losing my hair as I get older. But from time to time I still wear a ponytail...till they make me cut it off. And I wear an earring that is a tooth in my left ear. In a way it's my warrior symbol. Cause I can tell you now that you got to be a warrior to survive.

Where am I? I'm on Death Row here in Texas. I've been here for over 12 years now, I think.

Although I'm here now I'm still a man. I have the ability to love and care and respect others and things in life. I still think children and youth and dogs are the greatest things on earth. I still walk like a man, like I would be if I was out there. But all in all that doesn't matter here anymore. In here nothing matters except for me and my brothers that wear the same patch. As for the rest they are the enemy....

So by now you're thinking, "so what! Who is this guy?" Well, I'm the guy that you will have to answer to if you come here. If you're not kin to me, then sometime you will have to deal with me. This ain't Kansas anymore either. And if you can't fight, then you will take a few quick courses in fighting. If you don't know anyone when you get here you will have to take a side. And I can tell you now that there is no crying here. You will not tell on people and be a snitch or be nosey and get in other's business....

All the things and family you had is just a memory. Oh, they can come see you from time to time, but when they leave you will still be here. It's what we call, the Hotel Californa. "You can check out any time you like but you can never leave."

Funny, while I'm writing this I hear the guards hollering, Fight! That means someone is getting down with the knuckles and they will fight until about 30 guards break them up and beat them down their selfs and drag them off to solitary. Not a nice place. It's cold and dark, and the mind can really play tricks on you. You can't even kill yourself there to get out of it. I've spent endless nights in a dark cell wishing I could just die. And I know that in time I will be back there again....

We have groups here that you call gangs. We call them "Familia." And from time to time we war against each other. I've seen men get cut and bleed to death before they can get in here and get them out.

I've been here in this prison ever since I came home from Nam. Oh, I got a few years on the street. But it's that life that got me here. Maybe I'll share a little with you on while I was out there, and what I did. Maybe it'll help you picture me in your mind.

I admit that I wasn't the perfect kid. I say kid, cause when I came home from Nam I was still 19 years old, for six months before I turned twenty. I can honestly tell you, if I would have listened to my parents I would not be here now. I had good God fearing parents too. They raised me right too. I could blame Nam on all the things that has happened to me, but I won't. I had a choice in all things. I was the only one riding my horse. I just made the wrong decisions.

I love to ride Harleys. Also I rode with a couple of motorcycle clubs too. I associated with a bunch of other clubs also, and that was pretty well my lifestyle. I tried to get away from it a few times because of the people and the trouble it brought. I was always around drugs of all kinds and carried three guns at all times, when in some neighborhoods on business trips. And I can tell you now that at times it was a close call to just get out alive in some wars on the streets with other clubs.

I did drugs, and I never let my family know. Of course I was never around them much. It's that way you know. We do drugs and we start falling away from our loved ones. And if someone approaches us about drugs we get all up in the air and run off. It all starts with just a little to be like everyone else. I had to fit in. It was that or be an outcast. I can tell you that before my year was over I had a serious problem. Yes I came home and tried to go straight, cause you couldn't be a Foster and do those things. But I tried, and

I had every chance a fellow could have to get life on the right track. But I failed. Even when I came to prison the first time and got out, I had it together. But there was always that first joint or that little bit of speed to do just for a night. It does not let you go just one night. We always think we can control the drug. It doesn't work like that. It controls you and gives you nothing but a false sense of security. Everything about a drug of any kind that is illegal puts you in a position that is not real, and so many things come with it. In time you start to lose everything that you thought you were, and all the things that are so valuable in this life such as real friends. Maybe you start to lose communications with your parents. Maybe you lose your job, your car, or house. Believe me, these things come with this territory....

I guess if you're one of those that don't listen or learn this about drugs and alcohol and what they do to you, then you will just have to learn the hard way. I guess you'll have to come here and get to know me or go to some other prison and you'll meet someone just as bad....

I set here and watch the news and read the papers and I see all the different drugs and how it is killing people and destroying their lives.

If you don't know who your enemy is by now you better have your parents explain that to you. We definitely have an enemy that comes to kill, steal and destroy you. That's another story for another time from me. Even I, at this time, am battling a force that is trying to destroy my life. And it's not a physical thing either. It's spiritual.

You got a chance if you haven't messed up yet. I have so many regrets in this life. I can't change it now. All I can do is survive. And this monster that has me does not let me live in a normal manner. Just think, I can never ride a Harley anymore. I can't be with the woman that I love. I can never go home. And I stand in line to lay on a table where they will kill me one day. I have watched so many people and some were brothers, leave here in chains and have ten guards around them taking them to die on that table. I've cried a million tears over people that I got to know here. The ones I knew didn't belong here. They could have been released and made it out there in the world again. But its too late once you get here.

People can care about you while you're in here, but it doesn't make any difference. You still have to walk the walk in here. You may even have to fight till you kill someone. It's no game here. We play for keeps. I'm not saying that it's right either. I'm just saying it happens.

My name is Richard Donald Foster. My number is #815, and they call me Stoney Armadillo. I am the president of the Brazos River Bandoleros . Want to know where I wish I was right now? It's not here. If I could be anywhere in the world right now, it would be setting in the park in Walters, Oklahoma. And after all I've learned about life and drugs and alcohol I'd never leave that town again… unless it was to warn others about what I know of this world and its ways. All I've got left to say is, "Don't Come This Way."

December 15, 1996

Donnie wrote:

I was thinking of things in the world we live in," I pretty well know how things are, and how they work, and what people think is right and normal. Mainstream is a good word. Whatever course we're on, it is all out of whack. We exchange pain for pain. It's like a continuing cycle that never ends. People with blinders on that never see how this world works is destroying people. I think, we as people, don't understand how our own minds work. We're that off and I can see how today's kids grow up without a conscience. I see it in myself in a lot of ways. We're off. And it didn't start out this way.

Annie, in your world there are people such as yourself and

other God fearing Christians that know all these things, but it is a small minority.

I know that our children are the most important in the world and it kills me to see them suffering from abuse and hunger all over the world and it happens here in the United States and people know it. They just don't want to see it.

Pro-lifers everywhere kill us here, and feel satisfied and justified and it's so easy for them. Confusing world. How can you be pro-life and yet kill? Just some thoughts. I try so hard to understand how and why. I guess satan would be our only cause for all this. We can know all these things and yet we fail in all we do. —Donnie

December 18, 1996

As Donnie continued to blame the world for much of what was happening to him, his anger seemed to worsen during the Holidays. Donnie wrote:

It's the worst time of the year for me, Annie. Veterans Day, and Thanksgiving, then Christmas, then the New Year.

Continuing in his seemingly never-ending anxiety and anger, Donnie wrote:

Long day. Wired up most of the day. I'm a hyper dude. Close to rockin and rollin [fighting] today. It's gonna be one of those Christmases.

Annie, do you realize how hard it is to live this way and stay in control? I wonder how long it will last. You got to fall sometime. At times I need to talk, but you can only discuss so much in letters.

Hey Annie, when you talk to Cody and Cory [author's grandsons] or anyone about me, never avoid the truth of the life I have lived or what I am now. They gotta know. There are so many lives one can live. I know mine is not a good one. My lifestyle of drugs, guns and outlaw biker got me here. I didn't know then what I know now or it would have made a difference. Maybe something good can come out of my life for my kin there.

Ya know, no one in my real family writes me. Dad does every few months, but he does come to see me. I have friends who know me better than my family. You're the only one in my family that writes. I just want to say thank you for loving and caring about me. I guess God does hear me sometimes.

I think this will probably be my last Christmas and you know what? I'm glad. You live here and it's a battle not to hurt anyone again. I may try to explain a few things to Stacy, [author's pastor] when he comes. It's hard to talk to just anyone. I know I'm ramblin again....

I'm glad that you enjoy Christmas. I love trees and the scenes and all. I love a house full of people and the smell of food cooking and talking to everyone. Mostly just watchin. I wish I was there. We could walk and talk too, like you and Sandy and Bev [author's daughters]. But I am blessed to have you to talk to this way, just to share my thoughts and all. I have no reason to fool anyone about my life. I'm not proud of my life at all. I've known for at least the last two years that my life is limited. I have shared much with Glenda. But it is important to me that I have someone that is family know me, who I am, right or wrong. The problem being here on Death Row is you're automatically a bad guy and it doesn't matter how the system got you here, you're here. I'm no saint, Annie. After Nam, something changed. I played rough. I feel so many times that I owe everyone an apology for my life.

I am a good man though. I care so much, and I can love and have compassion. I care for children. They are the center of my heart. At times in my cell I just fall to the floor and cry over a child that I don't even know. I ask God why these bad things happen to these children, to such innocent lives. I still care but I can make no difference.

I don't know what's really going on with me this last year. Facing death does weird things to ya, Annie. I play hard and for keeps. I have no choice and yet I don't lose what I really am inside. I'm hanging on Cous, yet I'm also drowning. I see no reason to be good here. I'm good to my own.

I feel blessed to have you in my life, and thank you for being there for me. I don't feel so alone now with that. But it has been a rough go lately. Wars, always wars.

Donnie wrote this piece of poetry:

> Mountain tops, desert plains,
> Full moons and darkness,
> Lone howling coyotes, and winds
> That sing in the days and nights.
> Waking emotions and feelings
> That soar through the body's soul.
> Rising anger and hate that crushes
> The hearts of lonely men.
> Desolate minds, empty thoughts.
> Journeys that never start or ever end.
> Time that passes and goes nowhere.
> Spirits that float over empty voids,
> They rise only to fall.
> Fluorescent green, pouring into past lives.
> Regret and rivers of deceit and despair.
> Thoughts that have no vision.
> Memories that fall into abyss.
> Loneliness that covers the spirit,
> And soul like a fine dust. Numbness!

Banks that keep the love,
Never to be used again. Locked away.
Hands that can't touch,
Feet that can't dance,
Eyes that can see,
But have no picture.
Blindness with no light,
And wings that have no flight.

SA
Richard Donald Foster #815
Texas Death Row

I reminded Donnie that it was because of the sin in all of us that Jesus came, and because Christ knew no sin, only His ultimate sacrifice would do. It was God's plan, because He loved us so much. That's what it took. Donnie and I had many discussions on just such as this. He loved for me to talk and remind him about Jesus and His love. Donnie knew the story of Jesus, and He knew it was true. But he wanted to be reminded often. I think Donnie almost began to predict what my response would be to each of his letters and comments.

Chapter 4

Ready To Die

"I've had enough...."

January 5, 1997

*D*onnie wrote:

This has been my roughest time yet. The tension over here and a clash [confrontation] came about and we made it through okay. Solved a few problems. But I stood my ground and it will be one way or no way at all. So the holidays here were bad, is all I can tell you.

Donnie would not go into detail in letters about the clashes, but he would talk quite freely during visits. He admitted much of the conflicts among inmates were from race and gang related tensions. Continuing his letter, Donnie wrote:

But what has been going on inside me is where the real battle lies. I can't tell you that I'm saved. I want to be honest with you about this. I can with my thoughts say that I am and almost believe it. But in other times I feel that I'm a loser in that. And yes it's all me. And it seems that it would be my decision and all. But I'm not sure about me anymore. These things happening in my life are real and believe me I do the best I can in it all. Annie, you know there is a time for everything in a person's life. And there are seasons that we go through. I'm asking you to understand me when I tell you these things. I've tried to tell you about my life all that I can, but it can't be done in letters. Just prison stuff that can't be done anywhere but among our own kind. The loneliness is enough to let you know that one can't survive here forever with that. Not me anyway.

I'm tired, mentally. I can't even talk to anyone here anymore. Not even my brothers. I just shake my head or walk away. Even the bosses know that I've had enough. I've been working here at night on the wing. I go out and clean up the day room and showers and stay by myself. I like that. I set and look out at the yard at night. Sometimes I can see the stars and see the moon. Something I haven't seen in a while. But I set and think about this life and try to sort things out, but I can't anymore.

I very seldom ever get to look into the eyes of the ones I care for and without that you got nothing. I have to get on out of here. I need this judge to rule on me and I'm gone. It doesn't mean that I don't care about my family. But I don't plan on sharing any of this with Cliff. How I love that man. I want not to hurt him or anyone. But this is why you're in my life. I needed someone to help on my way out of here. A comfort or nerve. Call it what you will. I'm no brave man about dying, but I think I'm ready.

I'm sorry for what I've been in this life. Maybe when I'm all alone in that final hour something will come to me and let me know it's going to be okay. I'm looking for it. —Donnie

I believe that Donnie received Jesus Christ into his life in 1985 on the night he called out to God in that shower in the Parker County Jail. I believe that God is faithful and keeps His promises. God's word says that whoever will call upon the name of the Lord will be saved (Romans 10:13). Donnie's friend, Glenda told me he was close to the Lord for a long while. It seemed to me that somewhere in Donnie's life he began to believe that it was up to *himself* and his behavior to keep his salvation secure. Oswald Chambers wrote in his journal, *My Utmost for His Highest*, that it is never our obedience that puts us right with God. "We are acceptable with God, not because we have obeyed or because we have promised to give up things, but because of the death of Christ, and in no other way," wrote Chambers.[1]

In *Eternal Security,* author Charles Stanley wrote, "God does not require a constant attitude of faith in order to be saved, only an act of faith in Christ."[2] Stanley wrote that we are not saved because we have enduring faith. But we are saved because at a moment in time we expressed a faith in our enduring Lord (Eph. 2:8-9). The apostle Paul writes at the end of this passage, "It is the GIFT of God; not as a result of works, that no one should boast."

January 14, 1997

Although it was difficult to hear about the hardships that he dealt with on Death Row, as our correspondence continued I asked Donnie how he managed to survive in hopes that this would prompt him to open up a little more.

Donnie wrote:

> In here, Annie, you take the part of the heart that loves and you put it on a shelf. From time to time you may take it out.
>
> I've learned to be gentle and tough. I guess it's good in a way. Kinda like fear, you have to have it to survive. But it can control you and ruin you for the kind of heart it takes to survive in here. Just funny how these things work in life, huh? —Donnie

January 15, 1997

> Slept till 11 a.m.. Got up. Sun was out, so I played handball. Did setups and crunches last night. Do an upper body workout tonight. I'm gonna get my waist in shape. Hard cause of my power-lifting before. Endurance for the long fights. Man who can

swing hard longer usually wins. Got my headphones on listening to Stevie Ray Vaughn. That's good for the soul, huh? Yea, right.

Maybe Dad will come tomorrow. I'm trying to get in a better mood for it.

I still set and talk to you. I just haven't been a good guy lately.

I wish we could talk right now, Annie. I got a real problem. Decision time among a vote here with the brothers [club]. I may step out of it all. This is what I see. My voice is only one in a vote. Weakness or strength? Smart or stupid? Always use wisdom and just do what's right. But here in this world a right is not the same as in your society.

What runs me and what runs the others are two different things, and in all this, this is reality here.

Funny, I was thinkin about the kids there and the decisions I make in all this. If they were watchin it would be for their benefit, but I'm not out there. —Donnie

Little did Donnie realize at that time, but he would be making the right decisions and my grandchildren would be watching and would benefit from the choices he made in the years to come.

Donnie wrote:

It's been so cold here lately, but I miss seeing frozen nights with ice everywhere. Makes the air clean and the lights reflect nice at night. I love a fire in the cold outside. I miss my life, Annie. And I'm so tired of hate and anger and the race stuff. I can't be me. Do you think of dying, Annie? What it'll be like when you pass from here to there? I have dreams at times and they mess with me. They're so strange and they stick with ya, too. Not like other dreams. But I am always laying there and I never pass on or feel anything and the people like Dad, my sister, and my nieces are there, but I never see you, Annie?
—Donnie

I replied to Donnie and told him that as humans we have a natural instinct to survive and cling to this life on earth. Death is certain, and I think about it, but I do not dread it. God made a promise to me many years ago in 1962 when I placed my trust in His Son as my Lord and Savior. And like the Apostle Paul, "...I know whom I have believed and am persuaded that He is able to keep that which I have committed unto Him against that day" (II Timothy 1:12 KJV) and throughout all eternity.

January 17, 1997

Donnie wrote:

I'm sittin here in my thermals and watching it get dark. It's getting very cold too. Suppose to get down to 19 degrees in the morning, and then sunny and warm up next week. Long day. I got up and waited for a visit like I did last Sunday. Guess Dad was busy. I don't want him out in this weather anyway. . . .

January 18, 1997

I'm sittin here listening to a Saturday night show of old country music. Patsy Cline. I love that stuff. Kind of makes me want to get the heck out of here and return to my childhood livin out by Corum and Comanche [rural Southwest Oklahoma]. I'd be happy just to be a dog or a monkey out there. —Donnie

January 19, 1997

Not a lot goin on here. I've stayed to myself. No fight all weekend! I had fun with Ms. J last night. She laughs like Snoopy the dog. She is less than five feet and runs death row (night shift). Smile. We're dangerous, huh? I've always wanted the lawyers to come in here and see how I live. I wrote Craig and asked him to check on getting in here with a camera. He did, but was turned down by the warden. —Donnie

January 21, 1997

Yesterday was Martin Luther King Day.... 'Where a man can live and not be judged by the color of his skin, but by the content of his character.'

I agree. It's not color; it's who you are, or what you are in your walk in life.

You know, Annie, I don't ever want to be responsible for someone getting hurt ever again. I pray things here change.

I've worked out hard all week. My stomach and legs hurt. I'm pushin myself harder than ever. Heck, I'd look like somebody if I had some of that Rogaine, that hair grower. Smile.

I keep a good attitude and outlook on things as best I can. But I'll never miss this place when I'm gone. Guess I won't miss anything, huh? Smile. I was thinking about your concern and mine too about bein sure I'm saved. I can imagine my last days and hours. I'll surely be talkin to God. That thief on the cross next to Jesus went, right? Annie, I can't help it that I'm selfish in ways. I do a lot of what I want to do. And I understand what Paul meant 'I do the things I don't want to do.' (Romans 7:19). The knots I get and the hand aches come from fightin. Frown.
—Donnie

January 26, 1997

My first adventure in Breckenridge was the bank [hostage] deal. The second is the escape with that gal. I got a lot to say. But I'm gonna just leave it alone until someone I know is right and good comes along and can research my life. I have never mentioned or told you all that I was involved in. They did a book and show on Young County. Law Officers and I was part of it. I was even snuck into a secret Grand Jury in Young County and was almost killed. Long story. Annie I was involved with one County Commissioner, a DA, and sheriff. And the days they chased me was strictly survival. I did what I had to do, to stay alive. But I've never told Dad any of this. TV doesn't have anything on my life.

Enough of that. It doesn't matter anymore. I'll get it out one day. Hopefully this cellie I got will be gone soon. I asked him to move. TV nut! He reads the TV Guide like I should read my Bible. I'm not a nice person here Annie, and I definitely intimidate the dude. You have to check people out here and see what they're made of. This guy don't share anything. I share all the time and have watched him eat my food. He saves his. Smile. So I told him it only cost me a little food to learn how he is. Now he wants to share. It's all new to him, so I'll teach him good ways and send him on his way. He can't stay here.
—Donnie

February 3, 1997

I just had a visit with Dad. We didn't have a good visit at all. It's bothering me too. I just wasn't in a good mood. I got too many things going on. He just doesn't understand. For all these years in prison, I have been happy when I wasn't; I smiled when I didn't want to; I said everything was okay when it wasn't, so he wouldn't worry. Dad doesn't know anything I did in Nam except about the murder trial I had there. He doesn't know what's inside me. No one ever has. As I set here today I know that my life has been one big waste. Dad is the only one left of this Foster family who cares. But I am going to do all I can to get this show on the road. I want to write him. I'm worried about our visit.
—Donnie

February 9, 1997

Hi Annie. I was just sitting here wondering what 'A' to use in your name, a or A. You can tell I'm bored, huh? I'd give anything to be out there. I would be there every morning on those walks with you and Sandy. I'd love to listen to you talk about God. It's in me, Annie. I just can't walk it here. My finger is a little broke up for the moment, so I am going to have to type the rest of this letter. More problems here. People never rest. Only way to handle it is to beat the heck out of someone. I do what I have to do, or let another group handle it. Annie, I know when I do wrong and I can tell you it affects me in the club at times. I want to do right and be honest in all things. I'm up front and straight all the way. I don't even lie to the bosses if they catch me breaking the rules. I just tell them I did and that's that. They respect me for that too. But we all play dirty in here from time to time. Have I been rambling or what? The reason I do that is because I never get to share myself with anyone else. I just like talking to you cause one day you will need to tell others about me when I'm gone. Nam is the main thing I have trouble with. But I know that's here to stay as along as I am alive and I've just tried to deal with it. I've had everything in life at one time or another. Material things used to rule my life. I've had family and I've been around the world, but I hope the kids can see that when you come here you got nothing. I had a guy do me real wrong and I'll have to tell you about it when I see you. It has nothing to do with God Annie. It affects all that I stand for here with my brothers. I pray that it gets right and I don't have to make a decision on this one. I knew this was coming. You know lately I've sense that the Lord doesn't want anything to do with me. I really believe He gives up on us. —Donnie

I responded to Donnie's comment by writing, "God doesn't stop loving us because we do wrong. He doesn't like sin! And when we finally get desperate enough to call out to Him in prayer the Holy Spirit brings to our mind those things that stand between God and ourselves. Is God waiting to hear from you, Donnie?"

As I think back, I know that I was in Donnie's life to listen, especially at this point in his life. I had to get to know him. I realized that if I had lectured him in all that he said and did, I would have served no purpose. He had been preached to all his life, and he probably had more Bible knowledge, and for certain more experiences in life, than me. But Donnie needed to know that I cared about him as a person. At this point the only way I could show my love is to give of my time to listen. I told Donnie when I disagreed with him. He told me that he expected me to do that and I held him to it.

I encouraged Donnie in the Lord as I felt God's leading. I was certain God knew Donnie's heart and He knew what He was doing. I prayed for wisdom and others were praying also. I trusted God for it. I didn't always know what God was doing, but I knew He did.

I often wondered if I had known that I would have to watch Donnie die on a gurney one day, would I have continued or would I have backed out of the situation? I thought about Christian writer, Lucy Swindoll's comments in *Moses' Choice-Your Choice*. I wondered if I would stay where things were nice and clean and comfortable, or would I follow God's leading? Like Swindoll, "I'd have to reach down into the part of me where my values lie. Such a decision would have to come from a sense of direction–from my faith."[3]

So by faith I kept listening, and Donnie kept writing and writing. He would say, "I don't know why I'm telling you this, it's got nothing to do with God."

I felt Donnie occasionally would make a statement to test me, like the time he wrote that he had used marijuana. My sister, Betty and I visited him shortly afterwards and he told Betty about my reaction. "I knew Annie would fire a letter right back, and she did saying, "Well, I hope it was worth it because I understand that every time you do marijuana that it kills more brain cells!"

I really didn't know if it was factual, and I was sure Donnie knew more about the effects of marijuana than me, but I could never resist the urge to make a point. Glancing my way, Donnie smiled and remarked, "And the last thing I need is more brain cells killed!"

The three of us got a chuckle out of the conversation, but I suppose those men on Death Row might try anything just to break the monotony. Donnie had remarked that he wanted nothing but my honest opinion, and I usually gave it.

With a son only a few years younger than Donnie, I began to feel that I could relate to Donnie as I would Steve. And like my own children, Donnie did not always follow my parental advice, but I believe he wanted that family concern.

February 20, 1997

Donnie wrote:

> It's been a hard month, heat of one kind or another, head-games, pressure. But I got some rest. Even got a few things ironed out. I've had my house tore up a few times lately. Then I have to come in and put it all back together. Snitches! They never stay out of your business. Always trying to get you moved, so they can have their way on the block. But it's good some bosses have respect for old convicts. Smile. I passed a kidney stone this morning. It had me up all night. I drank water and finally got to sleep. Then this morning I got up and passed it. I feel much better now. I can't describe the pain you get from one of those things. It made me sick almost to the throwing up stage. I don't even bother with the hospital. They do nothing for you anyway.... I have a good friend named Dave Herman. He's been pushed through the courts pretty fast lately. I've known this dude for years now and he's a good brother of the clubs. He lived with Blue [inmate friend] for a while, but he got his date set a few days ago and they will probably move him Monday. But I know his time has come. I'm real down about it. We all got together last night and had a spread [meal]. It's hard for me to

look at him now, cause I know he's goin to die. His date is for April 2. I just pray that something happens. We have worked hard and Blue has really got down for Dave to try and get him a stay. His lawyers wrote and told him he didn't have a chance and to get ready to die. Cold, huh? His appeal lawyer is the same one I had at my trial that threw a fit when my lawyers filed Ineffective Assistance of Counsel on him. I hate to lose Dave off this block and in life period. He means a lot to me. I have been trying to stay out of trouble, but as for things here, nothing is ever going to change. It's Sunday morning and I just got up and fixed some coffee and sat down to write you some more. I don't really feel too good this morning. I'm one of those that seldom get sick. But lately there is a real shortage of bosses cause of a virus or flu. All the guys on twenty had it, then it hit nineteen block. Now it has been over here for a week. I guess whatever it is it got me. My partner has it now. That's Martin Gurule. He's a Wop Dago. He's one of the best guys I've met here and was my work partner when we laid it down. He's got a heart and is solid as a rock. . . I know some think I should not worry people and just be happy that someone comes to see me. Is that right, Annie? I mean if I'm wrong, I'm wrong. I've never been too smart when it comes to others.

    I wonder sometimes how I made it this far. I can't count the times I have faced death, and even wanted to meet death. But people keep telling me that I am blessed to not have been killed. At this point I just don't see it that way. —Donnie

March 9, 1997

    Annie, I say a lot of things about God, but listen, I don't live the way I should and therefore I feel that God doesn't or cannot have any use for me. I'm worthless as long as I'm on my own so-called agenda here. I actually believe that I was very close to the Lord there for a while. I spent time with Him. I read and studied and prayed and was trying to just walk on faith. But the years went by, and the things I was having faith for just never happened. I'd get all excited about things, but nothing ever became of anything. I just got tired, Annie. I hear all that you tell me and I think about everything you say to me, but as for trust, I live in a place where you can't trust anyone. My brothers [club] yes but none other. It's just something I can't afford to do. My life has made me that way. —Donnie

In another letter, still feeling he should have been able to cut a deal with God somewhere along the way, Donnie wrote:

I can accept anything that He [God] puts on me and roll with it, but if I want something, it's still His way. Seems kind of one-sided to me. But then again I just come to realize that I'm actually a loser cause I can't be all that God wants me to be. I can't give in to it all. Why am I an individual at all if I have to accept whatever comes my way? Should I just kick back and say, 'Well, I guess it wasn't God's will?' Do we do that all the way through life? Listen, I don't kid ya, I have knowledge of God's ways and all. Prophesy and spiritual warfare, I understand it and how it all works. I understand where and who my enemy is in this world, but I don't understand God's ways of letting things happen, and as an individual it bothers me. I give up on God ever doing anything for me. —Donnie

I believe that even then Donnie knew that the worldly freedom he so desperately longed for wasn't going to happen. He knew God loved him. But there is a moment in every Christian's life when we meet God on His terms and by supreme surrender enter into *His* sovereign will. Donnie wasn't there—not yet.

Occasionally Donnie would admit, "Annie, I can believe for others but not for me. Faith the size of a mustard seed is sufficient, right Annie? If I can just get inside the gates of heaven, that is all I will ever need or get from this life, then this will all be worth it."

As Donnie's spiritual questions deepened, I searched for more theological responses. One author in particular, gave me much to tell Donnie. This author, C. H. Spurgeon, was an English Baptist minister who preached his first sermon at the age of sixteen. At the age of twenty-two was in the habit of addressing congregations numbering six to ten thousand. Spurgeon wrote that we should never make a Christ out of our faith, nor think of it as if it were the independent source of salvation. Our life is found looking to Jesus and not our faith. (Hebrews 12:2).

Spurgeon wrote, "Great messages can be sent along slender wires and the peace giving witness of the Holy Spirit can reach the heart by means of a thread-like faith, which seems almost unable to sustain its own weight. Think more of Him to whom you look than the look itself. You must look away from your own looking and see nothing but Jesus and the grace of God revealed in Him."[4]

As I sat and read Donnie's letters, I knew that God knew where He was going with this guy. And because He knew well in advance what was going to take place in Donnie's heart and life in the coming years, God must have smiled at some of the things Donnie would say. It was as if Donnie wasn't talking to the Lord, but he wanted the Lord to hear and find favor in him.

March 11, 1997

Donnie wrote:

> Listen Annie, like I said, I guess we make our beds and all that stuff like society says and by the way, I don't fit or believe in all the laws of society either. Therefore I'm an outcast and an outlaw. I can't make it with man's laws, much less God's laws. Know what I mean, Annie? As for life, I've been a round and I don't know many that has had a life like mine. Now I'm

not saying I had it harder, but it's been hard! I have to question the pain I've endured in this life. I've tried to bite my lip and go on but inside I cry out hard and ask, 'Why?' I need to know why. Maybe it has been something that has been passed down through the bloodline. I went through my whole life wanting to know what was wrong with me and why they gave us kids away like that. Hey Annie, I've really been just one lost puppy in this life. Yes, I had a good family adopt me, but this other always got in the way. I've bungled my way through it and wound up here. So I just get up and roll with it. I'm God-minded in many ways and my conscience works. But I'm not going to get anymore into this right now, Annie. I would just end up trying to fit a square peg into a round hole. —Donnie

March 12, 1997

I just found out that Dave Herman might get a stay [of execution]. Something about the date was set wrong or something to that effect. But I'm relieved. I am worried about him. He is taking it pretty hard. It doesn't look good for Barefield. Unless he gets a last minute stay, they kill him at 6 p.m. That is less than four hours from now.

The more I think about this execution tonight, the more I feel I should just try not to think. I've seen many a guy go over there and get killed. Some I have harbored bad thoughts about, them and their crimes. But then I just try to imagine the moment and what the guy is going through. I got moved back to my old cell yesterday. Don't know how long it will last. But I'll go as long as I can. Smile. I was on my fourteenth day in lockdown when the captain and lieutenant came by. I told them I had a raw deal. They said I'd be moving back tomorrow. But thirty minutes later they came back and told me to pack up. So now it has taken me a while to get settled in here. I'm going out at 10:30 and get a workout with Martin. It's Friday, so I'll have time to get over the soreness and do some stretches over the weekend. Monday I'll be back in the groove. I still have a cough hanging on from the flu. I hope I never get that sick again. I really thought I was going to die. I haven't heard if they killed Woods last night. Houston says they're going to get at least forty this year and that's not counting all the other counties. It's a real bad time here, Annie. I'll find out today if Dave Herman got that stay. My brother, Gribble, goes over there on the cleanup crew and he'll see Dave. It doesn't look like Herman's going to get that stay after all. Hopes go high; then we get shot down. —Donnie

March 26, 1997

I got in with this guy that is painting the wing here. We go out in the mornings and paint cells. Lots of work, but I did this so I can travel down to where Dave is. I got to see him Saturday and we had a good visit. Blue and Rex will get to see him too. Dave is getting a little shaky about things. I sent that witness card that you sent me to him on Saturday. I asked him to please read it, so I'm sure that he did. I want to try to see him again, but he said he didn't want us to see him after three or four days before his execution. I can understand that. But he will be out in the visiting room with his family and I will be out there. They will kill him at 6 o'clock on that day, but he will visit with his family until noon. I just can't get him off my mind. My little Jenni Lee is running around the neighborhood. She's hiding in one of the cells here and no one can find her. Maybe she's gone for good this time. But I'll leave her some food and water out tonight. I hope no one hurts her. So much going on around here lately, a lot of harassment. They're pushing hard and want us to go off [retaliate] for some reason. I think they want one of the bosses to get hurt so they will have an excuse to lock us down. They are expecting trouble because of all the killings that are going to start taking place soon. I just pray I can stay out of trouble this time. Dave Herman already marked all his stuff that he wants us to have after he's gone. He sent his wedding ring out to his Mom. Keep Dave in your prayers, Annie. Oh yeah, I told him what I believe about Jesus and what I hope for anyway. Also, the guy I paint with, JC Cockrum [death row inmate] prayed with Dave before we left Saturday. I joined in and we held hands in front of his cell. I could barely look at Dave when I left. Dave told Blue that the bosses were over there last night and shook all the houses [cells] down and tore up all the guys mail and stuff while they were outside. I don't know why they do that. That's personal mail. They dumped commissary all over the floors. It's a mad house here when everyone gets wired up. I hate to see Dave in that when he's so close to death. You wouldn't believe this place, Annie. People here don't even know when someone dies until they're gone. Also, it seems they have no respect for others at all. It used to be different here, when a person was going to die. Maybe you have heard it on the news that Dave tried to kill himself. I kind of knew it was coming. I am real down, Annie. I have prayed, but I have just had a problem with it all. Dave is back now and is out visiting with his family. He is not in very good shape. He has had a boss outside his cell all day and I can't get to him. It's been hell for Dave. He tried to spare his mom and dad and the victims. Believe me, Annie, I knew Dave well. I pray that he has peace. —Donnie

Dave Herman was executed April 2, 1997.

Chapter 5

Watching Friends Die

"It comes to me and I talk to God
about what is going on here."

Death Row

I cry out, but no one hears-
My face numb from all the tears.

I think of dying and long for it to come-
Just not my turn, but it is for some.

I see them daily and look into their eyes-
Wondering if I should say goodbye.

But I let them pass to go their way-
Not wanting to intrude upon their day.

All I can do is pray

Father in Heaven:

Be with these men that the beast will slay-
Protect them on their final day.
Comfort these men on their last few steps-
And walk them through this life's last door-
To be with them forever more.
Amen

How much longer, oh Lord?
Richard D. Foster

April 23, 1997

Donnie wrote:

I have watched so many go to die here. JC and I have been painting a lot to get around to see all the guys that have dates. We were worried about Herb. He hates anything to do with God. I thought about it a lot, especially since I'm not all that right with God either. But it was weird. We went over there just to wait on him and be with him. We talked and laughed and Herb run the preacher off that came by. I can't remember everything we told Herb, but it just started and I told him I had things happen in my life that had to be God. I never understood why. But I do believe God is real. It is my hope anyway. He wouldn't look at us, but JC said 'Man, would you just pray one prayer with us?' Herb said real slow, 'Okay…go ahead.' I reached through the bars and took his arm and told him I loved him. It just came out, Annie. I prayed and cried and told God about Herb's situation and told Him that Herb needs Him to be there when he passes on. Herb really broke down and cried. He was different after that. What was so weird, while we were praying the bosses just kept going around us and never bothered us once. They knew what we were doing and why we had come. It just seems it's our job now. It is all so strange, but it still seems I can believe for others more than I do for myself. But I do believe Herb is going to greet us when we enter heaven. Now some of the others are in line, and we've got to get over there and take care of God's business. Sometimes we can't get over there where we need to go, but God makes a way for those we need to get with.

I've got three friends now that are going and they are calling for me to help on this. It is so weird. I am seeing people out the door as they go to their deaths.

There is so much going on right now. Race stuff, and I'm in

the middle again. Another white dude was being preyed on by a pack of wild dogs [inmates] and they split them up some. About five of them that think they can do what they want with human lives. But now the one they moved over here is feeling what he has done to others. Funny how things work out. But it will all get solved. I'm the bonehead and JC prays about it all when he can. But we're alike in many ways. He really loves God.

I haven't felt right about telling about Herb, Annie. But it happened and I wanted you to know. It lifted me, yet at the same time I don't feel right. Worthy. I'm not reading my Bible and I don't pray a lot either. Just at times. It comes to me and I talk to God about what is going on here. So much, and it's like a battle is going on between Satan and God and you can see it. I'm still very much in things here and I refuse to let anyone be preyed on. But I am sure God will take care of it all.

Yes, some things are hard for me, Annie. So many dates getting set now and so many that came here when I did are going to die. My neighbor, Duke, is fixing to get a date. I get to see them, and I can see it in their faces. —Donnie

Although Donnie tried to remain braced for anything, the Lord was transforming him at His own pace. Donnie realized that God was working in situations around him.

I had taken a picture of my church's Wednesday night prayer group and sent it to Donnie. He had the picture in one of the albums I picked up with his property on the day before his execution.

April 26, 1997

Donnie wrote:

I always wondered what the people are like that send those prayer slips. Please tell them all hello and thanks for praying for me.

No race today on the Nascar Circuit. I've been waiting all day for this one race of the year and it rains. Bummer! At least I got some letters answered!

Donnie occasionally shared a correspondence he had received from another inmate. He would ask me to save the letters for him. In March 1997, a young man in jail in Texas wrote to Donnie:

What's up bro? I am locked down here in Parker County on a parole violation. My third.

At church here last night, I came across "Don't Come This Way" that you wrote and obviously sent here to Sonny [jail minister].

You may not remember me, but we were locked down in the same old Parker County jail in, I'd say in 85. I often wondered about you over the years because it is not every day that a man comes face to face with a man on his way to Death Row. I remembered the name, Stoney Armadillo. Each time I'd hear or read news about someone being executed or something I'd look or listen to see if it was you.

Your story has gotten around our tank and we've even had more copies made. It hit home for some of these guys as well as myself, because the misdemeanor charge turned into a felony conviction for me. Drugs. I am fortunate by the grace of God. I will be getting another chance back out there on those mean streets. The alcohol and drugs are a part of my past, and with the help of the great Lord above maybe it will stay that way.

I too am from Oklahoma. And I wish I had never seen the lights of the city. I know we make our choices and we have to live with them. But I pray that the Lord gives you peace in your heart. I remember how we talked and I know you have love and regret in your heart. That's what matters. We all make mistakes in life and I am sorry that yours got you there. May God have mercy on your soul. — Richard G.

This letter gave Donnie a sense of affirmation about his short story; apparently, it had far reaching effects.

In his book, *All of Grace*, C. H. Spurgeon wrote, "In the first place, nobody else but God would have thought of justifying these who are guilty. They have lived in open rebellion; they have done evil with both hands; they have gone from bad to worse; they have turned back to sin even after they have smarted for it, and have therefore, for a while been forced to leave it. They have broken the law and trampled on the gospel. They have refused proclamation of mercy and have persisted in ungodliness. How can they be forgiven and justified? Their fellowmen, despairing of them, say 'They are hopeless cases!' Even Christians look upon them with sorrow rather than with hope. But not so, their GOD! But even if anybody had thought of justifying the ungodly, only God could do it, and He does it to perfection!"[1]

May 11, 1997

Donnie wrote:

Right now, JC and I are getting geared up to go see guys that have dates, a day or so before they die. Yes, we have to tell them about Jesus and we will to as God open's the door for us to get there. I did get the list of execution dates for you. There are more dates too, but we don't know them all yet. Westley has a date for Tuesday and JC and I have been talking to him. We are painting the bars on all the cells now and we stay in front of his house [cell]. He wasn't eating up until yesterday and he was throwing up. Anyway, Westley did accept the Lord. Smile. He got a good night's sleep and even ate yesterday. JC and I sat there and explained the body, spirit and soul to him and the unseen war that goes on around us. JC read a lot to him from the Bible. JC really cares about these guys, as much as I do. But Westley is in God's hands now. . .I've got to get over and visit Cliff. He is my focus now. You have a picture of him, Peewee and me. He is one of my best friends from long ago. He is going to die Friday. JC and I got to pray with him and he already has Jesus in his heart, but he wants us to be there for him. It was so great, and yet it hurts and is sad for me. But I am praying for strength. I don't feel worthy to be telling them anything about God. A lot is coming back to me, and the tools for spiritual warfare is important here, binding and losing and pleading the blood of Jesus over things and these guys. The Lord, JC and I are having to use some strategy here to get to the guys. But some of the bosses and the captain are also hip to us and that helps. I am also learning more about myself. Smile. Although I am only human I try to do the right things. And I can tell you JC and I are under attack bad right now. No big deal though. I kind of like a little edge and excitement once in a while. Smile. —Donnie

May 14, 1997

Donnie wrote:

Westley is dead. I heard on the radio that his family had a hard time of it all. I imagine so. They loved him! They beat on the window and yelled, 'wake up!' It broke my heart. I've got to get back over and see Cliff again. They will move him tomorrow. They had a stabbing here the day before yesterday. Pretty bad one too. We haven't heard anything, so the guy must have lived.

JC and I went out and ate on the yard. He is steadily on me about God and His ways. And you know me; I'm a bone-head. Cliff is hollering at me. I will try and see him tonight and again tomorrow and Friday too until they take him away. I wanted to tell you about the captain here. He told us we had been doing some great work here with the guys who have dates. So that means we are covered here on the morning shift and the lady that is over JC and me when we paint is a Christian too. I was thinking maybe you could send the captain a card and let him know how much we appreciate him and say a pray for him. We need prayer power here. Just know that the battle here is great. Maybe this is what God has been waiting to use me for all this time, going on forty-five years, huh? But I am not ready. I am still so much of self, yet I fear God, but I have such a hard time of things between God and this life here. Also, Harris is calling for us too. He is beside Cliff. But Cliff will get moved tonight to deathwatch. Then Harris will be alone there. He and Cliff talk a lot and they hold each other up. One is black and the other is white, but all the race stuff is out of the way. Annie, I think I'd die for Cliff if I could. Maybe for once I'd do something good in life. —Donnie

Donnie and I made a plan that he would send me the list of scheduled execution dates, and I would send cards to the men to tell them how Christ died for the sins of the world.

II Peter 3:9 says that God is not willing that any perish. God chose redeemed sinners to tell others that He desires to save all people from eternal death.

II Peter 3:9 says that God is not willing that any perish. God chose redeemed sinners to tell others that He desires to save all people from eternal death.

Chapter 6

Final Visits

"God's gonna make a way for us"

May 14, 1997

I was relieved as I sensed from Donnie's letters that he had begun to focus on others' needs more than his own. Donnie believed God was using JC and him to witness to other inmates and encourage them as their execution dates were scheduled.

Donnie's letter read:

> In here my thought pattern is very limited, so to be kind of normal I dream or day dream that I'm with you guys and what I'd be doing if I was out. I know I'd be there with you all. I'd love to live close to the park or on the creek somewhere. I remember all that land around there and the tanks where I went fishing as a kid. What a life!
>
> Something happened here to keep us from seeing Terry before he died, but he was a Christian. Three guys here tried to escape coming back from a bench warrant and that locked us down for a bit. Now this stabbing and we got heat all over the place. But tomorrow is a new day and we will head out on another journey on the Row here. I'll keep you tuned on it.
> —Donnie

May 15, 1997

I just got in from playing some handball and doing some leg

squats. Been a busy day here. I got up this morning and JC and I went to the factory [prison garment factory] to take care of some business and then came back as fast as we could before count.

We were trying to get down today to see Cliff. The captain came by and we told him we needed to get down and pray with Cliff. He said he didn't have enough people. I was let down. But JC stood his ground and said, God's gonna make a way for us, just wait and see. Sure enough He did. An officer came by and said, You guys ready? We went and old Cliff was waiting on us and happy to see us. We talked and read the Bible and laughed and prayed and then he got a visit with his folks. But we'll get back down there tomorrow and see him again. He is in good spirits. He has come a long way in his walk with the Lord and it amazes me. But it is still hard on me to see him go.

They will get three more on Monday, Tuesday, and Wednesday. We'll go see them all. I know them all and one I am worried about. I'll just have to ask him out front on how he sees God. I've known him for a long time and he knows he's gone this time.

I'm amazed how the doors are opening up for us. And the captain is supporting us in this. I think even he is moving closer to the Lord. But I know he is in something great now and it's wearing him down. I will write him a letter tonight and pray for him.

Annie, I can't even begin to tell you how this killing is affecting everyone here. Some bosses are even sad. A nurse cried this morning and shook Cliff's hand. I can see this weighing heavy on most that believe in God. But still we have to do what we're doing and see these guys off. Who are we to be witnessing to the men with execution dates? But if God didn't want this to happen, it wouldn't, right?

There really is a handful here that care about us. But not all the bosses are sad. Some clap and rejoice that one is going to die. Going to always be that way I guess.

Annie, I need the last book of The Zion Chronicles series (The Key to Zion), and another copy of Within Heaven's Gates. Dave Herman took the last one. —Donnie

May 25, 1997

Donnie wrote:

I sat here and thought about all this, Annie. I want to run out and get something going and make something happen on my case, but maybe things happen just the way they are supposed to. I'm sure Craig and the lawyers are just like us, waitin on the judge to rule on my case. It really is doomsday for most all.

I just mainly want you and the family there to know what is going on with me and my case. I try to tell Dad but he doesn't seem to comprehend it all. Maybe he does but knows there is nothing that they can do about it.

Anyway, all the lawyers in the world couldn't stop God and what he wants in my life. I just want what God wants. Calling the lawyers and keeping up with all this here is not wrong. I think it is good that they know I have a family that loves me. But if I am going to die here, then I'll just have to get ready for that.

It has been a trying week for me. I got to spend time with the guys they killed. It was sad, and then again it wasn't. I can't explain it, but I'm trying. After they killed Cliff. Then it was Lackey. We got to pray and talk a while, but he was scared.

As for Bruce, he had the hardest time. He fought it all the way. Looking for a stay from man and those lawyers. He wasn't looking to God at all. He was scared to death and fought the drugs hard on the table.

Larry was a hard one. I stayed with him all morning for two

days. He never read his Bible and didn't know the first thing about God. But he was saved. He was so scared. I had to tell him what was going to happen after he died. It helped him too. He didn't know what to expect. JC prayed a lot and we read in Revelations to him. JC would read out loud and Larry shaved and got ready to go. JC stopped reading once and Larry told him to please not stop reading. So I watched him shave and JC kept reading. We prayed and then he was gone.

Larry told me one thing that got me. He said the VA people came down and told him he would not be buried with an X and his number. He would have a plaque, bronze on his grave. He was a Vietnam Vet. He also asked that he be buried in a cowboy shirt and hat and they assured him that he would get that. He was happy about it all. Then he told me he hoped that he could walk that last twenty feet to the table. He was afraid he would have to be carried. I cried on that one.

Now I am gearing up for Harris. I haven't been able to get over there. But I hollered at him and he knows we're coming. I've got to take him a few things. He's an old enemy of mine too. We have fought before, but after, we were fine.

Annie, no one is there, now. That is what gets me in all this. We don't get to see these guys until they get a date to die. They tell us we're the only ones there for them. I just tell them that God is always there for them and caring is all I can do.

Lil Jr. is up for next Wednesday, so we've got to see him. He has a strange belief. It's like talking to a happy demon. Hopefully he'll change and see things the way he is supposed to. He leans on people and soon he'll see that he is all alone. That's when the door will open. Pray that I can be there and God can use me to tell him the right things.

There is a guy here. He is a TDCJ spokesman. He comes over here with reporters and keeps an eye on everyone and what they do and say. I have got to know him good over the past year. I holler at him all the time and pull him over and pump him for info on the executions. He thinks I'm a wild man and crazy and bold. I say what I want and what's on my mind. But he likes me and he comes to me when he is here. But if my time gets close and you need to know anything, call him and tell him who you are. And I have a feeling that you will be talking to him one day. He's a pretty good guy, business and a company guy, but a good guy. I mess with him and get him in all the trouble I can when he's here. Smile.

As for all this stuff on my case, I don't want anyone out there trying to save me. I guess this is my way of saying that we'll let God do as he pleases in my life. I want to think God is going to free me from this place one day, but I see what's going on around me and it's not good.

I'll get you a new list of dates soon. Thank you for caring about us all here. I couldn't make it without knowing that you and the family and Dad and Glenda love and care about me. Also, save this letter and envelope. Larry gave me his Bible, this envelope, and a stamp. He didn't have anything. He wanted me to have it, and they mean a lot to me. I was looking at his Bible and it has Joe Lane's name in it and Gentry's and then Larry's. I'll add mine to the list and pass it on down the line. I have a good Open Bible. They are the best.

I hope Sandy and you are still walking together. Never stop that. I think if I was out I'd do my praying walking in the park there down by the creek. I could talk out loud and just let God talk to me. Maybe for once I would listen. And of course I'd have a dog. Smile. —Donnie

May 28, 1997

Jr. has a date this evening and he's already gone to the Wall's

Unit. JC and I got to go over and talk to him yesterday. I guess you have to know a little about Jr. Like I said, he has always had this strange belief. He says he believes in God, but I'm not sure. Anyway, he was saying he was going to get a stay and his lawyers told him that they filed some stuff and went back in the State Court. I knew right then what time it was. You can't go back into any court after you come out of the Supreme Court. He has been out of that now for two years.

JC prayed with him, and he was so confident about the stay [of execution]. I just looked at him and asked, but what if you don't? He just knew he would. I finally said that God has a will and I prayed for God's will and all Christians should pray that way. But I was so mad at his lawyers for telling him all that about a stay.

Lots going on about guys in death watch calling for JC and me to come over there. Some of the bosses don't like it. But the captain here runs this place, not them. I knew there must be a reason for not getting back over there to see Jr., so I'll accept that and will pray that Jr. is getting it together. I pray God will send someone to tell him more.

Also, Harris was glad to see us and pray. He was happy, but scared. I can't get over how people change when it is their time.
—Donnie

June 5, 1997

Donnie wrote:

It's been a hard few days here, four people dead in three days. They'll start again on the 11th. That's Duke's date. I was setting here thinking about him. I guess all of us here sound like terrible people to everyone out there in the world. But I know Duke. He is very close to God, so he is ready to go home. But I'll really miss him. He was my neighbor.

I was talking to Lasada the day he was going to die. He said he got a card from you and he was happy. Thank you Annie, for doing that. I still have the very first letter you wrote me. And the bookmarker (Footprints in the Sand) you sent, too.

I almost got into trouble today, but thank goodness just as it happened I got a visit from Dad and Diane, and it was great timing. I'll tell you about that next time we visit. They laughed about it.

I have got the last book of the Chronicles series. It is going to be a good ending. I love the characters. I've laughed and cried with them through it all. Some characters in these books have been my friends. I hope I don't sound stupid. I've got no life, Annie. Smile.

I'm having a picture drawn right now. My new cellie is doing it for me. I already drew up the plans for it. It's not something that you'd hang in your living room, maybe not even in your garage. Smile. It is a picture of my life story in many ways. I wanted you to have it to keep after I'm gone. Simple really, but I'll make it as nice as I can. —Donnie

In the drawing, Donnie's life-portrait begins from left to right with a back-view of him in handcuffs wearing a Brazos River Bandoleros Club jacket. As the drawing progresses to the right it depicts an armadillo…a woman…a human skeleton…then a helicopter. One large human skull with 'Vietnam' written across the forehead centers the drawing. Also representing his time spent in Vietnam are the 101st Airborne emblem and a map of Vietnam. To the lower right in the drawing is a man on a Harley Chopper wearing faded jeans and no shirt with Nomad [meaning wanderer] tattooed across his chest. Riding behind him on the Harley is a full human skeleton holding onto the man with all four limbs. As Donnie's life unfolds in the drawing it depicts prison bars. Above a map of Texas stands the prison guard's watchtower at the Death Row Unit...more bars...the death chamber...the gurney and a clock. Finally, Jesus Crucified with the word "Grace" carved in a stone at the foot of the Cross. The drawing reveals the shedding of Christ's blood as it drips down from the cross over the names of our family illustrating God's free gift of grace for us, as well as all humankind. This brought to mind a favorite scripture:

"For God so loved the world that He gave His only begotten Son, that whosoever believes in Him should not perish; but have everlasting life" (John 3: 16).

June 7, 1997

Donnie wrote:

> I guess Duke is getting ready for the eleventh. I need to get over there to see him, but things aren't right yet for traveling these tombs.
>
> Blue's Mom died a few days ago and he was just told about it an hour ago, so I have been busy. I went out and talked to Duke's close friends and made sure they were alright, and then Blue got the bad news. And today trouble between a boss and JC. Satan is using this boss to try to destroy what God is doing here. And I went all the way out. Why? Because I get respect here and they listen to me when I talk. But it has been a bad day and I hate worse than anything to get gruff or rough. I used to not mind and I still don't if I know that is all that person understands. —Donnie

June 11, 1997

> They killed Duke tonight. I know this guy and he was very close to God.
>
> Stan got a stay and West got a thirty-day setoff.
>
> I forgot to tell you, but I shaved my head before they executed

the last four. I hadn't had a haircut in three months and I was looking like Dad's dog, Kramer. I always have been ugly and this isn't helping matters. But these kinds of things don't bother me anymore. —Donnie

June 17, 1997

Donnie wrote:

There for a bit I was kind of screwed up mentally with all the executions. For some that I am real close to. I get where I don't know what to say when I look at them. I've always liked to look people in the eyes when I talk to them here. The eyes always tell me something about a person. They say they are the windows to their soul.

Funny how you was talking about shaking the dust off my feet and going on when someone won't listen. That's kind of what we had to do with Stoker and Eddie. JC sent Eddie a letter and really talked to him about God, but he didn't believe in God.

JC and I didn't see Stoker. JC and I knew at one time he was close to God, and he just changed. Got real bitter. We figured during these last days that he'd get it together. Stoker did ask Jack Wilcox [minister] to come see him and be his spiritual advisor, so we left that one in God's hands.

I got some news articles [on executions] I have been saving. Glenda sends these to me. I read them and all about their crimes. I think back on all the wars I've been in with other bike clubs and I tell you Annie, I may have done some rough things out there from time to time and I lived outside the laws or most of them I guess. But still in some self-righteous way I guess I believe I'm better than some here because of their crimes.

They say I belong here and I look at my life and think, yes, I am supposed to be here. If it wasn't for this case it would be another one in time. Just the lifestyle I've lived. But none of that adds up to rape and crimes on kids. It's hard for me to talk to some or even be around them because of the way I believe. But I'm in the same place as they are. —Donnie

June 24, 1997

I'm worried about JC. He may be hearing something on his case, and it's not good. It is a long story, but he admitted his crime and says he deserves to die. He was on 60 Minutes a while back. He knows his time is coming. Just keep him in your prayers. He'll die here one day because he admitted what he did. But just ask God to prolong it or lose his papers or anything to keep him here to do God's work. —Donnie

June 27, 1997

Donnie wrote:

Thank you and the church again for your prayers. I know God has looked after me because of them. I look at those prayer slips like get out of jail free cards. Too bad I can't tell you about some of the things I get into at times. Please don't stop praying for me.

I've really been struggling, and at times I just can't do anything right as for walking right and in God's Word.

I was convicted because I'm a bad guy in general. But I tell you that a lot of the early trouble I was in wasn't me at all. I actually got three years probation for something I didn't do. I don't want you to be in the dark about the things that I have done while I was on the streets. I'm not proud of it now, but then it was my life and it was a rough game. You need to know and I feel comfortable talking to you. As I said, I was headed here anyway. I need to sit down and write about some of the things I have done. I played some real serious games on the street with some very serious people and got into some real serious things.

Like many other times, Donnie talked and I listened. Jesus knew Donnie was burdened by his sins and situations, that's why He said, "Come to me, all you who labor, and are heavy laden, and I will give you rest" (Matt 11:28). As Donnie continued to focus on others instead of himself, he was more open to being used by the Lord.

"Come to me, all you who labor, and are heavy laden, and I will give you rest"
(Matthew 11:28)

Chapter 7

Saying Good-bye to JC

"There will be no more appeals for JC"

July 7, 1997

*D*onnie wrote:

I always felt misplaced or not really belonging where I was and I've always wondered why for so many years. I think it is the knowing you have been given away, and that the parents you have aren't your real parents that plays a serious role. No one ever knew the thoughts or feelings I had about it all.

Only my sisters Lisa and Mary and I talked, but it was always a dead end. I'd go home after seeing them and was always haunted by hundreds of questions, but there never was anyone to talk to about it.

Annie, if any of the family are ever through southeastern Oklahoma, do you think they would stop at my real mom's bar? I was just wondering if they could just go in, maybe talk to her and just see what she is like.

I have just been thinking about my family there in Oklahoma. They cared about me for a while. Things just got out of whack. They were there for my hearing and I was proud of them. But people just last a little while. They get tired and I become a burden to them and they just go away. I'd give anything if I were out of here. I'd just go up to them and look them in their eyes and tell them I love them and then leave. Then I'd go back and stay in the life God intended me to be in. I can't help it, Annie. Every now and then it just gets me down. I've got to break away from that.

Half my life has been around dying people it seems, Vietnam and now here. One thing about it, death is a certain thing in everybody's life. We all got a date to die. But lately I've just really been thinking about my life and all. I try Annie, but sometimes I wonder if any of what I tell you makes any sense at all?

I was lying in bed two nights ago and all of a sudden I had this guy here on my mind. West. He's got a date to die this month. But I dropped it cause he is not one of my favorite people. But again he came to my mind. I knew I was to get up and write this guy a letter; so I did. I prayed about it too and asked God to give me the words to say. JC read it and said it was good and he wrote him one too, so we'll see what happens. Tough case here with West. But what I told him will give him plenty to think about. All macho stuff aside, I told him and much more. He may call on us and if he does we're going to him.

Annie, could you look up my real dad in the Oklahoma City phone book; see if he is in there. I was just curious." —Donnie

My daughter Sandy brought home a phonebook from her work. I made a couple of calls to people in the city that I thought might possibly help me to locate Donnie's dad. The lady confirmed that the man in question did have a son in prison, but the man had died two years before. Almost certain this was his biological dad from the information I had heard on the phone, I ordered a copy of the death certificate and sent it to Donnie.

July 20, 1997

Donnie replied:

I want to thank you for the information about my dad. It played on me some there for a bit, and maybe you are right about it being normal for me to wonder about my real mom and dad and the rest of the family. I prayed about it and ask that it happen, and it did. But it has just not been what I thought. I guess it is not meant to be. I won't do anything else on this. It had just been bugging me for years. I didn't want to say anything to Cliff cause I didn't want to hurt him. But yes, Cliff is my real dad and the only one I ever knew. Now I can deal with it and end it. In my heart I have changed about it all. I had to. I block more than you would ever be able to imagine, just to survive and keep my sanity in here. I know I am cold in a lot of ways, but God will make me right in time.

One thing I remember so well about my life is when we lived on that farm out by Corum, near Comanche. That was my domain, Annie. I had it all. I had my tanks [ponds], my own creek, and fishin hole. I had cows and chickens and pigeons. I had all the animals a kid could have there. I even had my own mulberry tree. I practically lived in that thing. We had a giant garden every year, too. I pray heaven is like that, Annie.

JC and I are going down to see West Saturday and Sunday. We'll set up to paint in the day room while they are locked down for the weekend and spend some time with him. He got that thirty-day stay, but his time is coming up again. He is doing better. He was happy about the letters JC and I wrote him. He just didn't expect them. But he has been talking about the Lord to some officers. He must be changing, huh? —Donnie

July 29, 1997

Tonight is West's date and in about thirty minutes he'll be dead. He never called us. I know that the chaplain over there will be with him and I feel good about that. That's Chaplain Brazzil. Remember? I sent you an article about him. Please send me back a copy of that. The captain and a few other bosses are asking about this guy. —Donnie

July 30, 1997

Donnie wrote:

Another day. JC got a phone call from his lawyers today. They told him that his case in the fifth circuit had been kicked out and affirmed, so this ruins a good day. They will set a date on him now and kill him. Annie, I'm asking you to pray that JC not get a date and God uses him more. I'm just not ready for this at all. Maybe God will make a miracle happen here. There will be no more appeals for JC. He told his lawyers to file nothing else at all. Also, JC may move into my cell until he has to go to lockup. I can tell you now that everything has changed in just a matter of hours for him and me. JC is my friend. I can talk to JC about anything. I can't help but wonder why God is allowing this to happen. I guess I just don't want to lose my friend, Annie. —Donnie

In an article by Chuck Colson, "Exchanging Lies for the Truth, The Johnny Cockrum Story,"[1] Colson wrote how Johnny (JC) Cockrum received the death penalty after being convicted in the 1986 murder of a convenience store clerk. Then in 1990, his bitterness and anger towards the man whose testimony had convicted him drove him to stab a fellow inmate. The stabbing sent Cockrum to lockdown, where he realized he could no longer endure what he called the monster and hate that controlled his life. He cried out to God for forgiveness and accepted Jesus Christ into his life as his personal Lord and Savior. In his work, All of Grace, C.H. Spurgeon wrote, "Our Lord Jesus did not die for imaginary sins, but His heart's blood was spilled to wash out deep crimson stains which nothing else can remove."[2] The bible tells us, "For whosoever calls upon the name of the Lord will be saved" (Romans 10:13). Although Donnie had not seriously thought about dropping his court appeals, God had set him on a path that would change the direction he would take in his own life.

JC Cockrum was forgiven, and he began the legal battle for the right to drop his appeals, which meant he would be executed for his crime. As a Christian, JC believed he had to tell the truth about his crimes.

JC explained that he had to choose between going along with his attorneys, which meant continuing to lie or to totally trust God and tell the truth, even if it meant that he would die. So JC Cockrum was at this point in his life on August 4, 1997, expecting his execution date to be set at any time.

August 4, 1997

> Annie, I think it would be a blessing for you to meet JC personally. Right now I am reading a book he wrote on his life story. It takes all I got to keep the tears from my eyes when I look at him and hear him talk about God and his life. He says he has got questions he wants to ask the Lord. Smile.
>
> I bet Dave Herman will be waiting on the shores of heaven for JC, and me, when my time comes. Jesus has probably already told him and all of JC's loved ones to prepare for him.
>
> There is just a lot to JC and his life, Annie. He and I talked to the sergeant this morning and she began to move him right into my cell. So we have been moving him all-day and got him settled in. A minister, Jack Wilcox came to see him, too.
>
> Annie, JC may be the one dying, but it is me that God is working on. But I have so far to go in my walk with the Lord.
>
> I know that God is saying, now Donnie, I want all of you. Put yourself aside.
>
> Annie, you know I want to do right, but how can I with all I am into? —Donnie

I recalled Donnie mentioning that he needed to give up his club patch. That meant getting out of the club, which is not as easy as it might sound.

It is very hard for us in the free world to see exactly what all might be involved when a man on Death Row makes a decision to live for Christ. Donnie knew the image he had portrayed in the past was far from that. Remember that he is still a confirmed member of the Brazos River Bandoleros Club with their own set of by-laws, even on Texas Death Row. The bible reminds us, "I form the light and create darkness. I make peace and create calamity; I, the Lord, do all these things" (Isaiah 45:7). I reminded Donnie that God is with us in the darkest of times.

Continuing in his letter of August 4, Donnie wrote:

> Speaking of my human feelings, I finally figured out that these last few years that I have just layed down and depended on self. I distanced myself from God. I always went to Glenda to find out what God was saying to me. I could have been hearing from God myself if I had been in His Word. I mean look where I'm at, Annie. I can't even pass the smallest test that comes my way 90% of the time. —Donnie

August 8, 1997

> JC, the country boy. He and I are making a box for his daughter, but he is just not too crafty. Smile. I showed him how to make the flowers for the lid that I do with the wood and he likes that.
>
> We are spending some quality time together. He really loves God. He gets up early to study his Bible and pray. He studies more and then prays some more. He's always praying. I hope we can all have a visit together soon. Just knowing that people care helps a lot, believe me. We are expecting his date to be set soon. —Donnie

August 19, 1997

> A lot is going on here. JC is having a hard time. We have to stop and pray, and read, and cry some. The Holy Spirit calms us if we let Him.
>
> JC is going to go witness to some guys that God has laid on his heart to talk to. He doesn't want to leave the house [cell], but he knows he's got to go.
>
> Satan has done everything he can to get at JC and me, on an individual basis too. I want to sit and write you about what's going on, but I feel at times the things that happen to me are my problems and I have to walk them alone. I am in the battle of trying to give them to God and let Him handle it all, but that is so hard. Trust me when I tell you I am trying to please God and do the right things.
>
> I want to know who I am in Christ. That alone covers a lot of ground, important things to me that I am trying to leave alone and change in my life. In some ways I've seen that it is what God is telling me to do, but I just can't seem to do it. I see from past events where God just changed something in my life and I was relieved of it. I guess I just want God to do it all.
>
> Do you know what it is like to wear a patch on your back and be a part of something and not be able to get out? Just know it is not an easy thing for me now. I need my faith and belief to kick in. —Donnie

I realized at this point that Donnie was saying that as a Christian there were things in his life that he was going to have to set aside. He was very close to God for years after crying out to God in that shower at the Parker County Jail years before. But like Donnie said, "I have just laid down and depended on self."

As Donnie began praying and seeking God more, God began to work in his heart to bring about changes in his life. I was praying for Donnie, and God and I had many serious discussions concerning Donnie; I prayed if he were innocent, he would not have to die for this crime. Early in our correspondence, I made it clear to Donnie that though it was not always easy, it was always safe to pray for God's will for our lives. I told him that no one loves him as much as God loves him.

August 27, 1997

> Donnie wrote:
>
> JC is going through some mental things now, because of what is happening to him. I know this, when he is gone I will truly miss him. All this has to be for a reason and I am trying as best I can to catch on. God is preparing me for something, but when it happens I'll be by myself here. I know that I have no friends here. Some of my brothers are upset with me. I know that God has laid some of these guys on my heart to witness to, but I also know that they are going to have to see the change in me before it will ever affect them. But I am changing Annie, and if I have to leave them all I will. I care about them very much, and it hurts me. I feel alone, so alone at times. God had to know that I was serious about changing, and that I'd put Him first. —Donnie

I wrote Donnie the scripture, "For we do not have a High Priest who cannot sympathize with our weaknesses, but was in all points tempted as we are, yet without sin. Let us therefore come boldly to the throne of grace, that we may obtain mercy and find help in time of need" (Hebrews 4:15-16).

August 28, 1997

> Donnie wrote:
>
> I'm glad you liked the story I wrote about the little child. I still carry that around inside of me. What I feel at times is overwhelming for the children. Can you imagine all the children

in the world that has been born and wasn't wanted at all? And what about the ones that never had a chance to be born? It about kills me when I think of it or hear of it. I have been on my knees many times for those children. These are the things that make me not want to be a part of this world at all. Makes dying easier.

Gunter hung himself Sunday. JC and I knew him well. Sad.

JC goes tomorrow to get his date set. I think it will be within the next thirty-two days. He is hoping to get a contact visit with his mom and sister and daughter. He is happy and he knows that if that happens he has already had his prayer answered. We really have no other thought at this time than JC is about to meet his Maker. He said he actually got a little excited when his lawyer told him the news. But pray that he will get to stay over here for at least two more weeks or until he dies. He wants it and I know God is going to be talking to us two bucket-heads. Smile. Every time I turn around, he's on his knees praying. We've got a few specific times to pray and then there are those 'have to' moments when you are trying not to knock anyone out. It just kind of ruins the moment when you have to do that. I may sound hard to you, Annie, but here you don't tell on people; you just pay your debts and mind your own business.

On Aug. 29, Donnie wrote:

JC has been sitting here for a few days now during our piddling time working on a box. He said, 'This one's for Annie.' Hear me now, JC is not a good piddler. Just my opinion, but he loves doing it, and he makes all kinds of things. We made things for all his family. But I didn't help him on this box and you will treasure it forever. —Donnie

Author's Note: I picked up the box before leaving the Death Row unit, and I do treasure the box; it is displayed in my home among the many items I have received from Donnie and other death row inmates.

September 8, 1997

Donnie wrote:

Davis has a date tomorrow and I hope I get to see him in the morning. I hope he is saved. Maybe he will call JC and me out in the morning. I'll let you know.

There has been so much harassment going on here lately. Just makes the time hard for everyone. Football season is beginning so maybe some will get into that. Watching it seems to give them something to do, but then there are always people that gamble and cause trouble.

Well, they brought a paper in here this morning saying JC must be classified, so he will be moving on Thursday. To see him now I will have to go over there and paint like he and I have been doing for the others. —Donnie

September 9, 1997

I guess Davis is dead. I found out that he believes in reincarnation and thinks he will be coming back as someone else again. How very sad that is.

They moved JC Friday. So I have been just sitting here in this big old house [cell] all by myself. But I got the poster and the Sturgis Paper and the book Saga of the Sierras. That gave me something to do. I sat down last night just to read a chapter or two and now I'm halfway through. I've had comments from people who watch others for a hobby tell me, 'Someone out there really loves Armadillo!' I just smile and say, 'Yeah, my family loves me.' I am truly blessed, Annie. Thank everyone for all they do for me. —Donnie

September 17, 1997

> Dying is hard the way it happens here, Annie. I mean they kill you here; you don't just die.
>
> There are some problems here with one of the club brother, but I am going to leave it all alone for now. There are rules that say you don't mess over a brother, ever. I live by those rules and I expect my brothers to. Hey Annie, my world is so much different than out there. I see things here and live here the hard way, and I try to keep my sanity and still be a responsible person. I haven't changed that much in my ways; I just walk on different roads. But you know God has a strange way of doing things that just blows me away at times. I have to sit and think why it happened and try to make some sense of things. Once I see it I know God is showing me and curing something in me. Like I'm not angry anymore.
>
> Would you give this little religious tract to Cassie [Author's granddaughter]. She always draws something on her prayer slips to me. Smile. —Donnie

Sept. 25, 1997

> Last night they came in and tore nineteen wing up bad. They had lost a metal spoon off the chow cart and they were looking for that. Also, two gang guys on the program here got another guy. And another guy I know beat another one here that is a snitch. So now they are all locked up. The bummer was, they had all our water turned off for most of the night. —Donnie

September 29, 1997

The day before JC was to be executed, Cliff [Donnie's adoptive father] and I spent some time visiting with Donnie, and then I spoke to the warden's secretary about visiting JC, who was already in his cage in the opposite visiting area. JC and I had written a number of times since he and Donnie had become friends. Seldom did TDCJ allow a visitor to go from one inmate to another. But some allowances were made because of JC's execution the following day. They told me I could visit until his attorney arrived. Cliff spent more time with Donnie while JC and I visited. As the guards led Donnie from the visiting area, he stopped for a moment behind JC's cage and told him he loved him. Afterwards JC turned to me and said, "I love Stoney deeply and spiritually in one with the Lord. The Lord blessed Stoney and me in allowing us to come together in my last days. God allowed me time in my life to come to know Jesus Christ as my personal Lord and Savior. He took me, a worthless sinner, and gave me the heart of a saint. I feel sure, Annie, that God has given me the greatest gift He can give to His children, 'Absent from the body, and to be present with the Lord.'"(2 Corinthians 5:8).

Before JC was executed he wrote, "God kept me for four years after I dropped my appeals and I never understood the reason until this year. Now it's Stoney's time. God will do great things through him. I know this in my heart."

Before his attorney came, JC and I prayed together. I told him I loved him. And though I left somewhat saddened, I felt deeply blessed to have known Johnny Cockrum.

JC Cockrum was executed and went to be with the Lord the following day, September 30, 1997.

Chapter 8

A Difficult Time

"These walls are closing in on me"

October 5, 1997

*D*onnie wrote:

It's killer hot here. It's weird for it to be so hot this time of the year. More signs of the time, I guess.

The Star Telegram and the San Antonio Express were here on the Row taking pictures yesterday. They took some of Blue and me playing handball in our tattoos [no shirt]. One day you'll see my tattoos, Annie. You probably won't like them either. But I guess they're here to stay. —Donnie

After JC's execution came one of the more difficult periods of Donnie's life since our re-acquaintance. Donnie's attitude and spirits seem to go steadily down hill.

Although he chose not to involve me with the details, Donnie wrote, "JC broke some codes here that you just don't do with the brothers. It made me look bad and that's what got me, but they say pride is the last to go, right? It's just something we went through. It bugs me too, cause I'm sure I didn't handle it like I should have. I feel like a real loser at times and I just want to die.

I sent Donnie the scripture, "Trust in the Lord with all your heart. And lean not on your own understanding; in all your ways acknowledge Him, and He shall direct your path" (Proverbs 3:5-6).

Donnie responded:

Annie, I know that no matter what goes on I should be able to keep at a steady pace with the Lord, but it seems I can't. I don't want to be a burden, but remember just hearing from the family up there has helped me so much. Maybe you can't understand it, but having family that care means life or death to ones in here in this position. Just stand with me till my time comes. We'll make it with God's help. It was a joy to pray with you. And you are right about the moments on the mountain. It seems we are made for the valleys. I guess we learn more there.

We hear these comedians laughing and making jokes about executions, but it's sad really, because they leave out all the pain and suffering and every human emotion that one goes through in it. And they do forget that we all have a date to die.
—Donnie

October 19, 1997

Always shakedowns, fights and bosses getting told on for doing this or that and then bosses snitching on other bosses. I never know what is going to happen next.

There was a fight with a stabbing of the dude that snitched on a boss. There is never any peace and quiet, constant hollering. I am not in a good mood at all. I just would like to be human again. I'm thinking I'd like to get on the way out of here soon.

It's been raining here all day. The sun comes out and then it rains some more. Now they say a tornado alert is out. Hey, every time it rains I go out and I can only hope that lightning strikes me, but no such luck. I am just down. I have tried to pray and I can't get focused or stay with it. You know you get that unworthy feeling as always. I remember to pray about something when I get half way through taking care of it myself.
—Donnie

November 18, 1997

Donnie wrote:

Tomorrow they will kill Sharp. He is an old friend. There used to be a group of us. Now only two left. I have got to go see him. He has been a stable Christian for a long time now. He thinks he will get a stay, but I don't think so.

You know prayer is hard to do at times. I know we have God's Word and Promises, but still we falter and fall. I set here and stare at the walls for hours. I'm empty, Annie. I know Dad loves me, but the rest of the family, I don't even know them anymore. I am very blessed to have you all there caring and loving me. People who know me tell me I am so lucky to have family and it really is all so wonderful, but it's like a dream. All I can do is dream of being with you all.

Annie, it's not a sad thing dying; and going home to be with Jesus is our goal. Just getting there is the hard part. I've had dreams of dying like this. I've had fear too, but the fear is worldly fear. I just want to close my eyes and go to sleep forever. And I'll not talk or argue this with anyone but you, and I expect you to back me all the way in this. I knew when you came into my life you would be the friend I'd tell everything to. You would get to know me and let the family know who I am. I have been here so long that I feel lost at times and it's important to me that my family there knows me.

Hey listen, Cous, keep me in your prayers. There have been some problems here and all I can tell you is I'm trying very hard not to get into trouble. I am going through a few things and there is a couple that may have to be dealt with. But if I do, don't get all worried. Just something I may have to do. There are times when one stops holding back. I love you're preaching to me, too. It helps at decision times like this.

Trust in the Lord with all your heart and lean not on your own understanding; in all your ways acknowledge Him and He will direct your paths.' I'm trying, Cous. —Donnie

January 1998

You asked if God was waiting on me to do something? I had to sit a long time, and it turned into days on this one, Annie. I'm sure He is.

I have a couple of other things I wish we could talk about. But I will still be in the middle of it when I see you I'm sure. Yes, I'm sure God is waiting on me but I'll never make it. I'll never be what God wants me to be in here. I try to do right, then wrong, and then I usually do what I want to do. I'm very selfish, but I do fear God believe me. And I am trying to use a bit of wisdom here. Hope comes in so many ways.

I am glad you harp on things with me. I depend on you to tell me the truth in everything and anything. I'm the dummy here and I reckon you get to be the teacher. But if you only knew how stupid I am at times. I'm like having a dog with no legs, and you get to do everything for me. —Donnie

As serious as I knew Donnie was, I could not help but smile at his ways of expressing himself at times.

He wrote: "Everything is so screwed up now that I don't even want to breathe, but it just comes natural."

February 1998

Donnie wrote:

All this on Karla Faye Tucker was terrible. All the hate I saw on that messed with me some. What sense did it make to kill her? None at all! But we know where she is, don't we? I'm not saying it is wrong to have the death penalty, but some cases are worth at least taking a second look at. —Donnie

On February 3, 1998, Karla Faye Tucker became the first woman executed in Texas in over one hundred years. While waiting trial, Karla gave her life to Jesus Christ and during her trial confessed to the brutal murders she had committed. During her fourteen years on Texas Death Row Karla Faye Tucker became an ambassador for Christ, proving once again that God offers forgiveness and redemption to all.

"I will give you a new heart and put a new spirit within you; I will take away the heart of stone out of your flesh and give you a heart of flesh" (Ezekiel 36:26).

In *All of Grace*, the bold Christian preacher, Charles Spurgeon wrote, "Did you think that salvation was for the good and that God's grace was for the pure and holy who are free from sin?"[1] When Christians pray, the Holy Spirit of God will bring to our minds things in our lives that need to be dealt with or changed. Donnie knew he needed to choose to make some changes in order to be an effective Christian witness to others. But, these changes would affect the image he felt he needed to survive on Death Row. Sometimes when Christians are unwilling to make changes in certain areas of their lives, they often avoid conversations with God concerning these changes. Some might ignore those subjects or stop praying altogether. Donnie was still relying on his own strength instead of relying on God for strength to make those changes.

April 1, 1998

As things went from bad to worse, Donnie was sent to solitary confinement for testing positive for marijuana through a urinalysis, but they also charged him with possession of a controlled substance in a penal institution when they found a kidney stone on his top bunk that was thought to be cocaine. It was sent to DPS Lab in Houston for testing.

May 7, 1998

> Donnie wrote:
>
> Day 37 of solitary confinement with no privileges. I woke up this morning and my kidneys hurt. Please Lord, I don't want to pass a kidney stone now. —Donnie

May 15, 1998

> After 45 days confinement, Whitehead [investigator of TDCJ internal affairs] came to my cell and told me that the test from DPS lab in Houston came back negative. He wanted your number and the lawyers number too. So now I'm no longer considered a 'Crackhead.' Thank you Jesus! —Donnie

On May 15, Whitehead did call me and tell me that Donnie's lab test came back negative. Donnie had written about passing kidney stones prior to this and had saved them from time to time. Even on Death Row it was important to Donnie to get this off his record. He received the paperwork dated January 5, 1999, officially dismissing the charges and he sent them on to me.

Aside from the solitary, Donnie learned that his best friend, Blue, had cancer. By this time, he felt God was totally against him. In his frustration he wrote, "Don't talk to me about God, Annie, cause I can't tell He's doing anything here."

I wrote Donnie, "The Lord is the very best I have to offer you. He is your only hope, no matter what, now or in the future."

Evidently, Donnie had also told his friend, Glenda, to not talk to him about God.

Glenda replied to his comment, "How can I not talk to you about God?"

Donnie wrote back:

> I know I should never have said anything like that to anyone. It was wrong. I just get that way at times here. God has His

way of making me the fool, believe me. I know you are going to talk to me about God. Annie, I can pray for you and others and believe God will answer my prayers and He does, but I can't pray for myself. —Donnie

Donnie had spent the better part of his life working at being strong physically. But after 45 days solitary confinement and discovering that his best friend had cancer, Donnie was facing problems that human strength could not affect. When we cease to struggle against that which we cannot control in our own strength, are we able to stop relying on ourselves and draw on the supernatural strength of God. Often it is only at our lowest points in life that we can finally submit our will totally to God and it would not happen for Donnie for some time yet.

The Apostle Paul wrote, "I can do all things through Christ who strengthens me" (Philippians 4:13).

How very real this truth would become to Donnie in time.

May 7, 1998

Donnie wrote:

I really need to put my finger in the wounds of Jesus, Annie. I can't do this time any other way. If discernment and exhortation are spiritual gifts, then I have those. I can tell the kind of man I'm around and I can help another believer to have hope, but it doesn't work for me. There really are people like that, you know? I've read about them and I guess I am one of them. I really am losing it. I need to get out of this cell. These walls are closing in on me.

Annie, please pray for Blue. They've had to pull some teeth and they are saying they may have to cut part of his tongue out, but Blue said, no way! If treatments don't work, forget it.' He told me he is reading his Bible, too. —Donnie

May 17, 1998

Donnie wrote:

I know this guy that comes here and sprays for bugs every four months. A big guy and he always comes to talk to me. He knows a club brother of mine. We talk about this and that. But the other day he said, You know I'm a Christian don't you? I said, Cool, me too. The last time he was here he talked to me about God and I was so down. I told him that I just don't know anymore. But he talks and talks and he told me about this scripture. "It is the Spirit who gives life; the flesh profits nothing. The words that I speak to you are spirit" (John 6:63), and, "Let your conduct be without covetousness; be content with such things as you have. For He Himself said, "I will never leave you nor forsake you." (Hebrews 13:5).

I must be so hardheaded, Annie. It is not that I am going against God. I guess it may seem that way, but it is so hard living here. Hey, I wish I could throw these chains off and just run out the front door! —Donnie

July 2, 1998

It is killer hot here. If I were an old guy this heat would kill me. The water is even hot. I have to keep it poured over me just to breathe. I have a neighbor that is new here and he doesn't have a fan at all. And my other neighbor's fan went out on him. Maybe soon it will rain or something.

I got your letter and you didn't preach to me at all. I was disappointed too. You'll never know how much you all help me to stay in line and act right. Never, ever stop sharing with me what God shows you and tells you. Even if I say don't, still do. I hope I never say that again. I only have a few brain cells left. Smile. But I think, maybe God has restored a few of them for me though.

I thank God all the time for you all in my life and it is for a reason, I know.

Blue is back here now. But he looks so bad. I gave him my fan tonight cause someone stole his while he was gone. I just stayed awake. He was in real pain. I could feel his pain and it brought me to my knees for him. He told me he thought something spiritual had happened to him. I want you to send him one of those witness cards. They don't say it to him, but a nurse told me they didn't expect him to live. They burned his neck so bad with the radiation and it is worse on the inside. He can hardly swallow. He is two cells down from me and he can't holler at me. Blue is tough and he don't let a lot show, but he cried and I didn't know how to handle it. They are wrong. He is going to make it, right Annie?"

Blue doesn't need to be here. He needs to be in the hospital, but I don't want to let him go. I'm scared he'll die on me. He is my brother and the most trusted and loyal friend I have ever had within these walls and he is sick and needs a miracle. Just pray.
—Donnie

July 14, 1998

Please rain! I try to cool off with water and the water is hot.

My neighbor died on me. Poor guy didn't have a fan and he just died. He went to the hospital for a bad heat rash that everyone here has now. He came back and died. I wonder if he has family to come check and see why he died?

Makes me want to go off and do something stupid. This second shift has always been the hate squad. Annie, he was a little off, but he made me laugh all the time. Just a funny guy and I will miss him.

Proverbs 3:5, "Trust in the Lord with all your heart, and lean not on your own understanding." Maybe one day, Annie.

Donnie needed to trust the Lord for everything, especially in these difficult physical conditions; sometimes the Lord uses the most difficult time to turn us towards Himself and His will for our lives. Donnie was feeling much frustration and fear within those prison walls, but the Lord was changing his heart, day by day.

Chapter 9

A Struggle With Purpose

"...living in a closet"

September 2, 1998

Donnie sincerely believed that he was found guilty in his case and given the death sentence because of his background and violations of his rights during his trial. In his opinion, those rights that were violated should have resulted in suppression of the evidence that was used to convict him. Later at his competency hearing, Donnie's attorney spoke of how more than half of his trial was used in trying him in regards to a totally different crime in which Donnie admitted being involved but was not prosecuted at all. He believed the crime was used to poison the jury against Donnie.

In August 1998, my sister, Betty, and her daughter, Sherry, began writing Donnie also. Concerned that he was innocent in his case, Betty wrote Donnie that she had heard of a ministry that sometimes investigates questionable convictions. Donnie wrote the ministry but later was informed they would not be able to look into his case for reasons that he had a past record of offenses plus an escape on his record earlier in his life.

September 20, 1998

Donnie wrote:
> Cruz has a date to die. He only has ten days left. I didn't know him before he got moved over here. I told him about a lot of

things and that he needed to trust Jesus now and take care of all those things. He is going through a lot. He wanted to see his daughter real bad. And he finally got the visit. He came by here and was so happy. He is working hard to get some things made for his family before his time. I haven't looked at his crime at all. It's just that some affect me more than others. —Donnie

October 13, 1998

After a visit Donnie wrote:

I hated to see you all go today, Annie. You guys are the only church I have here. Only time I get to talk about God to anyone other than people that die. Well, I talk to my neighbor some about God but he is so off. He seems like a nice guy, but so misled. He killed his whole family, Annie, said God told him to. If God told me to do that, I'd know it wasn't God. Do you wonder why I want out of here? These people and this place are driving me.

I expect Gribble will be getting a date to die anytime now. If he does, then I'll be out of close friends. I think I'll just withdraw all the way from everything. —Donnie

October 16, 1998

I have been here so long I'm just numb. As you can see I haven't given it all to God. I'm running on self. Yes, I am God conscience, but I am not sure who I am in Christ. I can't remember a time when I have been this down. Doubt seems to be a major player in my life. I am just out of gas, Annie. JC's death made me set and think harder about dying. You know you get that unworthy feeling as always. But one thing comes to my mind always, and that's the thought that I can do something about all this about anytime I want to. —Donnie

Comparing his doubting to Christian author, Hannah Whitall

Smith in *A Christian's Secret to a Happy Life*[1] I wrote Donnie that he could not keep doubts from coming to him any more than he could prevent another inmate from swearing at him from another cell there in the prison. But he could refuse to listen to the one swearing at him, and he could also refuse to doubt. In her article, Smith wrote that the doubts are not a person's own doubts unless they accept them as his/her own. So I reminded Donnie to put his headphones on to block the noise that he so often spoke of on Death Row, get his Bible out, and begin renewing his mind in Christ.

Smith wrote that God knows about our weaknesses already, but in prayer we should tell Him anyway and ask Him to help us in this weakness of doubting. We must look away from ourselves, rely not on our own faithfulness, but on God's, 'the Author and Finisher of our faith' (Hebrews 12:2).

I reassured Donnie that if he had ever given his life to Jesus Christ then it was up to Christ to keep his salvation secure.

"Let us hold fast the confession of our hope without wavering, for He who promised is faithful" (Hebrews 10:23).

November 3, 1998

After reading the ministry's refusal to investigate his case, Donnie wrote:

> Annie, this will always be the way the world sees me. I wrote my lawyer last night and I had a talk with him. I want him to see about pushing my case harder and getting that federal judge to rule on my case and get me going here one way or the other. I told him I was tired and wore out. I really do want him to help me get this thing going.
>
> Annie, you and I talk all the time about this and I know that you guys want me to be tough and hang in there, lean on God, and see what happens. Well, I've been trying to do that but I have had my fill of this. And somewhere along the line here you

have got to know that I am tired and this is very hard on me. One day you are going to have to want what I want for me. I just want to go home. I don't say that for attention. I say that cause that is what I feel and want. I'm overloaded right now and I see no light at all.

    Annie, can you imagine setting in your closet for days, then weeks, then months, then years, and you can't go anywhere but there. That's it that's your life forever. You eat there, you sleep there, your life is that closet. If someone cares enough to come see you the guards come get you, take you out to see them. Then they're gone and you never know for sure if you'll ever see them again or not. Then they take you back to that closet. Could you do it? —Donnie

November 1998

    Annie, I know you must think I'm stupid at times from the things I say. But I tell you things and I'm really saying it to see if I'm wrong or right or see if I am normal. I'm just used to being wrong so much of the time. But God looks after me, if he didn't I'd be in trouble all the time. Thanks Annie for putting your self out there for me with these people here and this place. It makes a big difference if we have family checking on us. You remind me of Esther in the Old Testament. I'm sending you a picture of what I believe heaven may be like. Look at the trees, the river and the mountains. Of course there will be no darkness or shadows or dust there.

    I think I'll just sit here until my birds eat all that bread I put out there. They eat until about 6:30 or 7:00 and then roost. Neat to watch them. —Donnie

December 1998

    I guess you know by now about Martin Gurule escaping from Death Row. The Texas Monthly is doing a story on him now and they heard that we were friends. They want me to answer some questions. Like, did he ever talk about escaping? All I can tell them is we were friends. We just got separated somewhere down the line. I really liked Martin. He was a good workout partner too. They said he drowned after escaping, but I don't know what to believe. But I believe the boy was a survivor.

Because of the escape we had a major shakedown yesterday. It's been going on all week actually. We have been through the grind here. Man they tore this place up bad. But things are slowly getting back to normal if there is such a thing. The shakedown was all across the state in every prison. But please pray that they don't move us and discontinue the work program and the piddling program [crafts]. I know my problems are nothing compared to Sherry's cancer but it's a real problem for us here. —Donnie

January 5, 1999

Donnie wrote:

Yesterday a boss here refused me rec for a dumb reason. I wrote the guy up [filed a complaint]. But anyway, it's about 30 degrees in here and I'm waitin to go out. I'm dressed and the guy walks by my cell and I say I'm going out. He said I didn't have my shorts on. He has problems with people all the time. Creates chaos everywhere he goes. Can't do that with me. I told him to get someone down here. The sarge told the guy, Old Stone don't mess with anyone unless there is a good reason. And he left.

Then today I go out and a few of them act like they're afraid I'm going to jump on them or something, stepping real light around me. Hey, we got ten people in my group and I don't have but one friend. The rest I just get along with. But McGowan, a guy in my group came to me today. I asked, what's going on?

He's my bud and he tells me, Stone, man, people are scared of you. When you come in here people are just waiting to see what kind of mood you're going to be in. It hurt me Annie.

I know I push people to the side at times, but Roger said, Stoney, you don't want anyone getting close to you at all. And you know, he is right. But I didn't know it was that bad. I kind of demand some respect, but that's just being a man. I give it to get it. Pray for me that God will change that in me.

Craig and Alexa [attorneys] came to see me. They told me to tell you hello. Craig and I talked alone. He won't drop my appeals. But we talked about this place and my case and just things in life. It was a hard visit for me and I know it was for him. No one knows what to do. But I know. And I want to get out of here. He wants me to convince him about dropping my appeals, I think. He said he would go back and do some checking. He can't call the judge but he may call his attorneys and see where we are in this case as for the federal court. I realize I'm just one little drop in a monsoon rain, but I hope to hear something soon.

I'm not trying to hurt anyone or worry anyone. I just need to move on. I still wonder at times if God cares about me at all, or maybe He can't until I turn it all over to Him. I don't know if I can do that, or even really how to do that. Can anyone on this earth really do that? Have you? I just want to be right in all I can for God, but I'll never get that done on my own. He always has to intervene.

I got your letter and the pictures today. I just laid here and looked at everyone and dreamed how it would be to be there with you all. I'd love to hear that Christmas story. I know Dale did a good job on that. And the picture of the red cardinal in the snow beside your pond; so beautiful just sitting there. Thanks for sharing all that with me. —Donnie

January 11, 1999

Donnie wrote:

Just sitting here looking out the window. The suns out and it's supposed to warm up to 70 degrees today. Weird weather for January.

I didn't tell you that we have been getting Cheerios for breakfast twice a week. They come in this little plastic type bowl with a cover on them. Just peel it off and pour on some milk. Not much in there, but it has been years since I had something like that. And I was glad to get that apple and orange for Christmas, too. We only get an apple or orange maybe three times a year. I think we are blessed with one or two bananas. We don't ever get sugar anymore. They stopped that. So if you want to sweeten your cereal you have to use one of your syrup packets. I now have two extra syrup packets and I'm going to save them for cereal, or put some in my peanut butter. So I got a big decision on my hands here. I can have peanut butter now and no cereal, but they might give me cereal Saturday so what do I do? Smile.

Annie, I am working on this pattern. It's the centerpiece of the drawing I've been working on for so long. but I need some copies of this. I know it's an awful picture, but they [skeletons] represent dead Vietnam veterans in my life's portrait.

I am trying to pull closer to God. But now I've got so much trouble. Tests. And I don't want to hurt anyone or fight, but this is a very hard world. It's easier to hurt someone than it is not to at times. —Donnie

February 9, 1999

Donnie wrote:

I was just sitting here thinking and it came to me that you, Betty and Sherry are what I would call pretty established in the things of God. You seem to be. Know what I mean? He uses you in so many ways. So there has got to be a reason why we are all together, right? All this is going to come to me, Annie. But it's like God can somehow use us in this family. Something is going on. Wouldn't you agree with all that has happened since you and I started this relationship?

I've not been much of a person in life. But one thing I am is honest with you and everyone around me. I've always thought that I'm going to die here. And that there was really no one that knew me at all and I mean family wise too. Glenda knows me, but not as good as you know me now. I could finally for once tell someone everything about me and hide nothing. Easy to get lost in conversation here. Smile. So many memories and thoughts that come and go in me.

I am pulling closer to God again. I feel bad that I'm not what I should be, like in learning more about Him and all that. I felt bad while I was thinking this today. I'm here not doing anything, just waiting to die and go home to be with Jesus. I'm not even taking the time to do anything more. Like I've got a free ride or something, huh? Do I ever make any sense, Annie?

I have been reading my devotionals every day and I'm sharing them with two others here. We just pass it around.

I love this new Nelson Bible Sherry sent me. Nicest Bible I ever had. I worry about Sherry with the cancer. And Betty, I worry about Betty. Is she all right?

I talked to a guy here today. I usually stay to myself and he respects that. But he is a Christian and he felt like there was something different about me and he knew God was dealing with me. We talked and decided we would start going outside everyday, and we are going to pray before we go out. The guy is a big black dude about six foot seven and weighs about three hundred forty pounds. He asked me about my visit. I told him I love my visits with you and Betty, because I get to talk about the Lord and what is going on out there in the world.

He said, hey, we can do that here. It just caught me off guard, but we talked a long time. He told me that I wasn't a bad guy at all, that people just don't know me cause I don't let them know me.

He said, you know when we pray out on the yard people are going to talk about us. But he said what people thought meant nothing to him. I was just reading about that too. I am just going to try and stay focused on the Lord and give Him more and more of me.

From the beginning when you first came here you wanted to know about my life here. I thought at last I have someone to talk to. It's hard to explain, but I don't want this life here affecting you in a bad way. I realize that a man wanting to die is not your average conversation. I am hard and I forget how sensitive you are and that this place is hard on you.

You know what I like? At 6 p.m. every day we watch the animals on the discovery channel. I love that show. Surely God is going to have animals in heaven. I can't imagine that we would not have that. You know heaven is going to be just like this earth, but all light and clean and no dust and no shadows or stuff like that. And animals will have the same ways there, as here. We can go here and there and see them. I worry about that for some reason. I mean, I know God has this thing the way he wants it, but I'm counting on the animals being there. I know it is going to be so amazing and our little brains can't imagine it, and how awesome it is going to be. But there just has to be animals, Annie! And wouldn't it be great if we can communicate with them. I know I'm stupid, but I get lost in that show everyday. Smile.

Well, I was just sitting here dreaming and then I saw them

move Barber down to two cell. They're going to kill him on the eleventh. Poor guy. I never got to know him.

I get so lonely at times. And where I live, Annie, I have to be careful to protect my heart. I long for freedom so much and to be normal again back in the world with a life. And at times I have to block all that out just to survive in here. And hardest of all is to hang onto my sanity. It's not a nice place. But then I always have to remember who I am in the world. I'm a gentleman. I have beliefs and morals to live by. Don't get me wrong; I'm not saying I'm an angel. And I guess I wasn't even a citizen or a rule abider by society's laws. But remember there are all kinds of societies and I went where I fit. —Donnie

As Donnie struggled with his own need to fit in and his own doubts about the Lord loving Him, I gently reminded Donnie that we are in the world but we must not be of this world; his letters began to reflect that he too was accepting the fact that we must not feel comfortable with the sin all around us. Donnie began to see heaven as the place where he would finally belong.

Chapter 10

Giving God Control

"...I wish I had it to do over again"

March 7, 1999

*D*onnie wrote:

Dead end. I mean look where I am. Texas Death Row. Look how I've been in my life. I'm the worst of the worst in the world's eyes. So bad that they feel they have to kill me and rid society of me and that I don't deserve anything ever again but punishment and death. I'm at the very end of my roads in life.

At first when you began visiting me I was ashamed to be seen here, but I don't feel that anymore. God truly loves me through you guys. Annie, I only knew one other heart like yours and that was Grandma Odie. I have wonderful memories of my visits with her. Oh, how I loved Grandma Odie. I visited her when I come back from Nam. She came out to meet me and was so glad to see me. I had been drinking, but I stayed a while. And before I left I looked around at all the places I had played there as a kid. Somehow I felt that might be the last time I saw that place. But I will see Grandma Odie again! I've been thinking a lot about my childhood lately. I was alone so much that I was in a hurry to grow up and never took the time to realize that I had it made. God, I wish I had it to do over again. So many memories. One minute I'm here doing time and the next I'm back in my childhood days.

Annie, did you know that loneliness is one of the most dangerous and widespread problems in America? I was just reading about it in my devotional today. I think loneliness is a real killer. The fear and rejection if it goes on will erode the emotional strength of this country. And it is not just unbelievers that experience this. I'm loved so much by all of you there, but this loneliness affects us here in so many ways. I mean it's like I've got all of this love in the bank, you know? It's hard to explain. I have it, but I can't spend it or draw it out of the bank. It's just there. So often I think about others here on the Row that are ignored and forgotten completely by everyone, even their family. I am so thankful I have you all. —Donnie

April 8, 1999

Referring to his best friend that he had accidentally killed in Vietnam, Donnie asked:

Annie, do you think I'm right in wanting to find Mike's folks or family? I hope I am not just being selfish.—Donnie

I wrote to Donnie and asked him to pray about finding Michael's family. I told him if he felt like this was what he needed to do, I would try to help him with the search. The subject came up only one time much later when Donnie said he just needed to let that go.

April 19, 1999

It seems the closer I try to get to God, the closer Satan gets to me and throws me on the floor. I keep getting up but it is getting harder. Satan uses the people here most to get to me and they get the best of me at times. This one dude that got to me is in lockup, so at rec. time I'll settle that with him. It never fails, Annie.

Last night I read that article you sent on letting God be in control. It is so hard to do at times. That's what I mean about my will and not what God wants. I mean, look at the position I'm in now. I wanted to know where I am headed? Which way? But I look to man and how the courts are on the death penalty and I think, well God lets me see the world for what it is, so that way I'd be ready to come on home. So do I get prepared to die Annie? —Donnie

It was obvious that Donnie wanted a closer relationship with God, but at this time he was still afraid of what God's will could mean, and so was I.

Donnie and I would have to be willing to accept God's will, no matter what. Donnie was willing before I was. I soon began to realize that all the scripture that I had been sending to him over the years were ones God had given first to me. I kept good records, too. I also began early to make copies of my own letters to Donnie, in case I needed to refer back.

Before Donnie began talking seriously of dropping his appeals, he would say, "What's the use of hoping, God doesn't care, He doesn't even listen to me." But as Donnie began to draw closer to the Lord, his relationship to God became more intimate and he began to hear God's voice more clearly. If we don't believe God cares, and that He doesn't hear our prayers and wants to communicate with us, we won't be apt to listen for him, but Donnie was still humanly afraid...because he knew the truth. One of the first scripture reading I sent to Donnie years before was Psalm 139. The author of Psalms writes of how God knows us inside and out. The Bible says He knows the number of hairs on our head. So whether it would be God's will, or God allowing Donnie's execution, Romans 8:28 says, "And we know that all things work together for good to those who love God, to those who are called according to His purpose." The Nelson Study Bible says this means, "All circumstances will work together in cooperation for the believer's good...."[1]

Donnie continued:

I need to sit and write all that stuff down about Jesus that I was telling you. Lately so many things have been coming to me that show me more about what He went through and how most people don't see certain things. They are living life as it is taught by the world, not as Jesus taught it.

Annie, I know that faith is the substance of things not seen. And I want my friend, Glenda, to know that not all God showed me through her went to waste. I did catch on to some of it. Only thing is some people forget that I have to fit all those lessons into a different lifestyle here. It's a real battle in here. One day I am praying for someone and the next I have things coming at me from all sides. When I wanted to fight I didn't have that much trouble finding one occasionally. But now that I don't want to it seems everyone wants to. Of course half of them I can't get to and they know it. Especially, there is one and I've had enough of him, but he is in lockup.

I forgot to tell you that I got to meet and talk to that Nun, Helen Prejean, that befriended that dude that the movie Dead Man Walking was about. She held my hand for ten minutes and asked, how could they kill a face like that? She said, they are going to stop the death penalty one day.

Then I met Bud [visitor]. He told me that his daughter was killed in the Oklahoma City bombing, and that he was fighting for the death penalty to stop. I just saw him on TV and he said the same thing. And he told me he loved me. Bud was a genuine person too, Annie. —Donnie

April 31, 1999

    ARMADILLO Z-MAIL

"For we do not have a high priest who is unable to sympathize with our weaknesses, but we have one who has been tempted in every way, just as we are, yet without sin. Let us then approach the throne of grace with confidence, so that we may receive mercy and find grace to help us in our time of need" (Hebrews 4:15-16).

Moses was a murderer, but God forgave him and used him to deliver Israel from Egypt.

David was an adulterer and a murderer, but God forgave him and made him a great king.

Peter denied the Lord, but God forgave him, and Peter became a leader in the church.

Look at all the things people did, such as Paul for example. He had Stephen killed. So many people that did so much wrong as many do today. But God forgave them and used them mightily.

Annie, I was reading my devotional today and I came across this Inordinate Fear of God. There have been many times in my life when I felt that God was going to punish me by causing me to lose all that I had, either because I'd done something I shouldn't have, or because I'd fail to do something I should have. This erroneous perception of God has driven me away from Him on many occasions when I've needed Him most, and it is completely contrary to the one that Paul has described as the Father of mercies and God of all comfort in II Corinthians 1:3.

If we have trusted Christ for our salvation God has forgiven us and wants us to experience His forgiveness on a daily basis. Look at the fellows above.

God rejoices when His children learn to accept His forgiveness, pick themselves up, and walk after they have stumbled. But we must also learn to forgive ourselves. Rather than viewing our weakness as a threat to our self-esteem it is God's desire that they compel us to move forward in our relationship with Him.

So now I just remind myself every morning that I have been forgiven by God. And because he has forgiven me, I can forgive myself. —Donnie

May 1999

I received a story for the family written by Donnie titled:

Family Thang

...I don't write these things to justify anything about myself or where I'm at. But I write these things because they are truths in God's word that we have forgotten, or maybe never learned. But at the same time in all that I share with you, God somehow makes me feel better about things. He somehow brings me closer to Him in a way that maybe most can't understand. But I want to share this with you. And I believe that the last thing that Annie may email to you all is "Inordinate Fear of God." And how God uses people such as Moses and David, and Peter and Paul. God used them to bring about His word and to carry out His ways and wills to be done. Awesome, huh? I mean here we have murders and adulterers, and even some that denied Jesus. Makes one wonder, huh? I guess there could be a thousand thoughts in that alone. At least there is for me.

I was reading and something dawned on me. I had thought of them before, but today they really made me see all this in a different light. Maybe it was a comfort for me from God. I don't know, but I do know that it is a fact.

People, and even Christians, do not believe in demons and that is the problem.

Remember the demon possessed man in Luke, Chapter 8:26-38? He is possessed by legions of demons. And they spoke directly to Jesus. "Have you come to torment us before our time?"

Do these same demons possess people today? This man that was before Jesus was so dangerous that he had to be bound in chains which the demons were able to break.

What was Jesus' action? Did He say, execute him, cause he was a threat to society? No. Jesus drove out the demons and scripture says that the man was cured. Jesus didn't condemn him. Satan does that. That's Satan's job to condemn man.

Jesus said He did not come into the world to condemn but to save it from sin.

Think of all the people that have been executed and put to death. Look at the crimes they were put to death for. People wanted revenge against the man that did the crime. But that is not the example that Jesus set as you can clearly see here. Christians, Jesus cast out demons. Satan condemns man, not Jesus.

It is a wrong assumption that a man will not accept the gospel until he is pressured by Death Row. Killing a man will not shove the gospel down his throat, but will shorten his life before God's appointed time.

And remember that God commanded His followers to visit the man in prison in order to share the gospel. It's the word of God that drives out these demons.

Just think, if the Son of God could become the victim of an over zealous prosecution gang, then I'm quite sure it still happens today. And it does. I mean, look at how we conduct the laws today. Always condemning people. What happened to Jesus still happens today. When Jesus tells us not to execute, He means in every circumstance.

Look at a juror who has a man executed on circumstantial evidence. That juror could be in more danger of hell fire than the man that gets condemned. Let's remember that Jesus was an executed man. He knows what it is like. Have mercy so you will get mercy.

Hey they're just my thoughts. But they are also my beliefs. I've changed. I see some here that I know will never change, and they are the worse men I have ever known. I've hated them at times and judged them. I don't want them around me and I cannot stand some crimes, crimes that are against women and children. Just some things that none of us can ever agree with at all. We even think the death penalty is the only thing for them too. I'm still that way from time to time about some people here. But it is true, it is not the man, but the spirit of Satan that is behind them all. Behind all of us if we stop and think about it. None of us are free from Satan oppressing us in our daily lives. None! If you are then you belong to Satan.

So many things are there for us to see about this executing man. I even think about when Jesus, Himself participated in a death penalty case. Remember the woman that was brought to Jesus in the Temple. All the people came to Him and He sat down and taught them. But those Scribes and Pharisees brought to Him a woman that was an adulterer.

They had caught her in the very act and the law was to kill them by stoning them to death. That was Moses' law too. They wanted to know what Jesus would say. Kind of testing Him. But Jesus stooped down and wrote something on the ground with His fingers as though He did not hear them. So they continued asking. Jesus raised up and said, "He who is without sin among you, let him cast the first stone at her." And again He stooped and wrote on the ground. And all that was there left from the oldest first to the youngest last. He said to the woman, "Where are your accusers? Has no one condemned you?"

She said, "No one, Lord." And Jesus said, "Neither do I condemn you; go and sin no more."

That was a death penalty case. From old law to new law, that was what Jesus was about and why He came to this world, not to condemn, but to save us from sin.

I look through my Bible and I see nothing but Jesus casting out demons everywhere He went. People touching Him and was healed by the touch. Lepers that were sick and Jesus healed them one after another everywhere He went.

Remember anything that is not from God is from Satan, and

Satan has a demon for everything that is not of God. And we all deal with demons every second of our lives in one way or another. We walk in the Spirit and Satan flees from us. I mean, let's catch on here. These are the true ways of God today and back then too. Nothing has changed. This is still Satan's world till Jesus comes back and sets His foot on the Mount of Olives.

Yea, we forget these things, or we have never learned them.

I guess in a way I'm comforted knowing that Jesus Himself knows my pain in all things. He experienced what I have and what I will.

Just thoughts. Isn't it hard to walk like Jesus wants us to? We're only human. We just try as hard as we can. I wished that I could walk over ten feet without falling down though. I'll try for twenty next time. Maybe I'll just go for eleven. I just wished life was a little easier. I'll just be glad to go home.

Love you all, Donnie

Donnie continued:

> I found out today that we have to get rid of all our piddling [craft] stuff So I'm getting all this ready to go out. I'll just box or bag it and tell them I want you to pick it all up on your next visit. I wrote the warden today and sent him also a copy of the Armadillo Z-mail. Smile.
>
> Annie, this is going to be a big change for me. I can't sit here and not have anything to do. I'll go to work on that (letter) tonight and get it ready to go out to the lawyers. I'll have to deal with the competency part of all this, but I can assure them, I am that [competent]. It's time for me to go, Annie. I do believe God should be the center of all things and I just need to get passed this last stop here and get going. —Donnie

Donnie was beginning to see the importance of giving everything over to God, and he knew that Christ should be in the middle of everything, but some days he had a difficult time letting go of his own desires; I tried to remind Donnie that every Christian struggles with fleshly desires, but when we do give the Lord that ultimate control, then we are not better than others, but we have a better life in Him. As God altered Donnie's disposition, I sensed that he was seeking God more as time passed.

The better we know God, the more we love him.

Chapter 11

A Request From Donnie

"...would you be able to be there?"

May 5, 1999

*D*onnie wrote:

    Yesterday I came in and I guess I was at a point where I settled a few things. Maybe God did. But again as usual I had to straighten some people out about this and that. But I had one old guy on my mind. When he came here eight years ago he was bout 53 I guess or older. Coleman, old black guy. All laid back, and didn't have a thing. Just lost to the world. He had one of those cases where some people used him and actually set him up. But we took care of him. We all got moved over time and old Clyde just got all the way in his world. Sleep and eat, that's it. But I have seen him here and there over the years. He's got one of those spirits that is so gentle. But I knew that his date was this week and they moved him to the deathwatch cell. I saw him standing there looking at me. I waved. I didn't know if he would know me, but he did. He had a sad look on his face and voice so weak I could barely hear him. But he told me they was going to kill him, and he wasn't going to get no stay. But it was his voice. He seemed so lost. Made me cry. I said, Man, I love you.

    I came in and I got to praying for him. I was wondering if he was saved and if he knew what was ahead of him other than this life. I asked a boss about talking to him and he said they don't do that no more. No visits [inmate]? I told him to just go tell his sergeant, and let me know something. He did, and they said no, but an hour later it was yes. I think it bothered the guy. Anyway, I got to talk to old Clyde and we prayed. I asked him a bunch of questions and told him that dying was nothing if he knows Jesus. I told him about Jesus and heaven, and it was our main goal to get there. I felt good about our talk. But after I got back to my cell Satan comes and messes with me and says I didn't say the right things and all that, but I shoved it aside and said, Old Clyde is okay. It's six-thirty now and I'm sure he's passed. I hate this place so much. Clyde was an old man, yet a child in his body.

Other than that, same old thing here, Annie. —Donnie

May 5, 1999

Donnie wrote:

I've been all kicked back reading this book that you sent [Left Behind]. I love stuff like this. It's all about the rapture, when Christians are taken up to heaven.

I've been thinking of so many things about the rapture. I used to think about it all the time. But these guys (Lahaye & Jenkins) see it as I do. But so many thoughts, ya know. Like babies in the womb, just disappear! Awesome! All the children gone!

There is still hope that some will believe, but I wonder if they can actually still feel God's presence here on earth. I thought God would pull His Spirit from the earth, but there will be some that will realize what has happened and will ask Jesus into their hearts. When you read on in the second book [Tribulation Force] you'll be reading more about the two witnesses, whom I have always thought would be Moses and Elijah. But the witnesses will brave many things during all the time of preaching God's Word.... Lots to think about. —Donnie

May 9, 1999

Donnie wrote:

I just came in from rec and watched the news and heard more on the Oklahoma City tornado. Man, I'm all freaked out. I don't know if you guys are all right and I know so many in Oklahoma City, or did. None that cared about me, but I cared about them. I just pray that all of you are okay. I need to hear something! I am worried cause the letters I have received are marked May 3 before the tornado.

I was just sitting here looking out my window. It's been cloudy all day but I am looking forward to our visit. I had forgotten to pray for your trip down tomorrow so I stopped to do that. Now you will have a good one down and back home. Smile.
—Donnie

May 10, 1999

After Betty and I visited Donnie, he wrote this letter:

I was so glad to see you guys today. But I don't feel good about the way I made you feel. The subject [execution] stinks I know. But it is something that is a part of me and my life that I am going to go through. I have to talk about this to you and Betty. I don't have anyone else. I know it is upsetting for you and it makes you sad. That is the last thing I want to do and I am sorry. I admit that ever since that federal judge granted that motion I've been feeling different about things. I think I am ready to go. I've been like, kind of packin my bags, ya know?

I am so close to death all the time. Felder has a date to die. I've known these guys all the time here. The deathwatch cells are full now. And I'm just preparing myself, and it's not easy either. I have so many things come to me at night when I lay down. I think and dream and toss and turn. I'm dealing with things that make me angry and mad at times. I even think I hate some people lately. I can barely hold and contain myself when a certain boss comes around. He laughs and mocks me and I can't sleep just thinking about him. Bad, huh? But he wouldn't shake my cage down. He let someone else do that.

I was so sad today when you guy's left. I wanted to hug you and say I am so thankful for you guys being here and loving me. But it seems that our lives revolve around me and me only. You're always doing for me and taking care of me. And I am doing nothing but taking up your time. I care about you all too. I want to know how you are and what is going on in your everyday lives. As for Dad, I miss him. I know me being here on the Row looks bad, is bad, and is hard on the family but I miss Dad.

I think what I was trying to say to you today in all this is, I don't know what to do with myself. As long as I have been doing time locked up I've never run into this. I would get down and sad and frustrated and depressed, but I would bounce back somehow and always find something to do, but now there is nothing to do. I spend 22 hours a day in my cell and on weekends it's 24.

Well, here it is after seven o'clock and I've said nothing but the same thing over and over. I couldn't keep a straight face today and again you cried. When will we ever get over all this and away from these tears? We didn't get to pray together today!

It is so loud in here I can't even think. I can't even talk to my friend, Thomas [inmate] and he is right below me." —Donnie

May 11, 1999

Yea, I fell out last night, or rather this morning. Smile. Been a long day. I read all morning and waited to go to rec. When I went out Little was in the single man rec cage. I went and talked to him after I worked out. I talked to him about going to heaven. His date is for June 1. He's ready, too. We talked about God. It seems we dug up everything about how God works in situations and just everyday life in the walk. My friend Gribble was there too and he used to not believe in God at all, but he seems quiet settled in the Lord now. Little and I used to have deep conversations about God, but he was surprised about Gribble. He said, Man, Gribble has changed! The weird thing was we got to stay in the rec yard for four and a half hours. That seldom happens. It was so good to talk and share God like that. I talked to Little about me being almost there and he said it wasn't my time yet. But I see nothing wrong with stopping my appeals process and going on home to be with the Lord.

    I'm putting the pictures of your pond where I can see them all the time. Can you imagine walking through the woods, and down by the lake with two Bengal tigers? Smile. And a bunch of little otters all over the place and dogs playing and trees full of all kinds of animals. God has so many animals. They don't have spirits, but they do have gray brain matter.

    Hey Annie, I saw the bug man last night. He comes to spray about every four months and he is a real strong Christian. He is leaving to go work on other farms [prison units] closer to his home. But he loves my brother, Hammer, out in general population of this prison, and me. He said he had been reading the Left Behind books too. Little said he had listened to the books on the radio. I want him to read Within Heaven's Gates.
—Donnie

May 19, 1999

    Well, first I want to tell you that Death Row is moving to the

Terrell Unit in Livingston about 40 miles from here. All single rec, no more group rec. They will start moving some right away.

You could be right, Annie. Maybe God does have some kind of plan for me, but maybe not. I'm not exactly the kind of person He can depend on. Too much of self and too many problems. So many things happening lately that makes me want to go on. And some things leave scars upon us in this life, but like John 16:33 says, In the world you will have tribulation. Some things make us feel that we can never be forgiven. Like that paper I sent you about the Inordinate Fear of God. That was for me, for you, for your neighbor, your pastor, your brother and your sister, anyone that comes your way.

I will tell Gribble about what you said, that he must accept what Jesus did for him personally. And no it's not enough just to believe. Satan believes! Maybe we will go out today, and I will tell him all that you said about our sins are not what send us to Hell. Jesus paid for our sins, but not accepting Him and what he did for us is what does that.

I have been thinking about some crimes of us in here. Annie, I don't think Vietnam and flashbacks could cause crimes like raping a helpless old lady. I think the drugs over there that get you hooked and dependent on them could cause you to do some things, but not those type crimes. I can see many things that could happen, but nothing like that. I've been there. I have covered 40 miles over hills and rough plains on speed. I stayed up 26 days straight to be exact. I did that before running into that bank [Breckenridge]. I know bad things happened in shooting Belinoff. We had a fight and I won, but I was wrong for being there. —Donnie

In early May 1984, while doing what he thought was a good turn for his fellowman, a meat salesman, Jack Belinoff, picked up a hitchhiker in Throckmorton County, who turned out to be a desperate Donnie Foster. Realizing his own desperation, Belinoff tried to overpower Donnie and take his gun. Belinoff survived after being shot several times.

Donnie continued:

> Everyone answers for what they do, no matter what. Yea, I had a tough time in Nam and I do admit that what happened ruled my life for so long. I have seen it from every angle. I've had years to see and know and understand every side of this. And the reason it ruled my life was that I wasn't walking with God or seeking Him. I may have believed in God, but that was not enough when you're riding on self. Like you said about Gribble, it's not enough just to believe. I better talk to that guy tomorrow. —Donnie

June 3, 1999

> Little was killed June 1. But he is home now. He whispered to them that he has been jealous of all those who had gone on before him. Smile
>
> Right now I need to get settled and in the groove. It's so hot and it's not even summer yet. I just got in from rec and we can't shower until late so I am trying to cool off. —Donnie

June 4, 1999

> It's rec time and we can't go out, just to the day room. They're putting up more wire on the other end of the building and they have the yard closed. Shortage of manpower, I guess.
>
> Thank you for that book Endurance. I have already started it. I can tell it is going to be a good book.
>
> I have so many thoughts lately. I sit and write them all down then erase them. I think about Michael and what happened in Nam. Thank you for putting my "Remembrance" of him on the

Veterans Memorial. I wished I had found his family, but I have to let that go. —Donnie

Author's Note:

On May 21, 1999 The United States District Court in Ft. Worth, Texas denied Donnie's appeal for a federal hearing. This meant taking the next step in his appeals process which was in the Fifth Circuit Court or stopping his appeals altogether.

June 5, 1999

Donnie wrote:

Annie, I want to ask you something and I want you to talk to me about it. Please don't think I am being selfish or thoughtless because I have thought this over thoroughly. Would you be able to be there with me when my time comes? Annie, I need someone from my family to be there to hold eye contact with me and say good-bye to, kind of like holding my hand, ya know? Seriously, are you able? I will understand if you can't believe me, Cous. I know you love me and care for me. There is no doubt in my mind about that. It hurts me to ask and I'm kind of embarrassed about it anyway. But remember this is not going to be easy on me either. Smile. —Donnie

Knowing that Donnie was very serious, I could not help being relieved that his request was in a letter instead of on a visit, face to face. I had realized that Donnie was on Death Row, but I had not allowed myself to dwell for long on the thoughts of it actually coming to the point of execution.

So like Oswald Chambers in *My Utmost for His Highest* I had to ask, "What line does my thought take now? Does it turn to what God says or what I fear?"[1]

I knew immediately what my answer had to be and that I could not hesitate. But I needed reminders and assurances from the Lord for myself now, and that I could do this thing. Knowing that God's Word is true I went searching.

Chambers reminds us, "It does not matter what evil or wrong may be in the way, He has said, 'I will never leave thee.'" For He Himself has said, 'I will never leave you nor forsake you.' So we may boldly say, 'I will not fear; what can man do to me?'" (Hebrews 13:5-6).

What a blessing to hear God say that He would be with me, so I wrote Donnie that I would not consider being anywhere else but with him when his time came.

Donnie continued:

> I just need to start getting my house in order. Get this all out of the way. We have talked about funerals and you know how I am about that. I know there won't be many there. But the kicker is I really don't know for sure if I have a burial plot there at Walters. I need to find out from Dad. If not I just want to be buried here on peckerwood hill. It really won't matter. We'll let the state pay for it. I'll get the paperwork done in all this. Anyway, let's get it all settled and out of the way so we will have time for other things.
>
> Hey Annie, do you have anymore books like Within Heaven's Gates? I really enjoyed that book, even if heaven may not be just like that, but who knows? —Donnie

June 6, 1999

> I got a visit from Dad. He has been sick and he told me all about it. He came by himself and drove all the way and I worry about him. He said something to me today that got me. He said, "I couldn't live in a place like this for very long." I just looked down and we were quiet, then I looked at him and said, "I have been here 15 years." I worry about Dad. I hear about so many old people getting neglected these days and it is so sad. Can

you imagine the pain and hurt they go through? I mean they don't fit anywhere and some families just throw them away or use them. They get old and lose their mate, like Dad. I was afraid for Dad when Mom died. He was good to her and took such good care of her.

He was real happy that I am going to get to meet Dale [Annie's husband] and Bobby [Betty's son-in-law].

I was looking at the pictures you sent of Lauren [Annie's granddaughter] playing ball. How I miss games in the evening. Do you think we will enjoy stuff like games in heaven? I guess that is dumb to think about. But I can't help wondering.

Hey Annie, did I tell you I received a letter from your pastor, Bro. Scott, there at Calvary [local church]? He said I was an encouragement to him.

Bro. Scott wrote:

> Sometimes when I think about Paul there in prison I get your letter out and read it again and you may be right; you may not be a lot like Paul, but remember Paul left everything in God's hands. He was content, no matter if he stayed in or got out or lived or died. He knew that God was in control and that someday he would be there with Him. But sometimes I wonder if there are any Pauls left in the world, so I get out your letter. Then I know there are people like you who depend on Jesus and look forward to the reward. And sometimes I think, "God, where are you, nothing is right." Then I get your letter and it helps me to remember that no matter how bad it gets I can still lean on Him. I very much appreciate your concern for the friend you lost in the escape attempt [Martin Gurule] and for your cousin, Sherry with cancer, even though your own situation is difficult. Many would think of nothing but their own problems. To be going through what you are and caring so much about others is a spirit that only

comes from God. The Greek word is agape. It is encouraging to see it in you, so I want to say thank you for that. God be with you, sir.

Donnie continued:

Annie, it is hard for me to imagine myself being an encouragement to anyone, but I appreciated his thoughts and him taking the time to write.

You know, I know it is not easy on people to have someone they know here on Death Row. It's embarrassing and I am so ashamed to be here. You'd have to be in my shoes to feel and know what I am saying, but I have seen people actually afraid of me. I've seen Christians that are afraid to be around me. I remember a guy once that came to the county jail and peeked inside and I got up and went over to the bars and put my hand out to him, and he stepped back. I just looked him in the eye and I talked on, but he finally did shake my hand. It was kind of sad.

Annie, I know I often look at things with man's eyes. I have been here so long and haven't caught on to things and I'm not the best at walking in God's ways. I struggle, I'm a bonehead, I'm selfish, and I could have been and should be closer to God than I am and in my walk here. I know you will be here for me in anything, but at night I cry and ask God to reveal Himself to me. I ask Him to let me dream about Him and talk to me so I can hear Him and know that He is here with me. Why? Cause I'm dumb and hard in some areas. I know that believing and faith is what we are to have, but I want Jesus to come to me and let me know assurance like I have never known before. Stupid I know, but I just need that so much. —Donnie

Considering Donnie's circumstances, I reminded him of John 20:27-28, and that Thomas also needed more when the other disciples told him that they had seen Jesus.

God understands the needs Christians have for a touch from Him at difficult times in our lives. Jesus was patient and loving to Thomas even though Thomas doubted. When Jesus' touch did come all Thomas could say was "My Lord and my God."

In a folder marked 'Favorites' in Donnie's property given to me after his execution was a story that a relative had e-mailed me, and I in turn had sent it on to Donnie. Although "The Smell of Rain," had no author name, here is a summary of the story:

Danae, born premature with little chance of surviving, did survive, and after five years showed no signs of mental or physical impairment. Sitting on her mother's lap during her brother's baseball game one hot afternoon, the little girl sniffing the air, asked her mother, "Do you smell that?" Noticing an approaching thunderstorm, her mother replied, "Yes, I think we might get wet." With her arms folded, patting her own shoulders, the girl said, "No it smells like Him, like God when you lay your head on His chest." Tears filled the mother's eyes as her daughter's words confirmed what her family already knew. The first two months of her life, while her nerves were too sensitive for them to touch her, God was holding her to His chest, and it was His loving scent that she remembered so well.

Donnie wrote:

> I got that story today, "The Smell of Rain." You know while reading it I actually smelled rain! I had to get up to see if it was raining. It wasn't. But I've been asking God to show Himself to me lately, and in a way I felt He did. Smile! —Donnie

On my next trip to Texas Death Row, I took my husband, Dale, to meet Donnie. After a visit, Donnie would always go back to his cell and write his thoughts in a letter to us.

June 25, 1999

    I guess you and Dale are about half way home by now. But I had a wonderful visit. I was very happy to meet Dale too. You are so blessed to have Dale in your life. God allowed me to see Dale's spirit today and he is a wonderful person. I loved the story he shared with me about his friend and it allowed me to see what a real and sincere person I had here in front of me. I am so happy to know him and I hope we get to visit again.

    I know how you feel in wanting to know if everything has been done that could be done in my case. What I wouldn't give to be free and be able to live around you and Dale and the family and enjoy life the way it was supposed to be. One thing about it, we've got another chance coming, huh? Smile.
—Donnie

June 29, 1999

    Well, I'm sitting here looking around and it looks like we're fixing to get shook down again. It's in the 90-degree range and we're burning up and they want to tear our cages up. Going to be a long night.

    Sunday somebody escaped from the Estelle Unit and we've been locked down since. 'Hello coppers' are everywhere. No visits here for anyone either, except Duck Tuttle.

    That's cause he has a date to die July 1. He said he got a witness card from you and to thank you. I am going to fix him some burritos tonight. It's about time for him to move to the deathwatch cell.

    I got up and just set here this morning. Most of the guards are out hunting the guy that escaped. They got the taste of blood too and can't wait to get off work and go hunting for humans. As you can tell it has not been a good day at all.
—Donnie

Sunday, June 30, 1999

I guess I have been getting pretty weird, but I get to thinking, what if I am not right? Then I get to thinking about going to heaven and I get excited. But I have a million thoughts that are dumb and not important, like will I know that I'm executed? Will I see my body leave? Will I leave with angels or maybe Jesus, Himself?' I've got to know I'm dead, right?

Then I get thoughts that say that I'm not going to heaven, and that Jesus won't have me. I know it's a lie, but I know I don't exactly do things right and I get angry about things and I'm lazy and I'm not that spiritual. I don't read my Bible like I should with a hunger that many do. But I've got to believe and trust Jesus for what he said, right?

Annie, I wonder if heaven will be like I have been there all my life? I can't help but wonder those things. Smile. —Donnie

I reminded Donnie that our feelings often fluctuate, but we are to keep on believing no matter how we feel on any given day. As Psalm 9:10 states, "Those who know your name will put their trust in you, for you, Lord, have not forsaken those who seek you."

Chapter 12

Family Visits

"...we don't belong to ourselves..."

July 3, 1999

*D*onnie wrote:

Thank you for all the words about David [the author of Psalms] and all that he did and went through. David wanted to please God so much. I beg the Lord at times to just not cast me away from His presence. And create in me a clean heart. And what you said about us not being our own is so right. I needed to be reminded of that. You know I haven't been praying like I should. But then I do at times just tell Jesus that I'm thankful and I praise Him. I get to thinking of getting out of here and going on home and I forget what I should be doing for others, especially praying. I do care about others and I don't want anyone that I know or anyone for that matter, hurting and suffering everyday stuff. I admit that I want some people that work here to fall over or lose their job. Actually it has been a long time coming. But at times I just want some to get right and know they may have to pay for the way they treat others.

I have changed a lot in these last few months, Annie. I don't even talk to most bosses like I used to. I try to just walk away when they come around. Actually I've got nothing to say to them anymore. But if one got hurt or something bad happened to him I'd feel like I do about others and hurt for them. Of course I still wish a couple of guys would lose their job, but someone else would just take his place. I was thinking about this little green plant that has been growing for months in a crack out in the yard. I watered it all the time and others did too. But this boss went out and broke it off and he knew what he was doing, Annie.

I wish they would come on with this chow. We are supposed to get watermelon. I'll be glad when we get an apple or orange again. I don't think we have had one since Christmas.

You know at one time, Glenda would pray that I would not get to leave here until I was right with the Lord? Yea and it used to burn me up too. She is a really good person, but as for this world's temptations, if she only knew the battles I face in here. As for drugs, well I admit there are times it is hard to leave them alone. But I'm glad to say those things don't mean anything to me anymore. I like myself and my body and I want to please God. I'm only human, but I may have changed more than most think. And I won't be left behind at the rapture. But I'm looking forward to getting out of here much sooner than that. —Donnie

July 8, 1999

After a visit with Donnie at the Ellis Unit, he wrote:

It was so great meeting Sandy and Cory [Annie's daughter and grandson] today. I had prayed about the visit and you saw how well it went. Sandy is really a neat person and she was so curious about my life here. I want to see them again and write them more and get to know them better. I owe Cassie [Annie's granddaughter] a letter, too. I know they know Jesus and have Him in their lives and I think, well, I'm leaving now. But I still want them to know something about me. I can't just be ashamed of who I am all the time and for being here. Facts are facts, Annie. That Cory is a heck of a guy. I was impressed! He's going to do something special. I felt two wonderful spirits before me today. I am so blessed. I came in and cried and I don't even know why. I think I wanted to go home with you today more than I ever have. What a blessed family you have! And like you said, I got to meet them in person with skin on. Just something about when you guys walked off today. I was okay for a bit, then in the hall and back to the cage. And it was so hot I couldn't breath and looked at my stuff all tore up, I just died a little more inside. It's a bummer; and we need to just focus on me catching the bus out of here.

I was so glad you came in with Dorothy [inmate's wife]. I was worried you wouldn't come in. I don't know why. I just let things work me over I guess. I know it all seems dumb, but I feel at times I am really a burden to you and I'll lose you all. It's happened to me so much in my life. People leave and go away and it hurts. I know that you all are not ashamed of me, but I guess Satan tries to use that against me. I have got to meet Dale and Sandy and Cory so far. I know that I am not the best guy in the world and have ended up here in the worst place one can imagine, but you all have allowed me to be me, and not hide anything in my life from anyone. Being able to do this has made up for all the lost years in my life somehow. Like I said, I can't imagine it now, but I do pray that my life can be used to help someone else along the way. What could be more important?
—Donnie

July 13, 1999

Donnie wrote:

I cried again when I got my letters from Sandy and Cory today. They touched the very heart of me. Cory wrote a very nice letter and I have never seen myself the way he sees me. I don't know how to explain it, but he liked me! He said that he was awed that I could live here in this place and still love

God and witness for Him. Your family's love for me just keeps growing and growing. And Cory loves you so much. He calls you Nana. Even that made me cry. He thinks I'm remarkable! I want him to know I'm nothing, but God loves me and if it weren't for God I would never have made it this far. I get over thrilled and excited about it all. It's some of what I'm going to be experiencing in heaven. Can you blame me for wanting to go on?

Annie, when you told me that we don't belong to ourselves, that really hit home with me. I know that only God is what counts, not me or my situation or anything about me. But I know He loves me very much and I am so grateful. I'm reading Charles Stanley's Early Light devotionals you sent. I seem to get slapped around more and more emotionally and spiritually lately and it about kills me, but then something comes to me and I'm selfish in many ways, but that hit home with me. I know that I want what I want and I don't know whether it is right or wrong, but I still want it. And that's to get out of here and go on home to heaven. Easy way out I guess, but I am going so why wait? I know as my time gets shorter there will be things we must talk about. I am just trying to prepare you, my friend.

Donnie continued:

Just sitting here in the dark. It's thundering and lightning and raining and it's actually cool. Time for a cup of java and to put my headphones on and block out this whole world here. I walked in the yard with Moreland and Gribble [inmates] today. Jim got kicked out of the Fifth Circuit [Court] and it's just a matter of time for him. All of us are close now after all these years, so we talk about dying and what it's going to be like.

You know Annie, I can be talking one minute about Jesus and heaven, and the next we're talking about these self-righteous characters running this prison. Kind of some mixed emotions there, huh? I guess I'm not as stable as I think I am at times in my walk with the Lord. But as I sit here now I see a deep need to get stable and be what I'm needed to be for the guys going before me. Like Jim and others who will come over here for an execution date. I know I don't deserve to be saved and to get to go to heaven but I am so thankful that Jesus made a way for me. And I know this life is nothing compared to where I'm going. I need to spend some time with Him today. —Donnie

July 16, 1999

Donnie wrote:

Hey I'm sorry to hear about Dale's dad. I know the feelings there and it just makes me sad, but it is all going to be okay. I assure you that his father is in my prayers and all of you as well. There are so many things they can do with the heart now. But one thing we all know as growing Christian followers of Jesus is everything is going to be okay and we are all going to go home one day. We'll all be together again for sure. So we lean on Jesus and all that He has promised us. I know it's still a sad thing if something does happen to a loved one and it really hurts. I just hope Dale is okay. I really love the guy and I know his heart. Tell him to not be sad and just give his dad to Jesus.

I was thinking of the kids and their lives and them just being in this world. I was writing to Cory and I told him how I don't want them to get hurt or suffer any kind of pain. But this world today is full of it and how he and I have our work cut out for us and we have to be in fervent prayer for one another. —Donnie

At this point, I was pleased that Donnie was stressing the importance of prayer to my grandson, Cory. Although prison life affected Donnie's mood at times, it was encouraging to read his positive thoughts on being in God's will.

July 20, 1999

Donnie wrote:

Annie, God does have a will and we have to be in that will. I've always had problems with that cause I have a will too. We've talked about that. But we can always look and see how dumb I am too and where I'm at and know that I'm probably not right. So the way it is, we go with God's will and believe what happens, happened because it was supposed to. If we are praying for God's will, then this is His will. It's so easy to say. Preaching is easy, but walking it is the hardest of all things in the Christian life.

I want to write Dale and he doesn't have to write me back, or just when he gets time. I mainly want him to know I love him and care about all he is going through with his dad. You are truly blessed to have a family that can love and are God-minded. Did you know that comes from prayers and years of it, and God does all the work? Smile. I just have to smile and cry at the same time when I think of you. I see the same kind of heart in Sandy that you have. I just praise God that I can be a part of this family. And Annie, I know about these things, because I believe my spiritual gifts are discernment and exhortation. Really!

Lately I've been trying to do the right things, but it's not so easy. Things just get to me at times in this little head I've got, and in this little cage I live in. Some days my cell is big and some days I can't breathe in here. But I will live and I will survive. I have to smile at times, because while others are kicking dirt on me and covering me up you're uncovering me. Smile.

I hope my mood swings aren't affecting you too much. Being a follower of God is not an easy thing, and He didn't say it would be. The battles are fierce and they are constant. But we do have the blood of Jesus that we can plead over our loved ones and all situations. We can rest and be assured that He keeps his promises.

I say, God, show me this and that and what I am going to do and where I am going. And I don't know if I'm hearing Him right or not. Is it God or self? You know Annie, as long as we are human we're going to be a little of self. Look at me. I live in a total world of chaos and I'm always on a path picking myself up from a fall. On people and situations in here, I just have to go with my heart. Emotions and feelings come to me and I know if they are from God or not. He just let's me know in my conscience. I don't know exactly how it works, but I do know God is here in the midst of it all.

I am glad you like my Life's Portrait. I was worried that it would be a little much. But it's about the life I have led. I wished that I could have framed it for you. That was my plan. But we had to get all that [craft materials] out of here. No more piddling on Death Row. I have bad anxiety attacks sometime and working with the wood and building Harleys helped. —Donnie

On May 21, after the federal court denied Donnie's appeal, he began, as he had said, 'to get his house in order.' One thing that would need to be considered was his burial place. His dad had told Betty and me that he had not planned to bring Donnie home, but if we wanted to we could have him buried on their cemetery plot. Dale and I, along with Betty, Bobby, and Sherry, made the decision to bring Donnie's body back to Walters for burial. It meant something that he would not be buried at the Death Row cemetery with only a number. Names are no longer put on markers because those of some notorious inmates were vandalized.

July 27, 1999

I'll get the paperwork in to TDCJ pertaining to who will pick my body and property up after I am executed. I'm sorry and I know this is not an easy thing for you to think about, but this part must be taken care of. I used to worry that no one would come for me at all. But we will get this all out of the way so we can think about more important matters. —Donnie

July 28, 1999

Donnie began to write more frequently as time went on. He wrote:

Blackmon will be killed on August 4. They just moved him over here and they locked him in the yard while they were moving someone out of the deathwatch cell. But he was hollering Armadillo! He said, I'm finally going home, Stoney. Just as happy as he could be. It made me sad, but I have to share in the joy with him. I'll get to spend some time now with the guys that have dates in August. I know all of them except for Dunn. But they'll all be over here soon and I'll try to be there for them, as best I can.

I have been so restless lately. I haven't been exactly the Christian with his light shining. But right now I'm thinking about Blackmon. His Dad was a hell fire preacher, too. And he loved his Dad so much. When he passed, Ricky [Blackmon] had a real hard time, but his mom has stuck it out with him. He asked me today to keep her and his sister in prayer. —Donnie

July 30, 1999

I die a little everyday in here. My want to come home and be loved and be something in a family is so strong. I have got to get some relief. But I'm not sure about out there anymore. Would I ever get any rest? I've just had enough. And in this time here God has let me see this world. He gave me a picture of it and only a few little pieces are missing, but what a sad world it is, Annie.

You remember what I was reading out there in the visiting room about God's will, and how we shouldn't go against it. Well, I believe that God is going to bring me home and I can tell you that I want it too. —Donnie

August 3, 1999

Donnie wrote:

Well, Ricky will die tomorrow. He got to come to my cell last night and we prayed. I am beginning to really realize the power of prayer lately, and I must watch what I pray for. But most of all I'm learning it's all in the heart, what we feel, and how we approach God. About being sincere. I mean I know that, but sometimes in prayer its just prayer. It must be a sincere heart thing.

I want to tell you a story, Annie. There is this one guy that ruins our rec group and he just keeps something going all the time. Well, I came in two days ago after listening to him all during rec time. I asked God why He allows this guy to get to me after I'd asked for help. I was so tired of being the way that I was about this guy. And he was responsible for me always falling or stooping to his level. And you told me that when I get angry that I should talk to God about it, cause He knows I'm angry anyway, so I did. I mean I was mad. I just told God that I was trying to be a good man and walk right and that I knew my beliefs were right and that it wasn't me being wrong, and this guy ruined everything and kept the group out of whack. I asked God why He allows Satan to always be at me with this guy and that I didn't want to do something stupid, which He knew I have a tendency to do at times. I asked God to move this man. I told God to let all the others see what this man really was and that he was the one with the problem. But I also asked God to bring him to his knees and then send someone to him to tell him about Jesus. On and on I complained to God about this guy. Then later I told God I was sorry for hollering at Him and that I was wrong in coming to Him in that way. And that I knew I should come in reverence and respect. Then I just left it alone. Anyway, today this guy comes in and he's been out in the yard always with the race stuff, and coming in he is mouthing and he yanks the cuffs and strap out of the boss's hand and hollers at him and they close the door. Well they move him 30 minutes later. Smile.

The last two weeks I had just stopped talking to this guy. I hate what his kind stands for. They can't ride alone at all. He'll probably get a class three [discipline level] now and that's bad, but God brought him all the way down. I did tell God if the guy hollers for me I would be there for him. I believe God heard my prayer. The guy is gone and I'm glad, and so are a lot of others.
—Donnie

August 4, 1999

It's about 5:30 now and I know Ricky is over there waiting to go home. I didn't sleep at all well last night, but I got up early this morning and went out. But Ricky and I got to holler at one another for about two hours and I got to see him off. It just affected me different this time. He prayed for me Annie, and we talked all about what we believed heaven would be like.

I think about these guys dying and I never know what their crimes are until the end. All I know is what I see before me, and it's not the same person as when they came here. Anyway, I just finished praying for Ricky and that is my comfort. We spread a meal for all those that come over here the night before. We do that for everyone and Thomas [inmate] heads that up. We all pitch in. But Ricky hollered out to all that gave him that meal and thanked everyone that had shared his last meal here on earth with him. He said that he wasn't going to eat anymore until he got home with Jesus. He said he was going to get in that river he read about in Within Heaven's Gates. Anyway, that really affected Thomas. He is a real caring person and these executions are really getting to him. I think Boyd is next and that's his best friend. He's a real skinny black guy that is real nice.

Well, I thought I didn't get any mail, but the other Foster got it and he sent it up to me. Smile. So in this letter I take it you're going to be here tomorrow. And the next Left Behind book is out! My friend Moreland is reading them now. He is on #3 of the series and he'll start #4 tomorrow. He goes to the Supreme Court and that is it for him. —Donnie

August 5, 1999

After our visit with him, Donnie wrote:

It was so good to see you and Sandy today. I knew today that her heart loves Jesus and I felt God sitting with us. Again I wonder why someone would love me the way you all do? Cory even told me the other day that, Yes, you are loved very much by a bunch of people.

We had a good visit today, huh? Smile. But when I left I went back and told the guard that next time to please give me the courtesy of telling me when I got five minutes to go, so I can pray with my family. He said, You wasn't told? And it bugged him, too. But I told him I would pray for their safety going home and that is the only church I get. He just looked down. I was hoping I was witnessing to him at the same time. I told him I pray for your trips before you ever come down here, so it was cool. But I don't want you guys to leave like that anymore. I'll just refuse to move until we pray.

I am so hot, Annie. I hate to keep saying it but I know I have not had over fifteen hours sleep during the last week. This building does not cool off at night. It may get to 75 degrees outside but it does not cool off in here. I need sleep.

I've day dreamed so much about heaven lately that I actually dream about when I pass, and how I just kind of walk onto some very beautiful grass and see the most beautiful woods and rivers I ever saw in my life. I just go from there and imagine other things that will be there and I even imagine I'll be the one to come back and get you, maybe even with Jesus to take you home to heaven. But I hope I will be there for you all.—Donnie

Donnie told us that after a visit he goes back to his cell and begins to look forward to the next visit. We tried to plan as many trips as possible to see him and continue to let him know that he was an important part of our family. At this point in his life, Donnie was writing a letter to us almost every day.

Chapter 13

The Confession

"What hurts and pains me is the human side of me…"

August 2, 1999

Donnie wrote:

What are you praying for me? What is it that you think God wants of me? All I can say is that if God wants me to do something then He has to set me on the way to do it. Do I try to fight or just go on? I believe that if I am going home, then He will make it clear what is to happen and we will be able to be comfortable with it. —Donnie

I wrote Donnie that I had been praying that God would show him His will for him. I prayed for God to reveal Himself to Donnie, so that he could tell others of God's love and faithfulness to him. I had asked God to make Donnie well spiritually and emotionally. I reminded God in prayer that although we do not deserve an answer He has promised if we would ask believing we would receive it.

August 8, 1999

Donnie wrote:

I look at my life now and I can say that yes, I have had a hard life. So many strange things have happened to me, and I have hurt. I have been in pain, physically and emotionally. I know what it is like to be lonely. I know what it is like to be away and not have all the things that I long for so bad. So many things, so many regrets and so many tears, Annie. But so many have it much worse than I do, and have suffered more than I could ever imagine possible. But lately in my dreams, I dream of being normal in life; yet I see myself dying. But at the same time I'm being filled by the things of God. Oh, I still want to go home and be free and have a life out there but I can't see that happening, so I see what I have left to look forward to, and that is to die and go home and live the real life that awaits me. Nothing in this world can compare to anything we are going to experience in heaven, nothing. And we could never suffer like Jesus did in dying for us. I have been loved, too. But what hurts and pains me is the human side of me. But like Sandy said, As long as we have this skin on we will be human. —Donnie

August 11, 1999

Donnie wrote:

I just came back from a really good visit with Sherry and Bobby [author of poem, *Accepted Just As I Am*]. It's just hard to get everything in on a two-hour visit. I was very glad to meet Bobby and see Sherry smiling and looking good, too. She is going to make it and I know that God will complete a full healing of that cancer in her.

I like Bobby and I was sad to see them go, but we got to pray and talk about things of God. I'm noticing that God is allowing me to fellowship more and more about Him. I've had more conversations about God and His Word with all of you than I have in the years here with anyone.

I just peeked into the sixth book The Assassins and before you know it I had read a hundred pages. And I am now about half way into the book Faith on Trial. She writes, Would the testimony of Matthew, Mark, Luke and John stand up in court?[1] Not bad, but I can sure tell a lawyer wrote it.

I finally got a pair of shoes that I like. They're white and a size 10. I've got two good pair of shoes now. Smile! I threw the blown out ones I had out on the run. I tore the insides out of them and the shoe strings to re-use. But I had no longer thrown the old ones out when someone yelled to Mark below me to get those shoes! He said, They're blown out on one toe, man. They said, I don't care, get em!

They killed Dunn yesterday and then today they get Earhart. Remember, he was out there next to us during our last visit.

Well, they just moved the next two guys they are going to kill into the deathwatch cells. —Donnie

August 14, 1999

Donnie wrote:

I was just going to lay around tonight, but I am so homesick. Some days I just can't stand it here. Everything just gets to me. And I heard they are going to move 105 of us to the Terrell Unit, so that is just another thing I don't need right now. I haven't been able to pray these last few days. It's like I took a few steps backwards. But I stopped and praised Him for the rain, and just loving me. But I feel so empty tonight. I get those dumb thoughts and fears. This place and life just gets to me. I mean I really don't want to be here. I just get overcome at times. Dorothy said you guys are coming this week, so that cheered me up.

Annie, sometimes things pop up that we think we have gotten rid of, like prejudice. It's right on top of the conscience all the time. Triggers easily. But I can leave it alone till it comes to my face. And then as usual, the one thing that gets us all, PRIDE! No one's perfect. I like to look at a person for who they are not the color of their skin. And I can do that, too. But so many here actually think they were born in the slave days. —Donnie

August 16, 1999

The family got together at our house in Walters to celebrate Donnie's birthday. Cassie made a banner, and Sandy got a cake with "Happy Birthday Donnie." We took pictures of the celebration. We sent the birthday banner, cards, and pictures to Donnie.

I had written Donnie that I had called a prominent defense attorney in Springfield, Missouri, for advice. I guess it was a desperate, last straw effort to see if something had been left undone in Donnie's case.

Donnie wrote:

Stop, Annie. You've got to let it go. —Donnie

August 19, 1999

My sister, Betty, and I had special visits scheduled for August 19 and 20. Special visits are two, four-hour visits over a two day period and are considered for visitors that travel over 300 miles to visit death row inmates.

On the first day of our visit, I could see Donnie had something on his mind. Often he would begin by talking about problems there. We understood and would allow him to talk and release his frustrations. After a time, he would apologize for his anger and ask about the kids, and we were able to even laugh and enjoy the visit. But this particular day, towards the end of the visit, our conversation turned very serious. Believing Donnie was innocent, we began to question him about the details of his case. We wondered if other individuals could possibly have been involved. He seemed to become somewhat irritated at first, suggesting that it would not be honorable or perhaps he would be breaking a code or something to mention others concerning the crime.

Seeming puzzled, Betty asked, "You mean to tell us that someone else could be involved in this crime and you have sat here on Death Row for nearly 15 years and are close to dying while others go free, and you're concerned about breaking a code?"

Realizing the conversation was going nowhere, the subject was changed, and before leaving, our visit had even become pleasant again. We prayed together and began to look forward to our visit the following day.

Later in our motel room, Betty and I discussed how upset Donnie had become during our visit. We fervently prayed for him and for our visit the following day before retiring to bed.

Anxious for our four-hour visit with Donnie the next morning, we arose early and went to IHOP for breakfast and arrived at the Ellis Unit shortly before 8 a.m. After being identified at the gatehouse, we went inside where we were assigned seat numbers and waited for the guards to bring Donnie down.

"What's goin' on?" He would always ask after entering his small cage.

After he was locked in the cage, Donnie would squat down and put his hands to a small hole behind him to have his cuffs removed by a guard. After his hands were free we would put our hands to the glass separating us and his hands would meet ours on the other side.

Donnie spoke up quickly. "I had a terrible night and couldn't sleep at all. And before we go any further, I have something to tell you."

Leaning close to the grill that separated us, Donnie said, "I did it."

Betty and I knew that we were back on the subject of his case again. But hoping she had misunderstood, Betty quickly leaned close to the grill and asked Donnie, "What do you mean? You were there?"

Recalling an earlier conversation with Donnie, I knew what he meant.

Approximately a year after my first visit with Donnie, he had commented that before he was executed, he wanted to tell me something. But after getting to know him I never allowed myself to believe he could be guilty, always pushing any suggestions of that aside. But when he said it that day, I knew it was true.

Donnie continued, "I mean I shot him," referring to Gary Cox, the man he had been convicted of killing. "But it wasn't murder. It was an accident. But the point is I shouldn't have been there."

Heavenly influence must have been on Donnie that night of August 19, 1999, the night before he admitted his crime to Betty and me. God wanted Donnie to know he was forgiven and free, but like J. C. Cockrum, he had to tell the truth. Donnie knew that Betty and I, as well as other family members, were praying that he would not die an innocent man.

In our conversation following his admission to Betty and me, Donnie quickly realized that his confession changed nothing concerning our love for him.

Donnie admitted, "Annie, I have wanted to talk to you for so long about this. Only one thing in my heart has kept me going all these years and that is I hoped the day would come that I could tell someone, authority wise, what really happened that day. The truth has never been told in this case and what it was all about. It's never been what it was."

The remainder of our visit, Donnie seemed more at peace. He had never told anyone the truth about the crime. I remembered Donnie saying, "Once someone admits his crime, he is gone."

From that day forward, Donnie began to talk very seriously about stopping his appeals effort. When Donnie said he wanted to drop his appeals, my only response was

"Are you sure, Donnie?"

I didn't like the subject because I knew what it would eventually mean that he would be executed. I had to remind myself that I had been praying for God's will for Donnie.

August 20, 1999

After our visit Donnie wrote:

Well, I guess you guys are well on your way home by now. I'm always so happy to see you and Betty and then I realize you are going to be leaving and it gets harder and harder. I look at you and emotions start rising up in me and I can't keep the tears back, so I have to stay busy talking and not thinking about you leaving.

Now, Annie, maybe you can be at peace and let me go when the time comes.

Somehow I feel that even my death will bring this family closer through it all. For once in my life I have a real family, real love. It's changed me in so many ways. You have done more for me than you will ever know. And it's not just me, but it's all of us. We reflect God to each other and He stays in our midst. I can't explain it. I only want to share in it all. Smile!

I loved my pictures of my birthday party! I was so lost in thought. I just sat here and looked at those for about 2 hours. This was the neatest thing to ever happen to me. And you said it was Sandy's idea? And Bev made the dirt pudding! I would love to eat some of that. I never knew they had gummy worms. I can't stop laughing about that. Bev must have a really good sense of humor. And that cake really looks good. The colors are so cool. I can't remember having a cake with my name on it. Hey, I thank you all for this party. Tell Sandy that was the best party I ever had in my whole life. I'll tell her too.

You know I have everyone's pictures here on my wall. I change them out as I get new ones, but I always have some of everyone up there. Sometimes I just look and dream and then I just get overwhelmed at times by all the love and it hits me pretty hard lately. —Donnie

I had previously sent Donnie a copy of an article that came out in the *Wichita Falls Times & Record News* about him. The article was published previous to Donnie admitting his crime to Betty and me. The article was in response to one that I had put in Walters' local paper referring to Donnie's trial.

The article by Joe Brown had mentioned that Donnie held an elderly ranch couple at gunpoint while making a telephone call.[2]

Donnie wrote:

> Everything that has happened in the past in this case, and in others, is never going to get right or be seen right anyway. I was reading this article again in this newspaper, and I was thinking of the rancher that old Joe was talking about. I didn't hold them at gunpoint. The day that I got there the baby sitter was there. I knew her. We talked, and I told her, Man I'm in some trouble now! The people were not even home. They came home and I told them who I was and what I had done and that I needed their car. And what happened after that was so weird. I remember the older lady had a cane. It was black and had a silver top on it I think. But she said, Before you go I'm going to pray.
>
> Now if you can imagine me outside the open door of the car, standing there with two guns on me waiting on her to finish her prayer. She and the other three were on the other side of the car. I believe I thanked them for the prayer. It's a blur now, most of it. But I do remember the prayer and the older lady well. I had been up for many days. But the prayer there, that day, and then in the bank with Randy Jordan. Man, miracles were happening all around me then and I didn't even know it. And Randy witnessing to me. I mean Jesus was at every point and every turn that I took.
>
> I do wish at times that I could tell the story from start to finish and get everything in order for everyone. Smile.

I can also tell you that God was not going to let me go without telling someone something about this case. But all these things wouldn't have happened if I wasn't there, right? I've told God everything about all of this and He knows anyway. But I believe that God has made me whole and complete again. He saved me Annie, and let me know who He was, and He made a way for me. He made me right. Now I am able to live in heaven when I pass from here. It don't matter anymore about what's happened in the past. I can't help but hope that some get what's coming to them, but then that makes me wrong. How God plans on handling it to the end I do not know. But I think now that we can all sit back and let me go on and go home in peace. One thing about all this is that this can be a learning experience for everyone. —Donnie

Romans 8:28 states, "And we know that all things work together for good to those who love God, to those who are the called according to His purpose." God may have even used the news article that I had put in our local paper to persuade Donnie to tell the truth about his case.

Donnie continued:

You, Betty and I have now talked about why I am here on Death Row. A day that something happened and it never should have happened. —Donnie

August 25, 1999

Donnie wrote:

McFarland has a birthday today and Gribble's is Friday, so I'm going to cook them up some roast beef.

Jones and Barnes have dates and will be moving over here today. Then Crane has a date in October. —Donnie

August 26, 1999

Donnie wrote:

It seems I always need a haircut! But if I let it grow out I look like a Cabbage Patch Doll and that ruins my image. Smile. I hope to get it cut before you guys come for the visit. -Donnie

September 1, 1999

Dale and I visited Donnie. "Well I see you got that haircut!" I commented to Donnie on our visit. He remarked that they should allow them to cut their own hair.

"How hard can it be to shave your head?" Donnie said.

After the visit, Donnie wrote:

I was so glad to see you and Dale. I didn't know that he was coming but I'm glad he did. I'm so glad that you've got him in your life and that you and Dale are in mine. Smile. I love you both so much. And you know what? I forgot to tell him Happy Birthday in person. I feel so irresponsible when I do that. I don't get to laugh too often but Dale had me laughing today.
—Donnie

Donnie loved hearing about the grandkids. Repeating what my grandson Trey had said to me, Donnie wrote:

Watch me spin out, Nana! Smile. Believe me Annie it was important that you saw Trey do that. It's cool to watch kids at Trey's age play. They keep you laughing. I wish I could watch him play. I can remember when I got that new bike and I was at Grandma Odie's that summer. I would pop wheelies and I'd want her to watch me. It's been a lot of years but I'll be glad to see her again. Lately I've been thinking of everyone I'll be seeing in heaven. —Donnie

September 7, 1999

    I was just sitting here watching all the little spiders on my floor. They're kind of cute the way they jump. They're the kind that are brown and eat ants and crickets. They're not poison at all. I play with them all the time. When I was moping under my bunk and I moved my shoes and there was all kinds of little baby spiders. But I just go on moping and if they get took out, oh well. We have sugar ants bad all over the place. I can sit here and watch them crawl out of my typewriter and they get on me at night. They don't bite but they're bad here. Between the roaches, ants and those spiders and the crickets it's a real circus of little things. I watch those little spiders go up and jump on the ants, so I let them stay. Nature is at work right here in my cell. Smile. I'm lonely, huh?

    I was talking to Gribble about his case. His lawyer didn't file anything on his behalf and he shouldn't even be here now. But Houge that got killed here last year filed a supplemental brief for Gribble and they sent it in to the courts. Well, they've been pondering over what to do and can't come up with a decision on it.

    So God has a way of getting people ready to come home. I believe that is what God done in Gribble's case. —Donnie

September 8, 1999

    I long to leave here and get away from all this. I try to find something good in every day here and I know I am blessed. There is no doubt about that. But in here something is always missing no matter what you have.

    I have read this book *Within Heaven's Gates* a few times now, and each time I read it I search my thoughts and feelings on it all. I pay attention to every word. But she [author] helps me dream and helps me to think about what waits for us in heaven.

And I know because God tells me the same things in His Word.

I was thinking this morning about the houses and mansions and all. They sound so beautiful. I thought, Annie is going to have a beautiful one! Smile. And you know what else? I feel like God may let me live next door to you and Dale cause of the things we have shared and gone through in this life.

So much in that book that I think about. I wonder if my real mom and dad will be there. I know Cliff and Bertha will be. I have a million thoughts on it all.

Anyway, I just have my hope and faith placed in God in all this. I feel that if anyone really knows me they know that my time here is up and anything further here is nothing but pain and heartaches.

I doubt that one can know what I feel inside when I have to look at you all through a window and not be able to touch you and give you a hug when I see the tears. And then watch you guys walk away and I have to walk back to this cage to just be alone again. I live in my mind, and dream that I am with you all. Smile. I guess that's all corny and dumb, but maybe not though. Anyway, I'm just talking Cous.

Well, I went out and got burned up and tired today. I weigh 255 and I'm going to get under 250 by the end of this week. I want to dump ten pounds fast as I can and work to get my strength back. I ran today and it was very hard on me. Smile. I did my stomach workout and then punched the bag and played some handball. I'm just an old, over weight guy that may never return. Smile. —Donnie

September 10, 1999

Hey Annie, I received the prayer slips from the church there and I read your friend Valerie's note. She wrote asking me to pray for her mom's family. Her mom's sister died and they are taking it real hard. Her funeral is today and I just finished praying about it. You know so many Christians forget God's word or maybe just don't realize that death is not an occasion where it should create so much sadness. I know it's hard to get around being sad because when you love someone and they are a really big part of your life. It does hurt I know. But we must cling to God's Word and that it is true and stand on that.

I guess they will kill Barnes today. He really thinks he is going to get a stay. He spent all that money and they didn't file it until yesterday. It just seems to me that he's not looking to Jesus. Maybe I sense it all wrong. But I can usually tell when a guy is really leaning on the Lord, especially in the last days. It's unlike any other days here. I prayed about it and it is definitely in God's hands, as we all are.

Donnie later wrote:

Well I guess Barnes is dead. He didn't come back.

September 12, 1999

Donnie had allergies and a doctor at the prison had given him some medication. He wanted to know if the medication prescribed was for allergies. I checked the Internet and sent him a copy of the printout.

Donnie wrote:

Hey thanks Cous for sending that information about the medicine. It really is an antihistamine! I just knew I had that guy in a lie. Smile. And it bugs the heck out of me that I can't drive or operate heavy machinery. When it comes time to cooking and opening cans here I tell Gribble, I can't do that, cause I'm on meds. And I show him the label that says I can't drive or operate anything. Smile! —Donnie

September 14, 1999

    Someone brought me a bird with a broken foot. They thought it was a sparrow. Well it was a Yellow Breasted Swallow and the little thing didn't have a broken foot. It was just locked on one side and couldn't set up straight. I prayed hard over it too and asked God to heal and make it new. I watered it and it was so tired. But its stool was weird looking. I think it had got some poison or maybe had internal injury. I checked it's feet and they were okay. It was paralyzed on one side. But it slept all night with me and this morning it was sitting there and it just kicked its feet out and died. It made me so sad, Annie.

    Today is Weed's day and he should be on the table right about now, or walking that way. I got to talk to him yesterday and he had also read the book Within Heaven's Gates. We talked about what heaven was going to be like.

    He told me, Stone, I'm ready to go. I'll take a stay, but I'm ready.

    He was close to God, too. He changed a lot over the years. So he will be with Jesus today.

    Sessions, a guy that I have known ever since I have been here, died of a heart attack two nights ago. He was in lockup in solitary for something stupid. But I had just talked to him last week. We was laughing and cutting it up. He came down and told Weed goodbye and went back and died. He beat Weed there! He told them he was sick and they took him to the infirmary and brought him back. He told them again. They did nothing and he died. They found him later, about three in the morning. They couldn't even get a key to one of the gates out here to take him to the hospital. He was dead anyway. —Donnie

    After Martin Gurule's escaped from Death Row in November of 1998, TDCJ had taken most crafts away from death row inmates.

They still were able to buy watercolors, but Donnie had written that he had a hard time controlling watercolors with his brush, so I sent him a book hoping it would show him how to correctly use watercolors.

September 22, 1999

> Donnie wrote:
>
> On the watercolors the problem is that we don't have but one kind of brush here. They're plastic and you can't get any definition out of it. I am trying to make a brush out of hair. So we will see what happens. But I thank you for that book. I may learn something. —Donnie

I didn't know that much about water coloring myself, but I knew Donnie wanted detail and after receiving the picture he did, I understood why. It is a picture of the universe with the planet earth in the background and another planet in the foreground with a man on his knees crying out to God of loneliness.

...As I was setting
here in my cage,
I turned the radio on
and a sermon was being preached.
I thought, I'll go to church.
But I was the only one in
the congregation as always
here in my cage,
and of course God was there too...

So, I sat in my cage
and I went to church.
I know I was the only human here
in this cage,
but spiritually,
we couldn't have got another person
in here I reckon.

Donnie
9/5/99

Chapter 14

A Family's Love

"...I can honestly say it was an accident"

September 26, 1999

*D*onnie wrote:

I stayed busy all day yesterday. I scrubbed my toilet out real good, plugged it up, heated water and laundered my blanket in it. First of all I bleached it good and it took me a while to get it rinsed out. Then I had to stretch it out and fold it in half and put it through the bars to wring it out. It was like wrestling a bear. I was tired out but I got it wrung out and hung on my line in here and put the fan on it. It dried in about three hours. So I decided to do another one and I got that done and then I washed a sheet the same way. So my blankets are clean. Smile! Also, and this is no lie; I sat there and watched the first one dry. —Donnie

September 29, 1999

Donnie wrote:

Sometimes I wished that we could just sit and talk all day about things, Annie. In this cage I just live in my head and think and even answer myself on any questions that come up. Too much time alone. If I was in population I could stay busy, or even if we had a piddling program again. This time here is just too slow and mental. I'm a thinker and my mind is going all the time. And these last few days I've wanted to see Jesus. Yea, I mean really! Before I go to sleep I ask God to show Himself to me and remind me He is there. I just wish Jesus would come to me in my dreams and talk to me. You know, and give me that assurance.

Well, the cleanup crew is here and I got to see some of my old dogs [friends]. They tell me Blue [inmate friend with cancer] is back from the hospital in Galveston. He told them to tell me he was doing much better and he has gained weight and is exercising. He wanted me to know that cause I stay on all my friends about working out everyday. That's why most of them run when they see me coming. Smile!

Say, Annie, write this name down. McFarland. If you can send him those devotionals like you sent me, or anything on the religious side. But he likes those devotionals.

I have not been doing that great lately. I'm tired and I'm lonely. I have had a rough few weeks. A few things going on that's had me a little off. At times I think about being so close to the ultimate in life. Killed. I feel it coming and dream about what's ahead of me. It's not as easy in here as one might think. This is not a boy's camp. I think I know a little about what Jesus felt now before He was crucified. I know nothing I go through could compare to Him, but what I go through is enough to get me off balanced lately.—Donnie

Referring back to our visit of August 20, Donnie wrote:

I vowed that I would never tell anyone anything about this case unless they took me back and dropped the case. But I have still not told them all that took place and what actually happened. But I told you. I did that because it was on my mind to do. God told me to. It was not easy either. But no matter what one may think of me I can honestly say that it was an accident that day in the feed store. —Donnie

Our hearts broke for the Cox family as Donnie described to Betty and me the details of April 5, 1984 when Cox's desperate attempt to avoid being robbed resulted in Donnie shooting him. I thought about the bad choices early in Donnie's life that led to his drug addiction. And how broken lives often lead to bad choices; then lead to desperate acts which ultimately, as in Donnie's case, lead to one's own death. I thought how Betty and I had discussed before what we knew of Donnie's life. He seemed to feel a need to be punished for the death of his best friend Michael in Vietnam.

Donnie continued:

> So many times I have asked 'why' about my life and the way it has been. But the one thing in life that has held me up is God and He has done it through you and this family. I love you very much and you are my best friend that I have ever had in life. I'm sorry I get down but I just want a life so bad, or to go on home.
>
> No need to worry cause God does take care of me and I get through things as they come. But there is something about dying and I'm getting closer and closer. —Donnie

September 30, 1999

Shortly after Donnie had told Betty and me about his crime, he proceeded to make plans to stop his appeals process. I received a letter from him along with his writing simply titled: Family.

Family

I know in my heart that the little child on this earth is God's very own, and that He loves them very much. I can see a child and especially one that is different than normal children. One that may be retarded or has Downs Syndrome or maybe they are crippled because of birth defects or born as crack or cocaine babies.

So many things affect children all over this world, abuse,

starvation, and loneliness. It's endless things in this world that plague them and when I see them, that is the moment that I know God is very real. It's that moment that I feel the heaviness in my chest and the moaning and the cries that try to escape my body. It's like God is praying through me for them, and hurting for them as I do. I'm 47 years old and I live in a cage and have for many years now. I'm not any good to anyone it seems, but at times God uses me to cry for the children. Actually people of all ages in different circumstances, but mostly for the children it seems. I know that God loves them so much.

So many times as a Christian I ask, Lord, why is there so much pain and why should the children suffer? And that's not all I ask God about. I ask about why there is so much pain and sorrow all over this world. You'd think God didn't care about them. But He does, very much. And although tragedy seems to strike every corner of this earth and we feel like there is no hope and that God has abandoned us. Its not so. All this suffering is for now during this time on earth and these things all have to come to pass before Christ returns.

It is up to us as Christians to be empty vessels for God, for Him to be able to use us at these times…. He does pray through us for these people and children all over this world that are hurting.

I can't get over the feeling that comes to me at times and I can feel the hurt and pain it seems. I may not amount to much to this world, but I know that God loves me the same as these little children.

Satan will not give up until the day comes when the One who is worthy comes to make it all right and take us all home, or one by one. I just pray that God comes and gets us soon. I know that there will be little children in heaven. We are not going to be all the same age. Without the sound of children's laughter and joy, that would be like taking music out of heaven. Smile. Those children will be there and they won't ever hurt again as we won't ever hurt again. Smile!

Donnie

Donnie followed his story with a prayer:

Lord, I don't know what You want for me, but I do know that I may be the most loved man on earth. That is truly a blessing, Lord. I must be selfish cause I want more than what I have. I'm sorry too Lord that I'm this way. But things that plague me have worn me out, loneliness mostly. And it seems I'll never meet the mark because of my selfishness. I try and yet I know I can try harder. But I am just so tired of this life that I have.

Please make things right for me. I know what awaits me in heaven, Lord. And again I guess I'm being selfish in wanting to come home, no matter what's here. I say I have suffered enough. I've been chained up for so long now. I've been beat and cussed at and spat upon by so many in this world. I've been left behind and forgotten by many. But then again You've replaced them all a hundred times over. You've healed my bones and bruises and You've mended the scars on my heart too. You've made me tough and able to handle it all. And yet at the same time, able to feel even the smallest hurt and pain in this world. A heart of flesh You gave me. And Lord I know that in no way could I ever suffer what You have for me and all the people of this world. Never could one do that. All I can say is I'm just so tired and lonely. I can't seem to live like I should or be spiritual all the time. This place I'm in is not good. I've had enough Lord.

I want to be right. But Lord, I think that as long as my spirit and soul is trapped in this body I'm not going to be what You want me to be. Forgive me for being selfish and untrusting at times and for not loving You enough. It's no excuse but I am just a human Lord, a human that wants to get on out of here. Give me the strength to go through what is coming my way. I'm sorry for being selfish, but I thank You and praise You for the family You have brought into my life. I know that's how You love me. And thank You for all the people that hold me up in prayer to You. If they only knew the many battles that have been won because of their prayers for me. And bless my family, Lord.

In Jesus Name

Donnie no longer doubted that he was saved, and it had nothing to do with obeying society's laws but accepting Christ's death on the cross as payment for his sins.

Chapter 15

Wanting to be Free

"...and finally, finally have a life in heaven"

October 5, 1999

*D*onnie wrote:

I'm hoping the lawyers don't file anything and they just do as I wish. One thing I would like to avoid is the competency hearing. Just would be nice if that part would go away. But I guess not.

I'm sorry Cous, I'm just not in a good mood lately and I want to talk to someone and I always run to you. I just want to get through the motions that I have to go through on all this and now they want to put me off for thirty days until November 11. It seems I can't get away from that day. Fourteen years ago exactly they sentenced me on Veterans Day.

Annie, this is the only way I am going to be free. I want to walk in the lush green fields and flowers where there are waterfalls and animals all around to enjoy and where I will be free to come and go and not ever be lonely again. I'll have a job and work to do. I can stay busy and not have all these feelings here to deal with anymore.

At times I still get scared and worried. But I feel if I stay here too much longer that I'll lose you all. I can't help it, it's happened to me all my life. It never fails that people get tired and go on and forget me here. I need to get on out of here while I'm still a loved man. I know this may sound dumb to you all but I deal with this at times. —Donnie

As I considered Donnie's feelings, I thought how we Christians often think that once a person is saved that we are going to be able to handle every situation with remarkable grace. Yet we are not always able to do this. It's not because God is not sufficient but because we are still torn between the natural and the spiritual.

Paul said, "For what I am doing, I do not understand. For what I will to do; that I do not practice; but what I hate, that I do. (Romans 7:15)

> I got a letter from you today with the pictures of Cassie in her homecoming dress. She's a beautiful lady. I'm proud that she was a good sport about not getting to be queen, but a candidate is quite a compliment from the team. Smile! I laughed when I saw her standing there all dressed up but no shoes. Thank you for sharing those with me.
>
> No date for Gribble yet. But things are moving in the Supreme Court now that they are back. And Jim is sweating it too. He's up there reading book #4 of the Left Behind series. Thank you for writing McFarland's name down too. He is a growing Christian and needs to be cared about. —Donnie

October 11, 1999

> Just one of those days here, Annie. It's a mad house and you can't concentrate on anything. Crane will get killed tomorrow and he bought us all ice cream, the whole wing. Smile. I wrote him a few days ago and he loves Jesus and is ready to go.
>
> I've been thinking about Dad. I hope he's okay. It's important that he has a life. I love him. I lie here and think about him getting old and maybe trying to keep up, you know? I just get these thoughts. —Donnie

October 12, 1999

> You okay? I just want to talk to someone. They're going to kill

Crane today and he just left for his last visit so we won't see him again. Once they leave the wing they leave from out there for the Walls Unit.

I got up and things are behind schedule today. I ate and then Gribble told me they kicked him out of the courts today so he's on his way. Say Annie, I was just thinking when they kill Jim and Gribble I'll be alone. But it's hard to deal with what they're going through and I'll be there for them all I can. —Donnie

October 17, 1999

I was so glad to see Sandy and Cory again and we had a great visit. Sandy is such a neat person and she is always interested in what is going on here. I don't want to just keep telling her more and more about this place and let it affect her. I want people to see and know to a degree, but not so much that it affects them in a bad way. I miss them already. I came in and didn't even workout. I felt so homesick after they left. You know Cory is like a little brother to me. I really love him and just want the best for him. Fun to watch him grow. He's such a good kid.

I have a million thoughts about these last few years in coming to know this family....

I guess everyone has hope to a degree, but I just got tired. I worry about this being too much of a load for you. And I know I drive you up the wall at times with my moods and all I put you through.

Gribble sent me a little book on Origami. It shows how to make things by folding paper. I made a teacup and a dove. It looks like a dead dove, but I was trying to make you something and it looks real bad but I'll send them on anyway. Smile.

I got a letter from Kitchens [inmate already moved to the Terrell Unit where Death Row was being relocated]. He has a date and will die soon and he wanted me to know. Remember

his brother Redbird that works here at Ellis out in the visiting area. You have met Redbird. Man, I've seen so many go to die.
—Donnie

October 28, 1999

Knowing there was a process to go through, Donnie wrote one of his appellant attorneys, Jim McCarthy:

> I wanted to end it all now. It's just a little longer this way, but I'll truly know this is God's will that I come on home.
> You've all been there when I needed you, but we're world's apart, Jim. I want to be right in this. I'm not lost to the attitude and outlook in the courts and justice system today and I just want to get in the Fifth Circuit [Court] by this month and knowing I won't be in there long, just get on out and down the line.
> We're all going to die one day, Jim. Even the people that kill me are going to die one day. And the way I live in this small cage here is no life. We have nothing to do anymore, too many changes here. Chains and cuffs all the time.
> I've just run out of gas. I'm desperate to get out of here by death and finally, finally have a life in heaven. I don't look for life anymore, nor do I have any hope in this world. My hope is God only.
> Thank you for writing me. Just file something and let me get on down the road. Please!
> Respectfully, Donnie.

After receiving a copy of the letter to his attorney, I wrote Donnie that it was a good letter, and I did not want to think of myself in this matter. I could not imagine this happening, but I promised Donnie to do my very best, and with God's help I would support him in his decision to stop his appeals.

I knew he was praying, and I was praying God's will for him.

November 1, 1999

Donnie wrote:

As for Gribble, he's up and down on things. People handle all this in different ways, Annie. It shows on some and when it gets down to that time and you know it's coming, it affects some in a bad way. But I can tell you he is trying, but he doesn't know the ways of God fully yet. He has a brother who is in need of a heart and Gribble wants to give him his real bad. He's tried to come up with a way of doing it. But he's not depending on God to take care of things. Baby steps, you know?

You mentioned that I might do more than I know down here as for God's work. Believe me Annie, I'm no light here. Only some see that side of me. Most still think of me as tough and trouble.

I hear what you said about our failures haunting us at times. But I believe that for the believer in God that memories are what keep us in line and growing. Romans 8:28 says, And we know all things work together for the good to those who love God. So no matter how much we hurt or regret the failures in our life it's how it affects us, and what kind of heart we have about it that counts. —Donnie

I had written to Donnie, I Thessalonians 5: 23-24, "Now, may the God of peace Himself, sanctify you completely; and may your whole spirit, soul, and body be preserved blameless at the coming of our Lord Jesus Christ. He, who calls you is faithful, who also will do it."

November 5, 1999

Donnie wrote:

I got the scripture you sent. I took the little piece of paper and I have it here on my wall.

As you can see, depression here is something that is common. I dread at times writing about how I feel about this place and how lonely it is because I know it only brings you down. But I have to talk to someone, and God sent you my friend. —Donnie

God sent Donnie a whole family of friends to listen, to love, and to encourage him.

Donnie wrote:

> Being blessed will always continue for you, Annie. Don't be scared of it. God knows that you have the kind of attitude and heart that you have and He trusts you. Therefore, He continues to bless you. And as you go through this trial He will see you through it, too.
>
> In my life here, some wanting me to live on means a lot to me. But I can't see that I could be that important to anyone, not with the life I have. I'm a drain I'm sure to many that love me. I wonder so many times if you really know what you and Dale mean to me.
>
> I lay in my bed at night and I just look at the wall and I pray, "Lord please make this all right for us all." —Donnie

November 11, 1999

Donnie continued to report as TDCJ moved more death row inmates to the Terrell Unit in Livingston, forty miles east of Huntsville. He knew it would be only a matter of time until they would all be moved there. He dreaded the change...the unknown.

November 13, 1999

> I thank you so much for caring and sending these guys things to read. I'm no light but they will listen to you. Around here I often see Satan at work. So much evil going on. Most Christians in the free world don't even know how the battle works. They don't realize that angels are fighting a war in the spirit realm and they get tired, too. They get overrun at times and have

to retreat, because they work by prayer power. Prayer is so important and the key to all battles. Remember in the book of Daniel when it took the angel 21 days to get down to Daniel. Why? He had to contend with the angel of darkness.

Annie, Satan is alive and well on this planet. The Bible says that our adversary, the devil walks about like a roaring lion, seeking whom he may devour [I Peter 5:8]. I know that today people hear what they WANT to hear and what makes them feel good about themselves. A man preaches the Word of God, as it is, and most will run away. God's Word convicts. And as for judging? We should learn that judging is not to be thrown at others but at one's self. We judge ourselves and that is what changes us.

Well, I get carried away. But we'll talk more about this.

They made 54 moves on Friday. Moved some to solitary and they cleared out 18 and 20 wing. It's empty. An old friend of mine, Jose Gutierrez moved over here. I saw him go by and it surprised me. He's on the execution list I sent you. That used to be my old workout partner with Martin Gulrule. He's one of the best people I know and I lost track of him. Real strong Christian too. I knew he had a date to die and was thinking he might get a stay. But he dropped his appeals. They killed his brother a few years ago.

But I got to talk to Jose Monday. I sent him a kite [message] and I got one back from him. I wish I had saved it for you. I'm so used to throwing kites away. Not to be read you know. Smile. But he wanted something to eat. Said he was going home to be with Jesus, and can't wait. Smile! I hope he is in my rec group so we can talk and pray some together before he goes. He used to stay on me about God and the Word, but I was so caught up in the wrong things as usual. He's a real inspiration to me. He might be dead by the time you read this. —Donnie

November 14, 1999

I have to tell you this story about Sonny Buckingham, the preacher at Parker County jail. I was going through some things to send home with you next time you're down here and I found some pictures. I found one of this old Ford Ranger truck that belonged to Sonny. I want you to save this picture, Annie. This is the truck that a guy gave Sonny. His old truck blew up and he didn't have a ride, so he prayed about it and told the Lord that he really needed a truck. So this guy comes to church and gives him the keys and says, God told me to give you this truck. Sonny told the Lord, You know I don't even have the money for the tags and registration. Then out of nowhere he gets a check from someone for two hundred dollars. It cost $198 and some cents to get the tags and registration. So this is a miracle truck, Annie!

I think the memory is going out on my machine here. It's been giving me some problems as you have probably noticed in my typing. I had to work on this thing some more. I'm afraid it is gone. Looks like I'm going to have to use the manual part on it.

I got the papers from the lawyers yesterday and they have put me off again for thirty more days. Will it ever stop? —Donnie

November 15, 1999

After Dale and I visited, Donnie wrote:

Sitting here sweatin. The weather is not hot but those peppers I put in that spread is!

I came in and went right to the rec yard and talked to Jose for about an hour. He is really ready to go be with the Lord. He sang me a song that he is going to do for his last words. Really nice song too. I had him sing it to me twice. I had chills all over. God was there. And then he helped me work out some and we just talked away about the Lord and this place. I fixed Jose a can of roast beef, some refried beans, one can of beef stew, hot sauce, peppers and Fritos. I spread cheese over the flour tortillas and made four big ones for Jose. Jose is built like a bear and weighs about 250. We were laughing about how much weight we had gained.

I cried, Annie. I have so much compassion for Jose. But we talked about all he was going to see in heaven.

He wrote a letter to the family and asked forgiveness and he's got his business taken care of. I wonder sometimes why God brings these guys my way and then they're gone. I want to go too. I'm sad.

I loved seeing you and Dale today. I love it when you preach to me and talk about God. That's why I've got you. Just like going to church. But two hours just isn't enough time. We just get wound up and our time is gone. —Donnie

November 16, 1999

It has been a rough day here. Jennings had a date with death and he refused to come out of his cell and said he didn't want to die. They sprayed him. I watched it all. Four of us were caught out there. So my day is ruined. But what got me most was the officers out in the hall afterwards, laughing and high-fiving. Some joke to kill a man. But the boy put up a fight and got two of the officer's mask off and they got out of there real fast.

Now what I was feeling inside for the people who hold us was not good, Annie. I felt hate and anger in me, and it brought a tear to my eye. But this guy must not have known where he was going when he died. I was sad and angry.

Tomorrow they kill Lamb and Thursday they get Jose. Jose had a visit today, so I missed being with him.

I tried to eat some supper, but I just fixed a soup. I think I'll just do some puzzles and leave it at that. I'm just mad! Like I said, we were caught out there and watched it all. —Donnie

Friday, November 19, 1999

I got my newspaper tonight and Jose was in it. I was waiting and he did everything he said. I cried, but I was happy. Jesus got the glory here. All that took place robbed the state of everything, in a sense.

Holy, Holy, Holy, Lord God Almighty. Smile! Jose sang that song real well too. I look forward to seeing him again. I told him God may let him and me go on some missions together and that we'll be busy in heaven. He liked that.

My friend, Jim, has a date now for January 27, 2000.
—Donnie

November 20, 1999

Thoughts: When I look out the window here, there's nothing to see. I try, but I see nothing. It's as if I look through things. Very hard to explain. I guess one has to be here to know. —Donnie

November 21, 1999

More thoughts: Today I saw what I had written yesterday. I look out my window and still there's nothing to see. So I'll read my Guidepost and do a few puzzles Annie sent me. —Donnie

November 22, 1999

Got two letters from you. I read the stories you sent and I read that Guidepost, too. I love those. I used to read them all the time. Thank you for them.

Annie, I get tore apart with this family thing. I know Dad loves me and I love him. I love my sister and the girls. I've really never stopped loving them and at times it hurts so bad. I get confused and it affects me.

Happy Thanksgiving to you all! —Donnie

November 23, 1999

    Gribble was asked if he wanted to go to an execution summary. He said no. Then he asks later why he was asked that. They told him he has a date. No one had told him court wise. It's March 15, 2000. He has a little time. —Donnie

November 29, 1999

    After Betty and I visited, Donnie wrote:

    Annie, I am so tired of being a failure, kind of like Jose said to me, Just tired of sinnin. I mean, Annie, I want more than anything to please God. I want to know Him more and more, but it is like I'm frozen in time. I can't seem to read my Bible and stay as close to Him as I should. And Like I told you today about laying down at night and I'm just talking to God and I ask to see Him in my dreams. Talk to me loud and clear, Lord! Then it comes to me that I'm not good enough to stand in His presence. I just need something to grasp and hold onto. Yes, I know we have His Word, but I'm just dumb and I need a little more than most. I get scared at times Annie. I think its time that I go see what's up in the kingdom. Smile. Like I said, We are all going to die one day. Ain't no getting out of it. I'm going to close and go to bed. I'm looking forward to seeing you and Betty again tomorrow. —Donnie

November 30, 1999

    Well, here I am just sitting here looking at my orange. So hard to let you and Betty leave today. I get back in here and I don't want to talk to anyone. Just want to be left alone.

    Just sitting there today looking at you and Betty and I thought, these are the best friends I've ever had in my life. I love you both so much.

    Today Betty was telling me what I needed to hear about those last few days and hours and minutes. How God would be strong around me and I need that now too. I did notice that when I left and I was back there being shook down [searched] that I felt different. And I was even talking to that cop different. I just feel that relief is on the way, Annie. I talked to him about the Lord and told him I was ready to go home, that this is no life. He just looked at me and said, I hear ya Stone. I can't wait to retire and get the heck away from here myself. Then I came in and talked to a nurse and she said the very same thing to me. But I tell them that I believe in Jesus and that we all have to die sooner or later. Smile. I hope no one gets into a conversation with me without doing some thinking later. I really feel that doing this [stopping appeals] is the right thing to do.

I just screwed this life up, Annie. I know I've missed God's blessings a million times because of self. I've just been so stupid and done all the wrong things. If I had walked a different walk in my beliefs I'd have been a different person no doubt. —Donnie

The regrets of his life weighed heavy on Donnie's heart; he knew he could not change his past, but believed his pardon was secure in Christ.

Chapter 16

Love Bears All Things

"I would give anything to be there with you all"

The Bear

A short story by Donnie Foster:

...*I* was standing in a forest, and there was pine trees so tall. And as I stood on a rock that was covered with pine needles and moss I could feel the moisture in the air. I held a tree branch in one hand and a knife in the other. I threw them down and stepped off the rock and into a thicket where I heard water running in the distance. I walked toward the sound and as I cleared the brush I saw a river that was shallow but running hard. I stepped into the water and felt the coldness of it, and I saw a fish that was swimming upstream. I looked down the river and I saw the most beautiful mountains so high and shinning at their tops against a blue sky. There was cotton like clouds that had a shade of purple around the bottom edges of them. Such beauty I had never seen before.

As I was looking at an eagle flying in the distance, I heard a crunching sound in the trees by the bank, and as I looked a tree was falling into the water. And then I heard heavy snorting and breathing in the brush coming toward me. I watched the brush move and then I saw a brownish that did not match the color of the brush and then the brush fell flat. It was a bear that was big as any bear I had ever seen. He looked at me and blew his breath at the ground before him and then stood up on his hind legs. He was as tall as ten feet and it showed his teeth and let out a growl that vibrated my body from across the river. Then he dropped down on all fours and stepped into the water. As he did I stepped further in myself and headed across to meet him. As we met in the middle, he looked into my eyes and sniffed at me. I sniffed back and I reached into the water; tried to grab a fish at the same time. As I felt the silk skin of one slide through my hand and I latched onto it and pulled it from the water and held it high above my head. The bear looked at it and he moaned as a puppy would. I held out the fish to him with one hand, and with the other I grabbed his ear and I scratched it slow. The bear took the fish and sat in the water and ate with both paws. I stood beside him and I whispered in his ear, Is this heaven? He looked at me and blinked his eyes, and dropped the fish in the water. We watched it float away down stream together, the water red around it. The sun glared off the water and it blinded me for a second. I looked around at the bear and he wasn't there anymore. I looked again and this time I saw a wall. On it I saw a calendar that had pictures of people that I once knew and loved. And then I looked back to my hand and there was no hair from the bear in it. And I realized that I had a dream. It wasn't real. I rolled over and looked at the floor and as I did I felt drops of water run from my eyes down my face. And as they hit the floor I rubbed them around where I had rubbed the other tears till they dried. I closed my eyes and cried and prayed that I never wake again till I meet the bear face to face.

SA

Richard D. Foster #815

December 3, 1999

Donnie wrote:

Almost Christmas, Annie. Smile! I pray that everyone will be together and close this year. I would give anything to be there with you all. I'd like to be standing in the back yard by your pond. I love that pond. I lay down at night and I talk to God and I am staying as close as I can to Him, Annie, but I have rough nights when I let a lot of the bad things come back and I just try to sort them all out. I talk to God about them too.

This worldly war and my worldly shield, I am laying it down. I don't mean to seem like a quitter or weak. Lots of people here look at it as being that, like I'm giving in to a fight, but I look around at those who say that and they are of the world.

I have a sense of belonging that I have never had and I will not get away from that. There will be those who won't want things done as I have asked you to do about my service [funeral], but we'll worry about those things as they come. And it's not for people to say, 'well he's dead, he won't know the difference and he was a little off anyway.' Smile. I assure them I am not off. Off to a better life that's all.

I was laying here thinking and listening to all the screams and hollering for some rank [officers], cause some dude didn't get to go outside. Then I smelled a certain smell. It's cologne, and no one wears that except Father Walsh. Smile. So I jumped up and looked around and sure enough there he was! He's such a grand old man. We don't believe the same, but he cares so deeply. —Donnie

December 5, 1999

Concerned about more death row inmates being moved to the Terrell Unit, Donnie had written Red Kitchens, one of the first inmates to be moved to the unit.

Donnie wrote:

I never heard back from Kitchens, but another guy wrote and told me you're all alone there. You hardly ever see anyone. You don't know anything and they don't mess with you. Your radio is your friend. —Donnie

December 7, 1999

Referring to his funeral services, Donnie wrote:

Cory and Annie, I know I am different and I have lived a different kind of life. But one thing for sure, God made a way for someone like me and He loves me too. That alone is a witness to some in life.

Having my funeral this way is my way of bringing joy to this family. I want everyone that wants to participate. But most of all I want everyone to know I'm free at last and I'm home waiting for the rest of you.

I had a love for things that was worldly I know. I loved Harleys and old cars. Things were just as bad then as they are now. Murder, rape and robbery has always been bad. They just show everything on the news now. What a rotten world this is!

Annie, just bury me in my tennies, unless someone wants them. They still have a few miles on them. I don't want new clothes, but just a tee shirt and faded jeans. Maybe Dale has an old pair. He's taller, but who cares how long they are. No one's gonna be looking at my feet. Also, Glenda has my belt buckle. Just use one of Dale's old belts, not a new one. I don't want new anything, except for the box I'm going in. It may be hard to find a used one unless they have some kind of racket going in the graveyard. Smile.

Please don't shave me Annie. A trim if you need to but I want my moustache and goatee on me. I won't need a haircut. I'll get that done here. Okay?

It may seem odd to some that I am dressed that way, but I don't want anyone changing me up to look like they want me to look. This is not a lot to ask. —Donnie

In early December, Donnie had asked that I contact his lawyers to see if they had filed for another extension in his case.

I wrote him that I was sure they had filed for an extension and would want to talk with him more face to face. I assured him they would want to know for certain that stopping his appeals process was what he wanted. His attorneys had not yet been told what Donnie had confessed to Betty and me about what had happened April 5, 1984, at the feed store. I told Donnie that I thought his attorneys were going to need to know about that.

December 10, 1999

After a visit with his lawyers at the Ellis Death Row Unit in Huntsville, Donnie wrote:

I have got to write a letter, stating in writing, that I want to drop my appeals, then it's a done deal, Annie. Craig said they could challenge my sanity and I may have to be tested, but after that I'm home free.

Craig was uneasy about all this, but he came to see me as a friend as well as my lawyer. He's also going to be with you at the execution.

I did all I could to get them upbeat before they left. I told them some old stories here and had them laughing. So they're okay. Craig is my friend, and Alexa has been there for me and she is pretty cool. So Craig is the man to the end. Smile.

If I could be held and hugged by you ever, I would need it today more than anytime. I'm sad but that is nothing new to me. I feel a little anxious and just a little hyper. I need to workout a while and try to calm down.

I'm going to get on that letter to the lawyers and drink some coffee. But I want you to know that every one in this family is in my heart more than ever till I leave here. I love you all very much. We'll hold each other up as best we can till it's over. And life will go on, my friend. So as of today let's start getting everything in order. I'll need your help and advice in all things.

I guess this letter they want is on the way. But Craig said he wanted you to call him. And let him know how you feel, so will you do that? It bothers me to be putting you in this position, but I have no one else to take care of these things for me. I know you'd do anything for me and I need to get some things done and rolling the right way.

Okay, I have a few things that I want to ask you and talk about. As you know, I have never told anyone about this case except you and Betty, not even Craig, or anyone in that firm. And now that we're closing this book on out what do I do? I'm stuck here, Annie. I mean something is going to have to be said. God knows my heart in all this. I don't know if I should write this down and let the other side [victim's family] have it or what I should do. I'll pray about it. It happened. You see, knowing there is a heaven is where being a Christian comes into play. Wanting to die is an admission of guilt in the state's eyes and most everyone else. So I need you to write me and tell me what I need to do in getting things going concerning the victims. You know they've got this thing where an offender can face the victims and say we're sorry. From a legal standpoint in fighting this case and trying to get out of here I've had to take the stance that I have all these years. But none of that matters now. Maybe I should pray that I go out quietly for the family's benefit. No media and all that. I've got to believe that God is going to tell me what to do.

I just got your letter. Made my night to hear from you. I'm sorry, but you had me laughing about you pulling something off the top shelf at Wal-Mart and bruising your lip. Take time to find a clerk next time, will ya?

Oh God, the hardest thing of all in this will be leaving you all.
—Donnie

On December 12, 1999, my daughter, Sandy, and I visited Donnie in Huntsville.

He later wrote:

    I came in from our visit and I cried. I thought about the prayer that Sandy said out there. Bless her heart. I love her very much, Annie. She is such a caring person. I need to spend some time with Sandy and talk to her, so please make sure that she gets down here again. I know people work and it's not easy for them to come but as you and Sandy left, I just wanted to holler and tell you I love you, even though I tell you all the time. And then I thought that you won't make it back home in time for church tonight. Annie, I'll be praying that God bless you with energy and strength. I don't want you to be getting wore down spiritually either.

    Hey my friend, I came in and I had this thick envelope on my bed and it snapped that this was the pictures you were telling me about! I pulled them out and started looking through them. I had so much fun just reading the backs and looking at them. But I had a sense of being there with Dale and it was so good of him to take the time to write all that on the backs for me. I loved it and I guess it is just a bad time, but it hit me so hard emotionally. I realized how much I love you and Dale. You both are so good to me and you make me feel so loved.

    Well, I guess I'll watch the Cowboys play today. Craig says I'll at least be here to see the Super Bowl.

    I was thinking about what all I was going to give to who. Smile. I started laughing out loud for a bit. Except for this fan, which is still a good fan, I got nothing! My worldly possessions are my pictures, watch, sun glasses and the glasses that you gave me, my coffee pot that I hope makes it till I'm gone. I got my billfold that I made at the factory and my alarm clock. It's old, cracked all over and been worked on a hundred times, but

it works great. It belonged to Pop Holland. Pop was a security guard at a bank. I forget where, but it got robbed and he was the one. He killed someone and came here. I liked him. He came over to the Walls Unit to be executed twice, but came back each time. Then they got him. He was tired too. But then the clock belonged to JC and JC gave it to me. Now I give it to Dale. I love my friend Dale. But all in all, I've got nothing Annie. It made me cry. I don't have anything, yet I have everything. Smile.
—Donnie

December 13, 1999

I wrote Donnie that I had called his lawyers on the phone, asking what the procedures would be in his case from this point. Alexa said they would get his medical records from TDCJ and did have to file for another extension.

I wanted Donnie to know that we would be here for him and asked him to write or at least make some mental note of things that he wanted to discuss.

I reminded Donnie that although we didn't always agree on some things, we loved him unconditionally and love bears all things. We know that love is the source of strength. We know that love is accepting the other person just the way they are without trying to change them.

December 14, 1999

Donnie wrote:

I am about as bored as one can get and just lost today it seems. I did some crossword puzzles, then I lay down, then I got up, then I lay back down, and then I got up and started going through some of my property and pictures. I'm keeping my pictures of the family here until I go, but I'll get those back to you the day I leave this world. The rest of these pictures and books I'm sending home with you right away.

I'm keeping my two Bibles and I bagged the other books except for a couple. Annie, keep this Nelson's Concordance out at all times. It needs another cover but perhaps you can repair it. But it is a very useful book. Put all these books in your library. And I thank you for them too. I enjoyed them and I tried to take care of them for you.

I would have given anything to just be there and just share some time with you all. From what God has taught me now I know that I could have made a difference in life and enjoyed it more. Being there for your loved ones is such an honor in life. Some of the smallest things in life can make such a big difference. Just taking the time to go visit a person you were thinking about or maybe just a phone call. It just changes their day and your day also. Smile.

Dorothy [inmate's wife] gave me the message that you're going to be here Thursday and Friday. I am so happy but I'm worried that you are going to get wore down.

Gribble is real down, Annie. He sent me a kite and wanted me to get the cell next to him. But the guy came back that was there. Maybe you could send him a card and tell him we love him. Mark was really up about you sending him a card. He said he was going to make you one. He's a good guy.

My hands are so cold. I can't get them to work right. But hey, I'm counting the hours until I see you guys. We got lots to talk about. Thirty more hours and you'll be here!

Yes Annie, love bears all things. I am so blessed. And although I want so much more, it is enough. Does that make any sense? You, Dale, Betty and Sandy and Cory are so much a part of me and everyone else there, too. It's as if I know them. Tell them I love them and I hope to get to meet them all before I go. I've had all my pictures of the family out and I look at them over and over.

I have a need to write, but I can't begin to explain to you how it feels to get ready to be killed and meet the Lord. Smile. But it's a mind boggling thing. —Donnie

December 17, 1999

After Betty and I had visited Donnie, he wrote:

Well, I guess you guys are headed home. I already miss you both so much. I didn't want you to go. I'm so glad that you stopped and waved at me again. It made my day for you to do that. After you left the lady next to us that was waiting for her visit was talking to me. We were talking about how we were so tired of all this here. I told her I was going to get out. She said, Well, my visitor isn't ever going to get out, he's on Death Row. I said, Me too. She just stopped and looked at me and said, 'And you're going to get out?' I said, Yes Mam, I'm going home to be with Jesus! She said, They're going to kill you; that's how you're going to get out? I said, Yes Mam. —Donnie

December 18, 1999

Donnie wrote:

Annie, you'll like Sonny [Buckingham]. You know some about him already, but he is good people. God used my friend, Glenda and him greatly in my life. Let me know what you think about the service. You have a say in this, too. But I wrote to Glenda and told her I'm comfortable this is God's will for me. God knows that I don't want to be out of His will. I told her that I'm preparing for my journey home, and I'm spending all the time I can with my family. I will always be considered one of the bad guys on this earth. But God made a way for me and He fulfilled everything that I have always wanted in a family, and that you all have loved me, and that God has been in everything in our lives. I told her that I am trying to walk with God and that soon I'll be with

Him and free at last, that it is nothing to be sad about and that it is a glorious occasion. -Donnie

December 21, 1999

Donnie wrote:

You may not even get this before Christmas. The holidays are hard here. But I got a card from Bev and I loved it. It had squirrels in a mailbox on the front. She probably knows how much I love animals. Smile.

Annie, all these years of time I've done I have always been protective of what I let in my mind. There is an art to doing time, ya know. You have to put the walls up and set your mind and not allow things to get in your head cause they make you fall. And when the world creeps in on your time it can become unbearable. It makes you mad and angry at the whole world. Am I making any sense to you, Annie? There are nine on the list to be executed in January. —Donnie

Christmas Day December 25, 1999

I wrote Donnie, "It has been one Christmas I shall never forget. I now know why you said you'd like to be standing out in my back yard by the fishpond on Christmas Day."

I explained that we had just finished eating Christmas Dinner and everyone was there when Betty and her husband, Hop, walked in.

"Come on everyone," Sandy said, "let's go to the back yard for some family pictures!"

I had just finished my last roll of film. I had taken approximately four rolls, a total of 96 pictures, counting Christmas Eve, but I followed behind. We were looking at the fishpond and talking about the Koi fish not hibernating this year, perhaps because of an exceptionally warm Oklahoma winter. My son-in-law, Wade, commented that I sure had some wild creatures in my back yard.

I looked around to see a large brown bear almost as tall as myself, carved from a tree. The bear was standing by my fishpond wearing a Santa hat and a large red bow around his neck.

I could not help but think of the bear story Donnie had written. He often sent me pictures of bears he had cut from magazines or calendars. Then I noticed a red gift bag tied to the bear's bow with a letter hand written and decorated by Donnie:

Merry Christmas 1999
My Dearest Friend Annie.

Guess you're standing next to the bear right now. I'd like to tell you Merry Christmas in person but I can't, so this will have to do.

Words can't tell how special you are to me, Annie. Even if they could there's not enough paper in the world to do so on. Same goes for all this family. How blessed I am by all of you.

I wanted something special for you, and without Dale and Sandy and Cory it could not be done.

I've been looking back in my life today, and I was thinkin what a strange and hard life it's been. I've missed so much. I've hung in there as best I can too and to make it this far God had to use some special people in my life.

You have loved me and taken care of me. You've made me feel for once in my life a part of something. You accepted me for me. And I am just me Annie. I doubt you or any of the family there will ever know how complete you all have made this man and his life. My cup is full now. I've forgotten what it's like to be hugged or to hug someone you love. I won't be able to hug you down here, but when you get to where I'm going I'll hug you then and all the family.

I am ready to go home. A life here is no life my friend. If I can't stand where the bear is standing then there is no place left for me on this earth.

    I'm asking God to bless this bear too and everyone who sees it. Also, it's so you'll never forget me. Smile. Just smile every time you and Dale look at it. Now if I can just get on my way home.

        MERRY CHRISTMAS, ANNIE!

At the close of his letter, Donnie wrote a prayer for the family.

    Father in Heaven, bless my Annie, Dale and family. Strengthen them in the things to come. And Father I plead the Blood of Jesus over them all and even this bear. I praise You for these people that You put in my life. Keep them all safe, and please Father, bring us all home. LEAVE NONE UNSAVED and Father, thank You for my friend Annie.

    In Jesus' Precious Name. Amen.

How wonderful I thought it was of Dale, Sandy, and Cory for doing the legwork, the trips to find, order, and pick up the bear and allow Donnie to be a part of something that gave him so much pleasure. Now as I work around the fishpond in my backyard, I occasionally imagine hearing a crunching sound in the bushes only to look around and see "The Bear" innocently gazing my way.

Father in Heaven, bless my Annie, Dale and family. Strengthen them in the things to come. And Father I plead the Blood of Jesus over them all and even this bear. I praise You for these people that You put in my life. Keep them all safe, and please Father, bring us all home. LEAVE NONE UNSAVED and Father, thank You for my friend Annie.

In Jesus' Precious Name. Amen.

Chapter 17

Family

"...I've wasted my life"

December 27, 1999

*A*fter Dale and I visited him, Donnie wrtoe:

I just didn't want you all to forget me, and I know you wouldn't, but the bear will leave its mark for sure. Smile. I had made plans with Dale to give it to you after I'm gone, but they thought it would be better as a Christmas gift from me. Without Sandy and Dale and Cory I could not have done this. And actually everyone got to be a part of it. That old bear will have a story behind it.

Well, I got to see you and Dale today. I needed to see you guys, too. Although I don't think I was much of a visitor. When you left to go to the front I couldn't even talk to Dale. I could barely hold back the tears, and I hate for other visitors to see me like that. But Dale made this man's day and put a period on my life by doing this bear thing for me. I wonder all the time why I could not have known you and Dale all along. Just my life I guess. But we're all going to make it in everything just fine. And Annie I love it when you pray. That meant more to me than you will ever know when you prayed for us all today. Nothing is more important than families making God the center of all things that go on in this world.

I'm so sorry for the way that I am and just about my life. I feel like a total loser. Like today I was telling you about my neighbor here. It's not right the way I felt about him. I lose patience with these guys. I was convicted about it too. But it's just the way here and dealing with all that goes on.

I wished God had done me like Saul [Acts 9:1-9]. After his conversion and his name was changed to Paul, he said, I press on to take hold of that for which Christ Jesus took hold of me. [Philippians 3:14] —Donnie

December 30, 1999

Well, January is about here and I'm sure the lawyers are going to have no choice but to get on the ball for the courts.

I wrote my sister Lisa today. I told her I loved her and that we would know one day why things were the way they were and are in our lives. I told her if she had any pictures of her and me when we were kids to get with you and you could get copies made of them. So we'll see how that goes.

Say I was going through some things you sent last night and found this little booklet, pertaining to facts in the Bible. I needed that last night too. It has some really neat stuff in there. Like, I didn't realize that the stone David threw didn't kill Goliath. It just dazed him and David took the giant's sword and cut his head off. That's what killed him! Odd how I missed that.

Well Annie, I imagine they'll be moving Jim and Larry this week and all that have execution dates in January. Gribble won't move until February. But most of the guys are already down there. Before long we will need to check about my visiting list and change that the way I want it in my last days. We need to see how all that is going to work. The warden's secretary can tell you that I'm sure.

I did go to the store today. [Inmates call ordering from the commissary, going to the store]. I tried to buy some photo albums to start putting my pictures in for you. They're easier to look at that way too. But they were sold out. I love my pictures. I keep them sectioned out, and I'm always pulling them out according to the thoughts I have. Smile. —Donnie

December 31, 1999

I'm listening to some real old country music, I'm Wondering Where You are Tonight, and There Stands the Glass. Remember those? I love old, old country music, even older than Porter Wagner and Dolly. Hank William's days, ya know? And I love the old blue grass gospel music too.

I was thinking of my mom, Bertha, today. When I see her it'll be great won't it Annie? Will I have two moms in heaven? I have weird thoughts, huh? Bertha was a good woman. We didn't get along too well cause all our lives she stayed uptight all the time. I had some pictures of her and Dad when they first married. I thought Bertha was beautiful in her younger years.

I'm glad you got to talk to Dad. I miss and love him, but most of all I don't want him worrying about me at all. I will be fine in all this. We need to let him know that we love him and will get it all taken care of. I have a lot of compassion for Cliff. I always have. You know why Annie? It may be hard to explain, but I'll try.

When I came home from Nam, I saw Dad as a man that was nieve to the world and its ways. I saw him as a good man in a dirty world. Kind hearted Cliff always smiling and loving and caring. Then I saw the world around Mom and Dad changing. I saw it Annie, and it bothered me too. He came from simpler times. But I got out in the world and saw it for what it was, but Dad never saw what I did. He still lived in the 50's. Dad has lived such a good life. I wish I had been a better son and done everything right to please him. I just blew it. All we can do now is just use what I have learned and know that you don't do it this way.

Tell Dale I love him and he did good reading the Christmas Story from Luke on Christmas Eve!

I think about writing my brothers. I'd like for them to come to my funeral.... —Donnie

January 4, 2000

Annie, do you realize that I've wasted my life? I ruined it, messed it up bad. I don't have a life here really. I spend my life waiting to see you guys when you come here. Then when you go I begin to wait again till the next time. —Donnie

January 6, 1999

I wrote Donnie that I had called his lawyer's office and Alexa had told me that she had his papers in front of her and ready to go to the courts that basically stated that he wanted to waive his appeals. She told me they had to have the paperwork in by January 10, but she was waiting for his final decision. I had told her that I was waiting for Sherry and Bobby Nance to return from their visit with Donnie with one last confirmation from him that stopping his appeals was what he wanted.

"No, Donnie has not changed his mind," Sherry explained to me after their visit with him. So I confirmed to Alexa to go ahead with the paperwork to the courts.

I wrote Donnie that Betty and I would see him on the following Monday and have a two-day special visit.

January 7, 2000

Donnie wrote:

Annie, I have worried about you lately. You've got to be strong and you must know that God has a reason for everything. Even today and last week I'm beginning to see things. Things like the prayer that I prayed and asked God to use me mightily in my last days till I go. Then witnessing to that dude out there that day after you guys left, then the lady waiting the next day. And then the day as I visited Bobby and Sherry. Oh, we had a good one too! It was so good to see them. I realize that I have to hold you all up and be strong. Keeping our eyes on Jesus and in his Word. The gift is called exhortation. You know that's one of the spiritual gifts that some are given when we are saved.

I know that God is doing something in this family too and rest assured that He is doing it for a reason, maybe something for the future. Maybe you are to learn something about certain things. But in it all I feel like family and I feel I belong. For once I'm not scared that you're going to run out on me or forget me. I just cherish that feeling too.

But at times it hurts so much. The loneliness hits hard and I start to want to go home. That longing to be normal. All these years I have waited to be free. But my hope for life here on earth is gone. I could go on and on in my feelings but there's no need for that anymore, not where I'm headed. I know that you will back me and support me in my decision. As for here, I just don't want to be here anymore.

I feel like I'm somebody now with you and Dale, Sandy and Betty, and all the kids, and everyone. I have love that is awesome. So I can leave here satisfied that my life is complete.
—Donnie

In the meantime, Donnie was still dealing with the frustrations and effects of life on Texas Death Row, and he wrote about it often. Donnie continued:

I get so frustrated at times with these yakkers here. You know what a yakker is don't you Annie? That's someone who is so busy looking at other's problems and keeping the light on others so it won't land on them. In other words they think they never do wrong and are so great that they have no problems and it's always others, not them. Smile. That's a yakker.

A stressful night. Then a long day here. They seem to get longer and longer and all we hear is that we're moving. It's starting to play on me.

Just pray about this place and things for me in these last days. Get these lawyers moving. I am trying to be nice Cous, but I am very worried that in my last days I may not be a very nice person here. I may take a few beatings but they won't kill me. They got to keep me alive till they kill me. Just pray Annie. I know me, okay? I know I'll fight if pushed. —Donnie

January 10, 2000

I wrote Donnie to remember that Satan wants to use this time to stop any witness that he might have with others there. We must remember that our thoughts determine our relationship with God. Donnie had told me on different occasions that he could not be what he needed to be for God because of where he was. I reminded him that we have a choice of what we are going to think. When we decide to think about God's Spirit living on the inside of us, it will determine our outlook on everything. "For as he thinks in his heart, so is he" (Proverbs 23:7).

I reminded Donnie to think about Paul. He persecuted Christians before becoming a Christian himself. But when he accepted the Lord as his Savior his purpose and mind changed. He was in prison facing death when he wrote, "I can do all things through Christ who strengthens me" (Philippians 4:13). Adversity does not mean defeat. You are not to let the negative people around you determine your thinking. When we do this our actions are affected.

God's Word tells us what to do in order to be saved and be forgiven, and God is faithful to keep His promises. So no matter what the world had suggested to Donnie about himself, he was a child of God and that made him a huge success. I reminded him to "set his mind" on the truths of God's Word, make a point of going to sleep with Jesus on his mind and wake up each morning and ask God to give him what he needed for that day. We have to choose to do this.

January 14, 2000

Donnie wrote:

Sometimes my feelings and emotions overwhelm me. I can't breathe and I just want to yell out to the world.

It's a longing that is always around me, a feeling that I never stop wanting but spend all my time blocking it because I know it doesn't exist in my life or could ever happen to me and that is to be held, or hold another....

Its like nothing is real in this world. Only when my family comes to see me do I feel human. But it let's me know what I've missed and will miss as long as I'm alive here on earth.

Father, why keep waiting? Someone sent me this article Away to Arabia by Charles Stanley and it spoke to me. He says that God's love doesn't stop with the act of salvation but continues throughout the wayward times of your life when personal failure seeks to rob you of the sense of His presence and His ultimate devotion to you.[1] Every trial, every heartache is a point of potential blessing, because it is a place where we have the opportunity to submit our wills to God. Paul measured his life with one statement, "I have been crucified with Christ; it is no longer I who live, but Christ lives in me; and the life which I now live in the flesh I live by faith in the Son of God, who loved me and gave Himself for me." (Galatians 2:20)

My hands are freezing. I just got through washing my gym shorts and socks and the water is ice cold. But I save some of my old peanut butter jars. I fill them with hot water and use them to warm my hands on cold days.

> I was reading an article in the newspaper on Heiselbetz's execution, and the picture wasn't even of him. It was the last guy they killed. Weird, huh? Guess we all look alike. Smile.
> —Donnie

January 16, 2000

I wrote to Donnie that I liked the Bible Scriptures from Jeremiah 29 that his friend, Glenda, had sent him. It says, "I know the thoughts that I think toward you, says the Lord, thoughts of peace and not of evil, to give you a future and a hope. Then you will call upon Me and go and pray to Me, and I will listen to you."

Glenda told me that she had always believed Donnie would be freed from prison one day, and I wanted to believe that for him as well, but God had not confirmed to me that he would be free here on earth. So I tried to prepare for what was ahead of us.

January 21, 2000

Donnie wrote:

> Annie if you ever get a glimpse of true loneliness after I'm gone; maybe then you can understand what it's like here for me. Don't be sad either about me. But take all the feelings and emotions and just remember them. You'll see them over and over in people's lives and when you do you'll know what to pray and who to pray for. Experience. —Donnie

January 23, 2000

> Annie. I know I am a disgrace to some. Actually I've known all along. They made it clear that I am a real blemish on the Foster name. Someone made that statement years ago, and I have never forgotten it. I embarrassed them. Annie, I don't mean any harm or to be an embarrassment to them or anyone. But what can I do now; what's done is done? Dad's name could be in the paper or even yours for that matter. So I'm praying there won't

be any media there or anything about me in the papers.

Just some thoughts, Annie. But if it were not for you and Dale and the family there I'd be buried here. No one would come for me. But I just lift my arms to Jesus and praise him for everything that He has done for me in these last few years in making me a part of something.

But I must have been a really rotten person, Annie, and I let this and even things from birth get to me at times. I mean I grew up knowing Lisa and Mary [sisters]. But we knew we were just kind of passed down. You just wonder why?

I was sitting here and this guy comes by. Big guy. Lots of bass in his voice. Looks you square in the eye when he talks to you.

Anyway, he just looks at me. I look back, and I ain't smiling either. He says something like, Has he seen me before?

I said, yea, when Jose died.

We small talked some then he says something about Jesus. So we cover some ground spiritually, and about being with Jesus. I had questions and he helped some. Anyway, we talked on and I tell him about dropping my appeals and going home. He realizes I do know Jesus, but I'm telling him I am not able to walk right and sin all the time. On and on, but in the end I'm not feeling too good about myself as usual. But we pray and he tells me Man, you gave me what I needed today.

I didn't give him anything! Matter of fact, I feel I am not close enough or pleasing enough to God at all. But I felt Jesus was with us in prayer. And the guy says he's coming back too. Jesus is getting me ready, Annie. Smile.

I want to talk about heaven. Now we know that Jesus has the rapture. We are caught up in heaven with Him. That's phase one. Phase two will take place at the end of a seven year period after the rapture, when Christ returns to reign over His earthly kingdom.

When Christ takes His own to heaven (Christians who are already dead, and those who are alive at the time), they will stand before the Judgement Seat of Christ.

Some ask, if there are so many to be judged then why aren't they judged as they die, immediately after their death instead of letting those millions pile up at the last minute? Answer is we don't finish our work even when we die. It lives on after us. What we did here if it amounts to anything continues after we die physically. Our influence we had over friends and loved ones and people we knew during our lifetime does not cease when our obituary appears in the local paper. Right?

Anyway, I've been thinking about passing from here to there. I think about the place where the rich man was and the poor man. I think of the thief on the cross that day Christ died.

Well, We got things to talk about on this next visit like when you wrote, Death, where is thy sting?

Well Cous, I'm going to read a bit and get back in this book Escape the Coming Night. It's on Revelations. I didn't know that they called James and John to Sons of Thunder. That's what they called them when they were young, but as John grew older he became known for his softness. Smile.——Donnie

January 26, 2000

More thoughts:

Will there be snow in heaven? Will it be cold to the touch?

Sometimes time just don't pass, it lingers and drags.

Jim dies tomorrow. Makes me sad.

Found out today that more ice is coming, and Annie and Betty can't make the trip.

Seems like a year.

I was mad about something here. And Alexander the coppersmith came to mind, what Paul said about him as he prepares to leave in II Timothy 4:9-16. ["Alexander the coppersmith did me much harm. May the Lord repay him according to his works"]. —Donnie

January 28, 2000

Well Annie, Jim is dead and gone to be with Jesus. I got to go see him the night before and visit. We just talked away. But he was happy and ready.

I missed you and Betty last week. All snowed in, huh? I saw it on the news. But I don't ever want you guys out in weather like that. —Donnie

Donnie had mentioned how he would like to see Walters again before he left. Little did he know that he would see Walters again.

My son-in-law, Richard, took Bobby Nance in a plane and flew over Walters to take pictures of our homes, businesses, places of employment, the Sultan Park, and anything they thought Donnie would be interested in seeing.

Continuing in his letter, Donnie wrote:

Well Annie, I got my mail and I had a letter from Bobby Nance and one from you. I cried a while. You had said something about a surprise but I forgot. And then when I got all those pictures I just looked at them for a while. It was so neat. Bobby and Richard did a good job. They made my day! Bobby spent a lot of time making little arrows and explaining each picture in detail. He had every one's house marked and I could even see the bear in your back yard. These pictures are awesome! God made a way for me to see Walters again before I leave. Smile.

I wasn't even sure that Bobby and Richard liked me! I guess that sounds dumb. But you know being here is a shameful place to be. I'll always save the letter Bobby wrote. It really got me.

Tell Dale I love and miss him, and I did get to see his shop! And that old bear really stands out, huh? Smile!

Annie, in what you was saying about faith and all? Well today I was praying in one of my desperate moods and I told God that I need to come on home and get away from this here and that I know that He had it all planned when it was going to happen. But I needed to hear something. It would be nice if I could get it set for March 15. That way I could be there for Gribble. Do something worth while, huh?

Did you get your feather?" —Donnie

Occasionally Donnie would send a dried leaf or something he had found in the rec yard in his letters. Once there was a cloverleaf someone had given him. He would gloss them and tape them where he had signed his letter. Once he even sent a feather. It's amazing how we in the free world take so much for granted.

Donnie continued:

Have you seen Sandy lately? Its strange Annie, how I can get to thinking of someone there in the family and I remember all the things that we have shared and talked about and it carries me through the day here. Call her for me and tell her and Wade I love them, please.

Well, I am going to stop here and look at my pictures again. I've got to get two more albums this week. Little by little I'm getting them. But these pictures of Walters are going to be so neat in an album. I prayed once that God would let me see Walters again. Bobby and Richard will never know what this meant to me. —Donnie

January 30, 2000

Annie, read the article about Jim and his last words in the Huntsville paper. He was singing and talking to Jesus. His heart was for real towards everyone. He apologized to the victims and said, My life is all I can give.

I will have to have a competency hearing, Annie. It's

mandatory now. Ever since JC dropped his appeals the laws changed. That's why I have always told you I would probably have to face this competency thing. I had just hoped to be able to avoid it with my medical records. But everyone has to go before a judge and the judge says whether he is right in the head or not. Then it goes back to the Fifth Circuit Court and it's a go ahead after that. So I guess I'll see the lawyers soon.

I was real down about this hearing but I guess I've got to go through it. But maybe, just maybe if I go back Sonny [Buckingham] can come there and meet you guys. Maybe we can visit and I can give you a big hug. I'm sure I'll see you all this week. I have prayed that it gets real warm and melts all the ice. Smile.

I'm going to watch the Super Bowl here at five. —Donnie

Donnie continued:

I'm real sorry about the problems with the guy at Dale's shop. So I sit down and I really prayed about it. I asked God to make a way for the guy to be saved. I know God doesn't force Himself on people. They have to make a decision to repent and ask Jesus into their life. But I asked God if the guy was not going to do that, then to please move him. I'll pray again and put that on paper so we can all agree on that together.

I have dealt with people like this before. Handling it my way only makes matters worse. You can break a man's arms and one of his legs and ribs and all and let them suffer that for their crimes, but it only builds a hate in us and makes the person worse. It's just wrong to do that.

You see Annie, some people only understand violence and I used to think it is the only way to approach them. This life here has been a rough one. But to be right in your walk with Christ you can't handle things that way. Love is the only way and the only thing that really heals. Love turns stone hearts to warm soft flesh. Smile.

Anyway, I asked God to make a way for the guy to be saved. I could be me and say, well, this guy is never going to change and he's got this coming. But we have to pray right for this situation. I know that I am to pray for him and I did. It's going to work out.

I dread this hearing. Please pray that the media not get in this and that it goes fast and smooth and I can get back here in one day.

I told you the other night I had just been sitting here staring at the walls and thinking. But I talked to God a lot and I told Him I need to hear something on this and if I was coming home I'd like to get on with it and to please let me know something. I told Him, Lord, I will accept Your way. I feel I'm coming home, but you do it all in Your timing and I'll know it's right.

Well, the next morning I got the paper from the lawyers and the Fifth Circuit saying there would be a hearing. Annie, I didn't want to have a hearing, so I got angry and upset and wrote bad letters and then had to tear them up. I did that after I said all that to God. Smile. But I caught it. He made time for me to catch it too. And I got to thinking, I just may be able to hug you guys! You never know what could happen. They may put us in a room and let us visit. Just never know, so be praying about it all.

Annie, thank you so much for taking care of everything for me. I really believe things are working out the way God wants it. Keep your prayers going on this hearing thing. I hope you got to talk to the lawyers. I'm praying that this will happen at least within the next couple of weeks. I'd really like to get my business taken care of.

I'm glad Michael Self [Donnie's friend serving life] wrote you. He has a case where he should have been out of here years ago, and is just trapped in this place. But I have gotten to know him over the years and he is a wonderful person. Please remember him in your prayers and also Reynolds and Henry [other inmate friends]. They are guys that have held me up for years.

It's good that we have to go constantly to the Lord for direction. I've been thinking about what to say and what to do at this hearing. God will guide me in it I know. Maybe I'm not to say anything, and maybe I'm to say everything. I don't know yet, but I will know. —Donnie

As a Christian in close fellowship with God, Donnie now believed every prayer is answered and was willing to accept the answer when it came as God's best for him (Romans 8:28).

"I can do all things through Christ who strengthens me" (Philippians 4:13)

Chapter 18

A Million Thoughts

"I wanted to be that little boy again"

"But I'm not the one serving the time on Texas Death Row." I replied, when Craig, Donnie's attorney, asked how I felt about Donnie dropping his appeals?

I had come to love Donnie as my own, and I knew my heart would break to watch TDCJ end his life, but I believed that if he were executed that God had allowed it. Donnie had asked us to be with him until his time came, and we intended to do that.

February 4, 2000

Donnie wrote about his different emotions concerning other inmates:

> I have been cutting some people loose here and staying away from them for reasons. I told one, I don't play the color game anymore. If you're a Christian, then act like one. Don't be wishy-washy. I got no time for games these days. I can't go into details but I had let my personal feelings get in the way. Then I had to realize that I couldn't let my personal feelings get in the way of God working with the guys here. I was wrong and God let me know I was wrong. But we talked and it was a good talk and I learned something in this.
>
> Annie, God has used you in lives here and I'm not sure you realize how much. Jim was really affected by your testimony

and words, and Tim too. Some I gave up on, but I was wrong. So keep sending anything you can grab up when you have the time. George said he reads those devotionals everyday.

I think mainly I just don't want anyone touching my family. I guess I'm protective of you all. But I have to admit I was wrong there. We'll talk about all this on our next visit.

I got a nice letter from Bonnie [Annie's sister] today. God is working in her life. I hope I get to see her before my time comes.

Sometimes I feel things, Annie. I can feel that I am a step closer to dying. It affects me for a time. But I want things to move faster. I have waited for years now, maybe always looking to man for relief. Every time someone said, This is going to happen, maybe I could even see it happening, but nothing. Now finally I'm committed to God, no man.

They still are saying Death Row will be moving. —Donnie

February 3, 2000

It's dark in here.

I feel tired today. I have a headache too. It's 70 degrees outside and they have the heater on.

I've been playing some with my pictures today. I was going to put my birthday pictures and the ones of Walters in an album, but I wound up putting the boys playing football on Christmas and Cory, Cody and Trey [Annie's grandsons] working out at the field house in the albums I had on hand. I am so glad Cory and Cody pay attention to Trey.

Annie, thank you for the pictures of Trey with his broken leg and his friends. Bless his heart. I hope he is hobbling all around by now.

God knows how to bless me and He does it through you and this family. I've got you all in my prayers every day. Tell Dale I love him too. Maybe you'll make it down this week.

Anyway, slowly and surely I'm getting the pictures in albums. Got five albums now for you. —Donnie

February 6, 2000

Well Annie, it looks like God heard our prayers, rather answered our prayers about the problems there at Dale's shop. I am so glad I used a little wisdom this time and not self-ways in getting things done. Who knows it may have been our prayers that have kept this man alive this long. In reality no one is driving this guy but himself and Satan. Just remind the guys there at the shop that we call out to God in all things, and we must cover everything, and our enemies fall in holes before they ever get to us. That's just how God works when we give our problems to Him to handle. —Donnie

Paul wrote in Romans 12:18, "If it is possible, as much as depends on you, live peaceably with all men."

Paul seemed to be indicating there could be times when peace may not be possible. So we turn it over to God and leave it there.

Donnie continued:

Annie, I wish I had been close to God all my life and know the things that I know now and have learned lately. Like my family there. Look at me! I'm on Death Row and you all have made me feel more loved than I have ever known and you have accepted me as a part of your family. I just get lost when I see one of you hurting in any way and I feel I've got to take care of it myself, but I know that's not the way. I believe that you have told me all this before somewhere back down the line there. Smile. But I never listen, huh? I wish I could have been what God wanted me to be. I know I failed in so many things and did just what I wanted to do. I still do that some too. I guess this will always be a long conversation, huh Annie?

But I know God really does listen to a sincere heart, and he knows when things are important to us.

It bothers me to see all these guys here wait on the courts and have all that hope for so long, and then nothing. It's bad too because it causes anger and hatred for so many. And it's hard to stay focused on God at those times. I worry about some, cause when it comes that time down here you're alone if you got no family to come see you off.

Be sure and get George and Gribble's devotionals to them, okay Annie?

February 7, 2000

Donnie had previously thought the competency hearing would be in Parker County, Texas. But after his hearing was set, I called TDCJ about clothes for the hearing and when he would be transported. I wrote Donnie with the details.

Donnie wrote:

So the competency hearing is going to be in Ft. Worth? And TDCJ transports me there and back. Only bad thing about that is the black box we have to wear. [Black box is a device attached to the handcuffs between a prisoner's wrist, holding them rigid for the purpose of preventing them from picking the lock]. They hurt after about ten minutes and kill you in four hours. Smile.

Whatever it takes. I knew that none of this was going to be easy when I made this decision. I just pray still that God uses me in many ways till I leave here and go home.

Annie, I know I told God that I'd rest in His time on this, but I want to get this hearing over with, and I just see no use in going on here.

I am very proud of this family. And I want Craig and Alexa to see who they talk to, and all that love me. Smile.

And I want them to see that bear one day, too.

I've got a million thoughts about so many things. Sometimes I look at myself in all my dreams that I have here about life, and being free, and I'm still that little boy I was on the farm in Oklahoma. Even after my life, the war, then home again and to the streets. I'm still a little boy inside looking at the world and wondering what went wrong?

I look at all the times that I would come home and I wanted to be that little boy again and be with the family. But all anyone saw was the outside of me. —Donnie

I would occasionally summarize and send Donnie an unsourced little humorous piece to cheer him that someone sent me in an e-mail. He enjoyed this one:

A thief had broken into a home one night. Shining his flashlight around to locate items he wanted to steal, he took a CD player and started to put it in his bag, a voice coming from a dark corner said, "Jesus is watching you." Whirling around in that direction he quickly turned his flashlight off.

After hearing nothing else for a time he promised himself a vacation, turned his flashlight back on and continued to gather more valuables.

Just as he was about to disconnect the TV wires he heard, "Jesus is watching you."

Completely frightened out of his wits, hysterically looking around with his light towards the sound, he saw a parrot in the corner of the room.

"Was that you?" he asked the parrot.

"Yes," the parrot squawked, "I just thought I'd warn you."

Calming down the thief asked,

"Warn me? Who are you to be warning me?"

"Moses," the bird answered.

"Moses?" the thief laughed, "What kind of people would name a parrot, Moses?'

The parrot suggested, "The kind that would name a Rottweiler Jesus."

Donnie later said that the guys got a laugh out of the parrot story and wittingly suggested that some might even relate to it.

February 9, 2000

Donnie wrote:

> Well, I started on that big book of crossword puzzles you sent, but they're too hard for me. It says for dummies. I really must be stupid. So I'm just going to do some stretches and go on out for a while. I'll try again when I get in.
>
> Annie, there is this song Your Love, Oh Lord, by a group, Third Day. Maybe you could listen to it for me. I want it for my funeral service. It's a praise song. I think you'll like it.
>
> I saved a few kites [letters from other inmates] that I have put in my Bible and in my files so you'll find them after I'm gone. Some things just mean a lot to me. I want to try to be some kind of positive model to these guys. I did pray that God would use me in these last days. I can see already that He is bringing some people around that I can tell about what I believe about heaven and being free because of Jesus. I guess all I needed, like you said, was to get my "want to" fixed. Jesus will do the rest. Pray for me, Annie.
>
> But save these kites for me. I know I'll never see them or read them again. Usually I just chunk things like this, but lately they just mean more, ya know?
>
> I have been going through some things. I love looking at my pictures. You know Annie, when I get to heaven I want a pond just like yours out back by the porch. Smile. —Donnie

February 13, 2000

I had written Donnie that I was sending him a news article about a moratorium on the death penalty; talk of suspending it for a period of time in some states. I wrote that I knew he did not want this to get in his way but to remember that we were praying God's will for him. I understood that some days it was easier to pray for God's will than others but that God's time was what we had prayed for, so I asked Donnie if we were sticking to the plan? No matter how it seemed for a period God always has our best interest in mind. He knows what lies ahead.

I had written to Donnie and told him I had talked to his friend, Ben Luna, a former volunteer chaplain on Death Row. Luna emailed me often to be updated on Donnie's situation.

February 18, 2000

Responding, Donnie wrote:

I know for so long many thought I was innocent. And I can tell you that it played on me too over the years, Annie. After a while I just sat back and let the courts take their course to see what happened. I always thought I'd beat this case anyway and by law I should have, and who knows, maybe I would have if I had went all the way through this. But I'd still be here and like I said, it plays on you. Once you really give all to God things like that change and you begin to see it all in a different way. But admitting you're wrong is a hard thing to do at times.

Annie, you know the day will come when all Christians will be outlaws? Naturally after the rapture during the Seven Year Tribulation, but even before then as in certain parts of the world Christians are being killed and persecuted for believing in Jesus. They're outlaws in that government's eyes. That was just something I was thinking about today, and I wanted to give it to you to think about. —Donnie

I recalled Donnie's comments later as I listened to the well-known pastor Charles Stanley, of Intouch Ministries, who tells that 389 pastors in India alone have laid down their lives for Christ.

February 14, 2000

I wrote Donnie that my grandson, Trey, had accepted Jesus as his own personal Lord and Savior the night of February 13. I explained that Trey began to ask questions about Jesus and forgiveness from sin. His mother, Bev, explained that Jesus had paid the death penalty for mankind. It is a free gift of God, but like any gift, each one must accept the gift for one's self. What a wonderful thing when parents can be the ones to guide their children in this salvation experience! In order to explain to Trey what he was feeling, she showed him how God convicts us of sin in our lives. She showed him Romans 3:23 in her Bible and explained how we all have sinned and need to be forgiven. And how we can have that by simply asking for forgiveness and turning away from our sins to Jesus Christ. Trey prayed the sinner's prayer asking forgiveness. Now his eternal life in heaven is secure. I knew Donnie would rejoice with us in this occasion.

February 18, 2000

Donnie responded:

> I am so happy about Trey. This is really an answer to prayer you know. Actually Annie, God is answering many of our prayers and I'm so grateful. I know that Trey will have the guidance he needs. But remember how we were talking about how we wish that when someone is saved they could instantly know all they need to know about living a Christian life? I know that is not possible. God gives other Christian's the chance to be blessed and to follow up and teach newborn Christians how to grow in their walk with the Lord. This is where many Christians fail.

They don't follow up with the newborns. The babes in Christ fall away before they have had a chance to grow and learn and experience the joy and peace in knowing what they really possess. I get so many thoughts at times I'm overwhelmed. Thank you for sharing all they do, and keeping me up with them all.

Annie, I heard TDCJ just moved 192 more death row inmates off to the Terrell Unit, and that we are all on the way soon. A boss was telling me today that we're out of here. So instead of rumors it looks like the time is coming. I just don't want things all screwed up in the last days for us all. I don't know what visits are going to be like there, but I'm going to keep praying that God will just handle all this and make it right for all of us. I'm praying about a lot of things. —Donnie

So Donnie would know that we were trying to keep him informed about the move, I wrote that I had talked on the phone to a warden from the Terrell Unit. The warden assured me that visits would be the same except we would be looking through glass and talking on telephones instead of through metal grills.

February 19, 2000

I called Donnie's lawyers as he had asked and told them he did not want the hearing date extended. Alexa told me that the competency hearing date could be set within the next couple of weeks. I knew Donnie wanted this hearing over. But I also knew the sooner the hearing was over, the sooner he would get an execution date. So, I was not so anxious. Donnie had become a big part of our lives over the years, and I was trying to take one day at a time with just Enough Light for the Step I was on, like Omartian wrote about, trying not to think about the following weeks ahead.

I wrote him that I had found the song "Your Love, Oh Lord" that he had requested for his service.

February 21, 2000

Donnie wrote:

They keep shutting the rec yard here all the time on us and it's like depression is over this place. You go out and look out the hall window to see who might be going by and you just can't get the workouts going.

They brought Gribble over at six this morning. His date is March 15. The guys, El and Mark [inmates] hollered and woke me up to let me know he is here. Did no good though cause he's in the far yard and I can't see him or talk to him. But when he came through we got to holler some. He was all smiles and said, Annie wrote me twice. He was happy about that. Smile!
—Donnie

Donnie and most other Death Row inmates were grateful for any small effort made on their behalf. Others wondered why you were there. Some have never had so much as a visit except from an attorney.

As I wrote this book, one of my friends commented to me how the Bible says that we are to visit those in prison, yet this particular thing Christians ignore so often.

I supposed that many Christians worry about the discomfort, some worry what others will think. But when faced with the truth as I was, we must ask ourselves, "What line does (sic) my thoughts take now?"

Christians have a story to tell, and as long as we stick with the plan of God we cannot go wrong. I tell inmates, "Jesus loves you as much as the best Christian in the world."

Consider Charles H. Spurgeon words in *All of Grace*: He that is a dirty sinner is the kind that Jesus came to make clean.[1] A gospel preacher on one occasion preached a sermon from, "Now also the axe is laid unto the root of the trees" (Luke 3:9), and he delivered such a sermon that one of the hearers said to him, "One would have thought that you had been preaching to criminals. Your sermon ought to have been delivered in the county jail." "Oh no," said the good man, "if I were preaching in the county jail, I should not preach from that text, there I should preach "This is a faithful saying, and worthy of all acceptance, that Christ Jesus came into the world to save sinners' (I Timothy 1:15). This is true. "The law is for the self-righteous, to humble their pride; the Gospel is for the lost to remove their despair."

February 21, 2000

> Donnie wrote:
>
> You know what, Annie? I know in my heart that I could never go back to a life that would not have God in it, not after all that I have learned and have been through and all that He's instilled in me. God would be and is my only hope in all things.
>
> Later. Well I made it back from rec. And I was blessed today Annie. Before we went out I saw another pigeon trapped in the yard. So I was ready. They roost over the single flex yards. They're all over really, but like the last one it got in and couldn't get out. But we chased it and finally caught the thing. It flew in the day room and I just picked her up. Pretty chocolate brown with white tail feathers. It had a violet color to her neck. Once I got her I just relaxed. Her little heart was beating so fast. But I held her and let everyone look at her and after a bit I got the picket guy to take her back on the roof. But it was good to feel her in my hands and feel her little heart beating. She was real calm and was just looking at me. Smile. But that was a blessing for me today. —Donnie

As I read Donnie's letter, I imagined how gentle he would have been to that feathered creature. He loved all God's creatures from bears to mice. As Donnie seemed to find the little blessings in life each day, I prayed he would be able to have as much happiness as possible during his final days on this earth.

I did so hope he would feel like a little boy again.

Chapter 19

The Move

"We were on our way, chains, cuffs, and the black boxes...."

February 22, 2000

*D*onnie wrote:

Been a long day here. We're locked down because of the hostage incident at the Terrell Unit. They cut our water off and tore our cages up. Took me a while to put it all back. But we'll be off lockdown tomorrow. I prayed for that lady who was the hostage. Everything went good too. Long story. The inmates just wanted to talk about the living conditions. You're just stuffed in a cell and that's it, no TV. You're just alone. But that lady hostage said they treated her good.

I prayed for Betty Beets also. She dies on the 12th. I saw her picture in the paper. She's sixty-two years old. What a hard life she's had. It makes me sad, Annie. —Donnie

February 23, 2000

I had a rough night last night. Not rough as in physical, but in spirit. And I grieved for others too. I grieved like the last two times I cried out to God to do something or show me something. And each time I have been awakened the next morning with news of a move forward. Kind of awesome cause I have learned something in this Annie and it is important that I share it all with this family before my time comes.

Last night when I was calling out to God I was very sad. I asked God to show me something and this morning I got the order as I'm sure you already know. March 9 will be my competency hearing. That is sixteen days away. So now I know I'm on my way.

But it's strange when I get these letters telling what and when something is going to happen. I get deep in thought. It's like a fear of some kind. I can't explain it, but you know...ya just know. Smile. I'm happy, yet I'm sad. I worried about you. But last night I prayed and asked God to take care of you and give you strength to go through this with me. One thing I want you to know in all this, no matter how bad I want out of here, and to go home to be with Jesus, a part of me wants to stay and cling to this life. But I know that as long as I have this body I'm going to be like that.

I struggle at times Annie with belief and trust in God, yet I depend on Him totally in all this. I begged Him to come to me and let me know and have something to hang on to. But I have to realize that God has done something here and has let me know a little of how He works, like those three times I was in His lap crying out to Him. He let me know He is here Annie. There have been other times that something affects my heart and I have cried out to God and asked Him to handle something and He does. Many prayers He has answered for me. But in it all I realize that it is how I am to approach God. It is then that He moves mountains in our lives. It's hard to explain, but I know you know.

As for these songs at my funeral, actually now there are only four songs I want played. I think people need to know how you felt in life and in your last days. I have always loved music. I believe that music speaks to the heart more than anything in the world other than God Himself. Smile. But add that song Thief by

Third Day and The Anchor Holds by Ray Boltz to the list. Bev said she and Richard would sing Go Rest High on the Mountain. And you pick one Annie.

In the end I hope everyone that attends my funeral will be witnessed to and will in turn be a witness to others all around. It should never stop. I want everyone, especially you, to realize that life goes on and this is actually a joyous occasion Annie. I want people to talk to Dad and love him and you all hold one another up. But remember the center of it all must be the Lord. I pray He will be there that day moving in hearts. —Donnie

February 26, 2000

Donnie had sent me a devotional page from a newspaper with a picture of Moses holding a rod high in the air Moses wanted to encourage the Israelites while they fought the Amalekites. The Israelites were winning until Moses arms tired and began to drop then the Amalekites began to win. Moses' brother, Aaron, and Hur saw what was happening and they set Moses on a rock and they held his arms up and once again the Israelites succeeded in the battle (Story in Exodus 17).

I wrote Donnie that although we could not physically hold him up, we were lifting him up to God daily in prayer. The Lord had used this time with Donnie to strengthen our relationship with Himself and through this situation had taught us that we can depend on Him for strength in all things. I pray we never forget this.

"I can do all things through Christ who strengthens me" (Philippians 4:13).

I realized several years ago that God allowed me in this experience with Donnie, not only as a mere instrument to help Donnie, but to teach me something about brokenness. I learned that God will not call us as we expect, but when He calls, we will not be able to deny it. It will have nothing to do with our goodness, or the lack of it; it will be for the purpose of being made useful to Him. It will be an experience that we could never create on our own. But if we will submit to His call, we will be able to praise Him for allowing it in our life for with it will come His most glorious peace.

Donnie had asked that I check on his friend, Gribble, whose execution date was coming up quickly on March 15. I assured Donnie that I was writing something to Tim every few days and would continue until his time came. I reminded Gribble that if we are a child of God, the Bible says, "Likewise the Spirit also helps in our weaknesses. For we do not know what we should pray for as we ought, but the Spirit Himself makes intercession for us with groanings which cannot be uttered. Now He who searches the hearts knows what the mind of the Spirit is, because He makes intercession for the saints according to the will of God" (Romans 8:26-27). Donnie and I were praying for Gribble, but the very Spirit of God was praying for him as well.

Donnie had asked that I frame his family picture when he was a small boy and have it at his funeral service and give it to Cliff afterwards. I enlarged it and sent Donnie a copy also.

February 26, 2000

Donnie wrote:

Thank you, Annie, for the picture of the family. It really got me just sitting here looking at it. So long ago that was. Things are so different now. But I somehow wanted my dad to know that was one of my favorite pictures and that I love him.

I dread the ride in the back of the van to that hearing in Ft. Worth with the black box and chains. They always make you sore, plus the attitudes that you come up against. People are real tough when you're all chained up. Smile. But I'll look at what countryside I can and know that it will be the last time I see some of this earth. I'm praying about it too. I'm asking God to just make everything happen the way He wants it to.

So many things I'm going to have to go through now that the ball is rolling. I know that in everything I go through I always want to run to you and talk about it. It makes me feel good to know that you're right in the middle of it all with me. Lately I feel so different about things of this life and of this family. I set and lay and think of God and all of you.

I actually get wore out mentally. So much to think about. Sometimes it's hard to get up when I fall spiritually, and at times I can't get rid of the sadness. Then it turns to praising God for His goodness. —Donnie

I admitted to Donnie that I knew the different human emotions because we were experiencing some of the same. As difficult as it was for me to believe what was happening, I ended up praising God for the blessing of being in it with Donnie.

Donnie continued to write about his thoughts:

I can look at the floor and just stare at it for an hour and not even blink it seems. But my mind is doing a hundred miles an hour. Smile. But I feel it you know. I mean I feel death coming my way, but I'm trying to focus on the life ahead of me. Smile. —Donnie

I often wrote Donnie about experiences here at home (and the shop) to help him know that our prayers were being answered.

I wrote that Dale had come home one night recently telling me they had a pickup at the transmission shop that was eating their lunch [couldn't seem to repair it]. They had rebuilt the transmission and then replaced all the parts one by one again, trying to get the transmission working right. Nothing seemed to work. I asked Dale 'Why don't you just start over with a completely different transmission?' I knew that occasionally they have done that and just starting over from start to finish fixes the problem. Dale told me they had to fix that particular transmission because they were very rare and hard to find.

I said no more at the time but included that transmission in my prayer the next morning, "God, I'm asking you to fix that truck today. The guys have done everything they could possibly know to do to it. Now I'm asking You to take care of it." Actually by night, I had forgotten my prayer, but that night Dale came in and asked, "You know the truck I was telling you about that we were having trouble with?"

I was sitting in the floor with my back to him doing some paperwork. I began to smile to myself and answered, "Yes."

Dale continued to explain "I just took that pickup out today and drove it and it started working perfect, and it has been working perfect ever since. We have had that transmission out several times, changed everything on it trying to get it working right and just didn't know anything else to try."

"You are probably not going to believe this," I said to Dale, "but I prayed this morning that God would take care of it, today!"

When we are overwhelmed and intimidated by the circumstance, what is our next recourse? PRAY.

I wrote to Donnie:

"Donnie, I pray each morning that God will bless their work at the shop. But you know if they never had any problems God would not have been able to do what He did today with the same results. The guys at the shop might even get to thinking they are pretty good transmission men…and they are, but God made it obvious who fixed this one. We are Christians, and we know that it is times like this that we see God more clearly. We seem to pray more in times of trouble. Had it not been for the trouble, I would not have prayed about this specific situation. And God would not have received the glory for this. The Bible tells how the Lord told Gideon, "The people who are with you are too many for me to give Midian into their hands, for Israel would become boastful, saying, 'My own power has delivered me'" (Judges 7:2).

March 1, 2000

Dale and I visited with Donnie at the Ellis Unit in Huntsville. As we prepared to leave from our visit, Dorothy, the wife of another death row inmate, pulled me over to the side. She told me she had heard a rumor that the rest of Death Row was being moved to the Terrell Unit in Livingston the next day. Before we left I told Donnie about the rumor. I knew that Donnie dreaded that move, but I felt it would be worse for him to be completely surprised by it.

When I got home the following day, I had an e-mail from Dorothy saying that Death Row had in fact been moved in a matter of hours.

I began to write Donnie everyday because I knew the inmates would be unsettled for a while, and when he began receiving mail at the Terrell Unit, he would be hungry for it. I felt it would be a major change from the Ellis Unit in Huntsville where he had been for almost fifteen years.

I finally received a letter from Donnie about the move to the Terrell Unit in Livingston.

March 3, 2000

Donnie wrote:

> Annie, I can't even see what I'm typing in this thing. It got broke during the move. Cracked the screen and I can only see half of it. I wrote them about it but they haven't gotten back with me yet. Probably won't do any good.
>
> The move was something else, Annie. They came in packed us up and by 12 p.m. we were on our way, chains, cuffs, and the black boxes I was telling you about, the whole works! They had

cops everywhere and helicopters. They moved everyone.

My cell is larger but there is no way I could just do time like this. I am really alone now. There are just walls. There is a very short window at the top of my cell, but it is so high I can't see out. But I'll make the best of it that I can. —Donnie

In her book *The Hiding Place*, Corrie ten Boom writes how her sister, Betsy, told her they should, "Rejoice always, pray constantly, and give thanks in all circumstances."[1] But Corrie saw no reason for thanking God for being placed in a flea-infested barrack in a concentration camp during World War II. Likewise, Donnie saw little reason for praising God for the move to the Terrell Unit where he would be isolated and more alone than ever before. Later Corrie realized that the guards seldom visited their barracks because of the fleas. This allowed the women more freedom to read scripture aloud to others confined there. And Donnie later admitted to Betty and me that his relationship to God was actually strengthened from more time in God's Word because of the isolated conditions at the Terrell Unit.

Donnie continued:

But I'm dreading that trip to Ft. Worth. It will be like the trip over here. The black box again. They really hurt you bad. Makes it hard for you to act normal and gives you an attitude. I hate for any of my family to see me all chained up at the hearing too. I'll be so glad to go home. I'll never have to wear another chain.

Please call and find out about the visits here, Annie. I was so sad to see you and Dale leave Wednesday. I knew that was about to happen and that I'd not see you that way ever again. I even thought that maybe I'd never see you again. Like a panic came over me. So right now I'm just not doing so well. But I wanted to tell you, hey, and that I love you all. I hope you're okay Annie. Be strong, and we'll make it through this my friend. I need to get where I can pray now. I was mad at God today and I let Him know it. Scares me when I get like that.

I had all these plans about writing a lot and now I can't see the screen on this machine. That property guy still hasn't come about getting it fixed. But even if they wanted to send it off to get it fixed, I'd be dead before it got back. Annie, sometimes I wonder if God is mad at me. Things seem to be getting worse.
—Donnie

Believing Donnie's time was getting very short, I called the Terrell Unit about perhaps getting his typewriter fixed, but I quickly saw that was not going to happen. After the hearing on March 9, his date could be as short as 30 days. So I told Donnie to get another typewriter from the commissary, and we would see that the money was in his trust fund. He proceeded to make the arrangements to do that.

March 7, 2000

Frustrated and angry about the move, Donnie wrote:

Hey Annie, I wanted to write and just talk some. I spent the day writing about the trip over here and how things are here and all. I have been asking for toilet paper all day. But I guess if God keeps listening to my prayers for everyone else I can take it. It's going to take some pretty big miracles to change all this. Right now my only prayer for some is the same as Paul prayed about old Alexander the coppersmith, that dude in II Timothy 4:14-15 and he's also in I Timothy 1:19-20.

Paul wrote, "Alexander the coppersmith did me much harm. May the Lord repay him according to his works. You also must beware of him, for he has greatly resisted our words."

"Having faith and a good conscience, which some having rejected, concerning the faith have suffered shipwreck, and

> whom are Hymenaeus and Alexander, whom I delivered to
> Satan that they may learn not to blaspheme." —Donnie

I knew Donnie was as serious as he could be at this point as he wrote about the changes at the Terrell Unit, but often Betty and I would smile at the way Donnie would express himself when he was angry. I never knew that much about Alexander the Coppersmith until Donnie pointed him out to me.

Continuing his March 7 letter, Donnie wrote:

> I hope tonight we finally get some mail. I can't see anything at all of the world anymore. So I just keep thinking of the water (Lake Livingston) that I saw coming over here. Brought back some old memories. I've been up and down that road a bunch of times. Now I know where I'm at anyway. I'll get to see that again before they kill me too and maybe on this trip Thursday to the hearing.
>
> Gonna be one heck of a ride this next month, huh, Annie? Smile. I hate everything about this life except for my family loving me. What would I do without you guys? As it is now in my last days I may just want to see you and Dale and Betty. I don't want anyone to see me this way or in this atmosphere. I don't feel right here. Just need some time I guess. —Donnie

March 8, 2000

I knew Donnie would not get my letter before the hearing, but I wrote him that we must apply God's word to every situation and circumstance. If we believe any of God's word, we have to believe it all. If we are children of God, we can call on Him anytime, and He is anxious to hear from us. I love my time alone with God in the mornings. I always have so much to say to Him after we had visited Donnie. As much as I hated to see Donnie moved, I was aware that the Lord knew Death Row was going to be moved and exactly when. Whether it was His will or not, I knew He had allowed it.

Not knowing how the move would affect our visits, Donnie dreaded being moved to the Terrell Unit and continued to complain and question why it had happened.

Betty and I were praying that the guards that escorted Donnie to the hearing would have caring hearts and that they would be effected in a positive way by the experience of transporting Donnie to the hearing in Ft. Worth.

Alexa called from the lawyer's office to talk about the hearing procedures and to try to prepare us for the chains and shackles the following day.

On the evening before Donnie's competency hearing, I informed Betty and Sandy that they should be ready to leave at 4:30 a.m. because we were going to be sitting on the steps of that federal building in Ft. Worth, Texas when they opened at 8 a.m. Betty and Sandy were ready.

March 9, 2000

At 11:30 a.m. the competency hearing reconvened after a short recession. Judge Means had recessed the hearing to allow Donnie time to rethink and confer with his lawyers about his decision to stop his appeals process. It was during this 30-minute recession that Donnie made his lawyers aware that he was about to confess his crime to the court. It was obvious that they were extremely saddened by what they heard. We, Donnie's family knew the heartbreak they were experiencing. Craig, Alexa, and Jim knew that they must now surrender in a battle that they had been determined to fight to the finish. But like JC Cockrum three years before, Donnie felt he had to exchange his lies for the truth.

THE COURT: Mr. Foster, could you step to the lectern, please.

I have given you about a half-hour or so to visit with your counsel and to think through your decision. Could you tell me the results of that thought process?

PETITIONER FOSTER: Yes, sir, I can. Are you allowing me to speak to the Court?

THE COURT: Yes, sir, I am.

PETITIONER FOSTER: Okay. First of all, Your Honor, I want you to know I'm a Christian. I believe in Jesus. I noticed that you opened your court with a prayer today. I appreciated that. As far as my decision, I've been advised by my attorneys in all the correct ways. They have done nothing but immaculate work for me through the years. I've had years to think about this decision. I've wanted to do this for years, Your Honor, through family -- which I have a lot of family, which love and care for me. I've done this time mostly for them trying to stay alive, but it's come down to this is my decision and the decision that I want to make.

You know, to be locked up like this for all these years is--you can have everything, Your Honor. I can have family, and I do. I'm the most blessed man on earth and the most loved man on earth, but, yet, to live in isolation like I do, it does me no good, and I feel like that---I could tell that you are bothered by my decision today. I could clearly see that. And I don't want you to be bothered by my decision, Your Honor.

I think in a man's life there comes a time whenever he must own up to what he's done. So today I want to do that in front of this Court. I can only tell you that what happened that day was not murder, Your Honor. It was an accident, and I live with it. It should have never happened, and it did. I feel like it's wrong for me to go on in this life, you know, dragging other people around fighting my case and my family believing in me and stuff, which I've already cleared this with my family. I believe a man owns up to what he does, and that's what I'm doing here today. So there is no sense in going any further with this process.

And I would ask, Your Honor, that you in your decision that you not delay me with the Fifth Circuit any longer, that you would help me move on down the road here. I'm of sound mind, Your Honor. There's nothing wrong with me. Like I say, I believe in Jesus. Although I screwed this life up, the next one that I'm going to I'm going to be a very blessed man. I do believe in Jesus, and this is not the only life, Your Honor. For me to move on is a blessing for me.

THE COURT: Let me say---

PETITIONER FOSTER: ---I appreciate you being bothered like you was. I could tell you were bothered by this case, and my attorneys have been bothered, too. I have never told my attorneys this, Your Honor, until today. So this is as new to them as it is to you in this court.

THE COURT: Mr. Foster, because I share your faith, it's probably easier for me than for some to understand what you are saying.

PETITIONER FOSTER: Yes, sir.

THE COURT: I don't want to make other people uncomfortable.

PETITIONER FOSTER: Yes, sir.

THE COURT: But I respect your decision. I believe it is knowingly made. I believe you have shown me and those in the courtroom that you understand what you're doing.

PETITIONER FOSTER Yes, sir.

THE COURT: You understand that by giving up your appellate rights, your rights to seek habeas relief, that you will eventually be executed.

PETITIONER FOSTER: Yes, Your Honor, I understand.

THE COURT: And I respect you for forthrightly stepping forward and saying what you have said, and because I understand and agree with your statement of your personal faith, personally I agree with you. Though, whether I personally agree is of no import legally. I personally agree with you and wish you well, and because of my faith, I believe that this decision, while painful for you and painful for all of us, has a rational purpose and a rational result.

PETITIONER FOSTER: Yes, Your Honor.

THE COURT: I, Therefore, will be making findings and conclusions that will be for the review of the court of appeals that you have made an informed, knowing, and voluntary decision to forego your right to seek any further relief from the penalty that has been imposed upon you by the state of Texas. Good luck to you, sir.

PETITIONER FOSTER: I thank you.

THE COURT: This hearing is adjourned.

Chapter 20

The Hearing is Over

"For me to move on is a blessing for me."

March 9, 2000

*A*fter returning to Death Row from his competency hearing, Donnie wrote:

> Hello My Family,
>
> I pray that this finds you all doing good. I saw you all there today and I could not hold back the tears. I almost broke down and started praising God right then, but they would have shot me. Smile!
>
> I wanted to write you all and tell you these things. I wanted to let everyone know how I felt today and how much I love you all.
>
> I had a feeling we would not even get to touch. Death Row dropping his appeals and they figure I've got nothing to lose. Just fear (on their part). They came and asked me if that was all my family. I said, Yea. Then they went and talked. Smile. Then said, when we went in there [court], no touching, and actually not to even look back there. But I did anyway.
>
> I read some and prayed before I left this morning. I knew this trip was going to be a hard one. I prayed and I just left it all in His hands. I asked God to use me today and He did in many ways. It was dark when we left here this morning to go there, but as the sun came up we passed this truck that said, Heaven Bound.

I had to smile cause it was at that moment I was talking to God.

But first, I was getting chained up to leave from here and this guard that was there had a WWJD [what would Jesus do] bracelet on. I had to smile at that. Maybe it means, What would Joe do? I felt his conscience, but the other one kept him off. In other words, he was not his own man. Sad.

When we got to the marshal's office I was already in a bad mood. Pants didn't fit and I had a headache, and I have not been asleep at all in three days now. I'm just running on pure energy. Not been eating well either. Just coffee mostly.

I pray that I have not let any of you down. I followed my heart and most of all, God's Word.

I knew nothing of what I was going to say. Nothing was planned at all. But as the judge was talking to me I saw something in him that moved my spirit. First of all he opened his court with prayer and I smiled at that. That is unusual. I think it freaked Jim and Craig out too. Anyway, after Means talked and said what he did I knew he wanted me to go on. But everything went down to the wire on what was my final say. Are you sure?

I told Craig then, what happened that day [at Cox's store] and I apologized for not saying so earlier in the years and wasting everyone's time. But as I did it I can tell you God was there with us and I could feel them. They do care about me. What I did today I did from my heart. I didn't want the judge stressed out over me or this case, or my lawyers either. Everyone needed a way out. I gave it to them and I took mine too.

I neither boast nor brag about this, but I can say that it was the right thing to do.

Before I came in there I had just started witnessing to two guys in the back. One black guy was waiting on a jury to come back in Means' court there and they would either set him free or give him life in a federal prison. I said, I hear ya man, I got this death penalty and I'm dropping my appeals today in that same courtroom. The bosses told him when I was visiting the lawyers that I was a murderer and that they might not want to talk to me. Smile.

But it only took a few minutes to get God in there and it was great!

After I went back I got to finish the witness and I knew that God was with me again and still. Everything I said to this guy, I knew that God was saying it to him. It was awesome. But then I left and I'll never know what happened to that guy. It's so easy to talk and not walk. Smile. But I have been down that road and it's a long one.

Anyway, that's what happened today. And right or wrong, like I told that judge, I'm the most loved man on this earth but living in isolation for years is not enough. Believe me, I would stay if I even thought I had a chance to be with you all one day. But I don't see any light at all. I can't go on living like this. And now it is even worse than ever.

But I love you all so much. It about killed me that you all were there and I couldn't even hug you. But it was a blessing the old marshal said we could talk right there [where we stood]. We just have to take these little blessings as they come. It's not over yet.

I need to get this date set and they will move me to a pod [separate building for inmates]. Then I need to spend my time writing you all as much as I can till I leave.

One thing I ask you all is that during my funeral you accept Craig and Alexa with open arms there in Walters. I've told them about you all and showed them pictures. This has not been easy on them either. I realize once again how selfish I had been and was being. I'm just cold I guess on this death penalty. But Alexa and Craig are going to be with you and Betty during my execution. It is not an easy thing I know. I have tossed and turned about whether it is right to subject someone to that. But I'll tell you this. I thank you for it cause I will need you in leaving here. It's not an easy thing, believe me. Annie, you know a little of what I feel all the time and in an awesome way too. Sometimes I get down at night because I just want to be with you all so bad that it drives me. I've just had enough. I have my pictures and my thoughts and dreams. I have my prayers that I say for you and that is my part for now in this family. Now I need yours more than ever, and I know that you're already there on that.

I'm going to close for now, but I will be writing. Hey, thank you for loving me. If you can, imagine me in a cage on the floor raising my hands and praising God for you in my life. You've all made everything in my life complete.

I've got to get settled down. But today was a must. Smile. Although I am in chains and they hurt and bruise me physically as well as mentally, and I'm treated as a bad monster; I realize in it all that I can never hurt like Jesus did. I really couldn't look at any of you today cause it was coming up in my chest and the tears too and I felt the Spirit there. More a longing I guess. I think the cops thought we had an escape plan going. Smile. And that maybe some old brothers off the street might come bust me out. Smile.

I got to hug Alexa today! Hey, I told you she was beautiful, huh! Smile. Craig was very emotional. And no one knew what I was going to do today on all that. That attorney general that I walked over to afterwards was looking at me like, Man, do you realize what you just said? But it'll probably do his future some good. How he got old Stoney Armadillo!

I hope no one in this family is hurt by anything that I did today. I got the pictures and they are nice. Bonnie sent some too. We've got to talk about her on a visit. She's changing and pulling close to God. —Donnie

My sister, Bonnie, had asked Jesus Christ into her life many years before, and had lived in close fellowship with Him for some time. She knew He had not left her, but as Christians sometimes do, we allow the world to creep in and take control of our lives. It is often a very gradual turning away from God. We hardly notice the curve. Our focus of Christ gets blurred, and after a while we hardly notice Him at all. But Donnie was right; God was getting Bonnie's attention.

Continuing his letter, Donnie wrote:

I love you all and thank you for being there today. I was glad to see Hop [Betty's husband]. Tell him thanks for all he did. I wanted to pull Sandy and Sherry up and hug them so bad. I don't get to see them that much. Annie, I can't wait to see you Monday. We've got to get things going, huh?

What was that reporter bugging you about? On anything like that, Annie, you just handle it your way. You do what you want to do.

I am going to lay down a bit. I am worn out. And hey, could Alexa and Craig stay a night with you after my funeral. I don't know if Jim will or not. I felt so sad when I saw them cry today. —Donnie

As I thought back on that time after the hearing in Fort Worth, I remembered that the family had hoped we would be able to visit Donnie and be allowed the only opportunity there would ever be this side of heaven to hug him. Alexa asked the guard as she stood near Donnie in the courtroom if she could be allowed to hug him and he asked, "Who, the prisoner?" She told him, "Yes." He said, "Yeah, go ahead." I wondered how long had it been since Donnie had felt a human hug.

I doubt that anyone left that courtroom the same as they came in. I saw attitudes and hearts change that day. Even the ones that were guarding him seemed to be affected as God answered Donnie's prayer to use him.

Except for special visits once a month, death row inmates with execution dates are allowed only one, two-hour visit per week until two days before his or her execution. After his hearing, we never missed an opportunity. Between visits, Donnie and I carried on a daily conversation by mail.

I reminded Donnie that Billy Graham wrote in *Facing Death and the Life After*, "The moment we take our last breath on earth we take our first in heaven. We are absent from the body and immediately present with the Lord."[1]

Donnie asked me to keep reminding him of that.

Donnie wrote:

> Know what, Annie? I think we better start getting everything in order and ready, huh? I told Craig I would like the family to bury me. He said that is the way his family does it. He said he would like to help. I told him that it's just like dancing man, you just cut in. Smile.—Donnie

March 11, 2000

Donnie wrote:

> I was just thinking about how love works. That's the way that I give, Annie. I may not be able to give someone something that they can see and say, look what Donnie gave me. I can only give in a spiritual sense I guess. I can pray for them, and hold them dear to my heart. But I can only give what God gives me to give them. Am I making any sense?
>
> You know last night I was thinking of Dale. I was looking at that old gas pump [picture] he restored, and I have a way of

dreaming at times. I may just set down and stare at the floor and get lost in thought. But I was thinking how wonderful it would be to have just been able to come to Walters years ago, like after Nam, or after I got out of prison the first time. I was thinking of how life could have been different if I could have simply come to Betty or Alma [Annie's mother] or you or anyone in Walters and said, Hey I need to talk to you, and I need help in getting my life turned around here. I'm lost and I need my family's help.

If only I could have done that. I could have got right and had wonderful friends as Dale to hang with all the time and Steve and Richard and just be a part of something. And I was so close, too. I remember one night I was talking to Bonnie [Annie's sister] right there in Walters and I told her I was looking for a Harley. She said, Dale builds old Harleys! See Annie, how close things come to making life different. Weird, huh?

I was just talking, Annie. I love Dale and I think he is one of the greatest guys I ever met. I'm so glad that he has you and you have him.

How's Bev? Would you bring Bev to see me, and Steve, too?

I was thinking about how blessed I am. I was thinking without you all in my life I would have been all alone in court that day. But I wouldn't have changed a thing. I think this is the first time I have been through something that dad has not been there, and I missed him. But I wanted to tell just you, that it hurt some. I know he had somewhere to be and all that. But oh how good God is to me. He showed me that too.

I need to write Sandy and Sherry. Would you please call Sandy and tell her I love her so much? Annie, whatever you do, make sure that you bring Sandy with you on one of our visits we'll be having before I die. I've got to talk to Bobby and Sherry too about things that are to come in heaven. We just got to get everyone we can down here to visit me. Smile. Steve and

The Hearing is Over

Cody should have all their sponsors after the first few races too. Smile.

I've been praying that God will let me go on missions for Him. I want to be the one that comes to get you and Dale and all this family as you come to where I'll be. Smile! Like a Wal-Mart greeter, you know? Smile. And like Frank, that lady's brother-in-law in that book Within Heaven's Gates. Her opening statement made so much sense to me. She said that not everyone's vision of heaven is the same. We all have different tastes and things we like. She didn't at that time have an earthly body, but spiritual. And like Jesus appearing with the disciples in that locked room showed he could walk through walls and eat and touch and all. Same as she was doing! Remember the water, and her being afraid of drowning? How nothing can be ruined? I have so many thoughts, Annie. Oh, how I've lost and missed so many wonderful things of this life that I could have had. But I'm going to do it right in this next life. I want all this family to live close so we can see each other every day. I know I'm so dumb sometimes thinking these things. But we can all go worship God and talk to Jesus together too. Hey Annie, I see things so different than most, but I hope that there are going to be all the animals that God made in heaven. I'll have a couple of Bengal tigers walking with me, and a big old bear, little otters all over the place, and lots of birds in my trees. I'll have dogs and mice and ferrets and monkeys, and every kind you can imagine around my house. I can watch all the little children that come my way play with them.

I'll have beautiful rooms of the most beautiful woods in the heavens. And in my bookshelves I'll have little creatures that are always there to love on and have them love me too. Smile. Animals are so neat. I can't believe that you and Dale don't have a dog. What's up with that? Smile.

> Hey Annie, I'm going to close awhile. Drivin you crazy anyway. Smile. I'm just glad I have you to talk to. —Donnie

I wrote Donnie that I do love animals and that Dale and I had fish in our pond, but we travel too much, and it wouldn't be a very practical thing for us to have a dog. I explained how we might settle down enough some day to have another pet.

Knowing how much Donnie loved animals, I could not resist reminding him of Rebecca Ruter Springer's book *My Dream of Heaven* (Originally known as *Intra Muros*). Springer wrote, "Do you know I think one of the sweetest proofs we have of the Father's loving care for us is, that we often find in this life the things which gave us great happiness below. The more unexpected that is, the greater joy it brings." Springer continued, "I remember once seeing a beautiful little girl enter heaven, the very first to come of a large and affectionate family. I afterwards learned that the sorrowful cry of her mother was, 'Oh, if only we had someone to meet her there, to care for her!' She came lovingly nestled in the Master's own arms and a little later as He sat, still caressing and talking to her a remarkable Angora kitten, of which the child had been very fond, and which had sickened and died some weeks before, to her great sorrow, came running across the grass and sprang directly into her arms, where it lay so intently. Such a glad cry as she recognized her little favorite. Such hugging and kissing as that kitten received, made joy even in heaven."[2]

Referring to Springer's remarks, Billy Graham wrote in *Facing Death and the Life After*, "Far-fetched? Why should it be? If to die is gain as Paul said, then why shouldn't we enjoy even more in heaven the things we loved on earth?"[3]

March 13, 2000

On Friday after Donnie's competency hearing, I scheduled a special visit for Betty and me for the following week. The first part of the two-day visit we discussed the details of the hearing. There was no doubt that Judge Means saw Donnie as competent and informed. Donnie talked about the different feelings of emotion he had been experiencing since the hearing.

He said, "One second I can't wait to go, and the next I cry cause I don't want to leave you all behind."

I reminded Donnie that even the apostle Paul was torn between the need to stay and carry on his ministry here on earth, and the desire to go on to be with Jesus, "…which is far better," wrote Paul in Philippians 1:23.

On his thoughts of animals in heaven, I told Donnie that I supposed it was pretty normal for us as humans to think of things in heaven in a natural sense, like animals, games, and who our neighbors will be. That's because we can only imagine what heaven will really be like. But I Corinthians 2:9 reads, "But as it is written: Eye has not seen, nor ear heard, Nor have entered into the heart of man. The things which God has prepared for those who love Him."

March 14, 2000

On the second day of our visit with Donnie, I got the opportunity to visit with Donnie's friend, Timothy Gribble. Tim's Dad allowed me to take his chair for a time. He had an all-day visit with his family since his execution was the following day. He was quite cheerful and assured me that he had made his peace with God. I smiled and told him, "Then I will see you again one day."

Donnie always wrote us after a visit:

> I'm a little perturbed today about this move and this place.
> I missed our prayer too and that makes me sad. They should have told us, you got five minutes. But the guy was real nice that come to get me. But I wanted you to pray today.
> I came in and went to rec I went to the dayroom and walked around some. Witnessed to a guy in one of the lower cells, a

youngster that just got here. I came in and checked my toilet paper and it was still there. I'm thinking about hiding it when I leave the cell. Smile.

Hey Annie, lets keep dad in our prayers too, okay? You know dad is the type that needs lots of love. —Donnie

March 15, 2000

Donnie wrote:

It's 5:10 p.m. and I prayed for Grib. In about an hour he will be in the presence of the Lord. I prayed God would give him the peace and assurance that he needs to sustain him in this hour and a sign that He is there with him. Tim assured me that all was well with his soul. I told him as I left, I love ya, Tim. I'll see you soon. He was all smiles.

Gribble has gone home Annie. I'm glad you got to visit him yesterday. I had a rough night and was in prayer for him. We were pretty separated already cause they put him in solitary.

How about you Annie? Strange and all talking to someone you know that is going to be executed, huh? Bet you never thought you'd ever in your life know people on Death Row and watch them die. I worry about you. God has used you mightily in some people's lives, more than you will ever know. I may not be able to do all that you tell me that's right but I listen and I try Annie, as best I can. What you see in me is what God put there through you. Never forget that my friend. God comes to me through you like a shelter to me. I can't wait till you and Dale come to see me again. I can't walk in the Spirit all day, you know? Smile. I get lost every now and then. I'm still human Annie. I pray that God keep us all standing and looking at Him. —Donnie

A prayer written on March 18, 2000, but found in Donnie's property after his execution:

Father in heaven, I'm so lonely tonight. I don't mean to say that You being here isn't enough. I'm human, Lord.

Yes, you've provided me with more love through my family than I've ever had. I'm just so tired of settin' in this cage alone. Please come get me. Please give me the strength to go through this execution. I'm a little scared. Actually I'm a lot scared. But I've got to leave here. I don't want to live this way anymore.

Forgive me for being angry and mad at times. I know this world is not important, nor what they do or say about me. But protect my family and friends in this all. And please make a way that I may see them all before I come home. Work this all out with the people here and the family. Thank you for Annie, Lord, and Betty in my life. I pray that they be blessed a million times over all through their families and lives. And bless my daddy too.

Lord let your Holy Spirit fall on them all that day even the wardens, guards and executioners. Use me to reach out and be a witness for you greatly until I die and come home. I ask these things in Jesus Name

Amen.

My sister, Bonnie, sent to me a small clipping with these words by Christian author, and missionary, Amy Carmichael, "Of one thing we are sure, prayer is heard; prayer is answered; forces are set in motion by prayer in the Name of the Lord Jesus which will not cease, but will continue until that which has begun is perfected. Love will perfect that which it begins. It will not forsake the work of its own hands."[4]

Chapter 21

Lockdown

"...fear coming at me from all sides"

*D*onnie had many things on his mind as he wrote to me after the competency hearing.

March 20, 2000

Donnie wrote:

> I'm not proud of me admitting my sins like that to the public. It was really hard. I had fear coming at me from all sides. I had so many things on my mind, yet I had God there too, and He was in control. But things such as hurting someone in this family and how they saw me, ya know? Then again it was a love in me for them, for my lawyers, and even that judge when I saw his spirit and knew that he was troubled. I did not want to leave no man struggling with anything that I had done. But also I was free. Yes I'm guilty, and yes I shot the guy over there and yes I killed my best friend in Nam. So I had to do this.
>
> Annie, I thought about trying to talk to Cox's wife and daughter [victim's family]. I know they hate me. But they have this program for guys about meeting their victim's family and all. Check on this and pray about it with me. —Donnie

As Donnie requested, I checked with TDCJ about the program called Victims/Offender Mediation Dialogue. The personnel in charge of this program told me the victims must request the meeting with the offender. I wrote Donnie and gave him the information I had received about the program, and we agreed to pray and leave it in God's hands if this was to be.

I was grateful that Betty and I had our two-day visit with Donnie when we did because the inmates were locked down until each cell was thoroughly searched and inspected because of the move of Death Row to the Terrell Unit. Donnie felt the timing of the move was bad for him because he needed to write letters and get things in order before he received an execution date. He was out of stamps, and they can only be purchased from the commissary. During lockdown there are no commissary privileges.

March 21, 2000

Donnie wrote:

> I got no stamps to mail anything, but I just got your two letters and the big envelope with another letter and the paper. I have been really disgusted with this lockdown. These lunches are nothing, peanut butter sandwich made out of pancakes. And then the other that should be some kind of meat is nothing I ever saw. I wanted to lose weight so I guess this is the way. I started working out a little more, but in this cage all the time is not good for you at all. I can't sleep. We can't go to the store [term used by inmates for ordering from commissary].
>
> Okay let me go through your letters here. I'm going to make the margin wider so I can get more typing done in this letter, if I can get a stamp. Smile. I'm going to have to go fishing again [death row inmates throw out lines to pass things from one to another]. No stamps is bothering me. I have letters to write.
>
> I so look forward to hearing anything from you. Annie, I know I'm a grown man, but I hang onto your skirt tail like a little boy. I can't help it. I have so much thoughts about all that

has happened lately. And without you sharing God's Word and everything with me the way you do I'd just be lost here.
—Donnie

I wrote Donnie that I had been calling the Terrell Unit everyday; they kept telling me the lockdown had not been lifted. The lady at the warden's office had told me that hopefully they would allow the sections that had already been inspected to start having visits next week.

I knew things were not well there for the inmates, but the Terrell Unit was probably dealing with many more inmates than they were used to having. While personnel are learning to do their jobs, the inmates must depend on them to supply their most basic needs.

Donnie continued:

> Annie, I know you said they would have to embalm me before my body could be transported across the state line, but please don't let them do an autopsy on me. There should be no need for that, huh? —Donnie

Although Donnie trusted us for the details of picking up his body and transporting it to Oklahoma, I sensed his need to know as arrangements were being made; therefore, I kept him informed of the details. I also knew that the closer it came to Donnie's time, the more difficult it would be for me as well as the rest of the family. But I assured him there would be no need for an autopsy. After he was executed, he would no longer belong to the State of Texas. He was going to Oklahoma with his family.

Betty and I had talked to Phillip Hart, the only funeral director in our small town of Walters. He had assured us that he would take care of everything and that he could even pick Donnie's body up after the execution. I told him about the jeans and tee shirt (not new), in which Donnie had asked to be buried. Phillip just smiled and gave me a hug.

The funeral home staffers are like family and are wonderful, caring people.

March 23, 2000

Donnie wrote:

> Although I had family and they came to me at times of troubles in life, they just came. We never had that talk or knew each other anymore after Nam. I just got lost. More my fault than theirs I guess. I'll take the blame for that and anything else. But people have a way of coming into your life and then just leaving. Its always bugged me. I was scared that you, at one time, would care about me for a while and then you'd all go away. This is the first relationship family wise I ever had that has made me feel human.... No one was trying to change me and cut me down and shove me to the side as a lost cause because I had a different lifestyle. Communications is the key to everything amongst people. Smile. —Donnie

March 27, 2000

Expecting Donnie's date to be set at any day, I called Texas Death Row, and they confirmed the lockdown had been lifted. Dale and I made plans to drive down to the Terrell Unit the next day to visit Donnie.

March 28, 2000

Dale and I were excited to see Donnie after the two-week lockdown and had an especially good visit. After the pancake and peanut butter sandwiches, he thought the sandwiches, chips, and cinnamon rolls from the vending machines were real treats. He wanted us to eat with him also. I believe I had a Coke and candy bar. We tried to stay cheerful and let Donnie lead in the conversation. Isolated in his cell during the lockdown I felt sure he had spent plenty of time wondering how quickly it would take the Fifth Circuit Court to accept Judge Means' recommendations and dismiss his appeal. We knew after the Fifth Circuit ruled, that the trial court would set his execution date.

As usual, after our visit, Donnie wrote us a letter.

> Man, I sure was glad to see you two folks today. I've missed you so very much. It was great to eat something too. Thanks Cous. You bought lunch for Dale and me and we got to eat together. I loved it! —Donnie

I thought about how such a small thing meant so much to Donnie, and how we take so much for granted.

Donnie laughed hard during our visit when I told him, "They had the drug dogs at the Walters Schools the day before and the dog went straight to Cassie's [Annie's granddaughter] purse. Cassie said she got all-nervous, then thought, "Hey, wait a minute, I don't have any drugs!" Funny, it was a Rice Krispie treat the dog was after.

Continuing, Donnie wrote:

> I love your humor Annie. I smile so many times when I know Dale and you will be coming to get me and take me away from here and I'll be free at last. Yes it's only my body, but still they will never be able to hurt me again, chain me up, or do anything to me. I'll never be able to tell you or show you all how much I love you and what you mean to me in words or in action, but I love you with the heart of Jesus. Smile.
>
> Phillip Hart sounds like a great person too. I loved that when you said he smiled and hugged you when you told him I want to be buried in Dale's jeans and a tee shirt, not new ones either. Smile. I came in from the visit and I memorized your favorite Bible verse (Gal. 2:20). I finally got it too! "I have been crucified with Christ; it is no longer I who live, but Christ lives in me; and the life which I now live in the flesh I live by faith in the Son of God, who loved me and gave Himself for me." —Donnie

The fact that Galatians 2:20 was my favorite Bible verse only caused Donnie to be more aware of it. Oswald Chambers, the author of the most popular book of daily devotions ever published, *My Utmost for His Highest* wrote, "What our Lord wants us to present to Him is not goodness, nor honesty, nor endeavor, but real solid sin; That is all He can take from us." Then Chambers asks, "And what does He give us in exchange for our sins? Real solid righteousness."[1]

Donnie continued:

> Lately Annie, during all the time that I spend listening to sermons and singing and all on my radio I get real emotional. I cry about people and how much God loves us. I know the Spirit of God is on me. Smile. —Donnie

"God is not dependent on us, Donnie," I wrote responding to his letter thanking us for promising to bring his body back to Oklahoma. "We are dependent on God! I imagine if I had ignored the call or made an excuse for not going to Death Row, God would have used someone else and I would have missed the blessing. I Thessalonians 5:24 says 'Faithful is He who calls you and He will bring it to pass.' He is fully able of equipping someone else for what He called me to do. But I believe that I am blessed with a closer relationship with God today because I responded. I didn't realize what was ahead of me because God doesn't reveal everything at first. I'm afraid we would often run the other way if He did. But like Christian author, Stormie Omartian, God gave me just enough light for the step I was on at the time.

"Therefore we do not lose heart. Even though our outward man is perishing, yet the inward man is being renewed day by day. For our light affliction, which is but for a moment, is working for us a far more exceeding and eternal weight of glory, while we do not look at the things which are seen, but at the things which are not seen. For the things, which are seen, are temporary, but the things, which are not seen, are eternal." (II Corinthians 4:16-18)

March 30, 2000

Donnie wrote:

Thank you for this scripture you sent. I needed this my friend, and it was so right on time too.

You have been praying hard for me, huh, Annie? When I came back in that night they said, Fill your commissary out, and we got that yesterday. Smile. Commissary came about 4 p.m. and I got busy. I washed all my clothes and cleaned up the cage. I got everything I ordered except for the illustration board [for drawing]. I got two more photo albums. Got nine albums now and another I already had, so that's ten. Probably have about 12-14 for you before I die. Smile.

But got some food and only 25 stamps. Smile. I can spend eleven next week so I'll get some more. I'll make it, but I had to catch up on things. I got a typewriter ribbon and the eraser tape and got two wash cloths too. The shorts they give us here are no good so I got my own. I got some more of that Tide soap too.

Hey, last night I fixed two soups with a can of roast beef and peppers and cheese for me and my neighbor. His money wasn't there, as usual. [No money in his trust fund].

Oh, I got two new pair of socks too, gave him one. So, I'm cool on socks.

I thought well, Annie must be really praying for me. Cause things just happened too fast, ya know? Also, I got your letter and two papers [newspapers]. And after that, about 30 minutes passed by. And the same gal passin out mail comes back and she's standing out there. But she has a box and she says she's got to open it. She does, and there are the books you were telling me about. One is Prophet by Peretti and Vanished Into

Thin Air by Lindsey. Smile. I was happy about that. But I got finished cleaning my typewriter up and changing stuff in it. I washed my clothes and ate and by that time it was 10:30. I felt tired. I had bought a box of antihistamine tablets and I thought, Hey, I'll take two of those tabs and read my new book. Smile, I was gone, Annie. I slept last night, at last. I knew God had made all that happen, time wise too. Smile.

I was going to tell you about this guy, Tiny. Guess that's his name spell. But he's a youngster and I talk to him every time I go out to the dayroom. He's new to Death Row really. But God kind of pushed me toward him. Anyhow we talk a lot, but it's been a slow witness. He knew Gribble in sol [solitary] over there. But he knew of me. He thought I was still the president of the club and the rough guy that I was once. Anyway, I told him about me and my case [competency hearing] and all. And I just started telling him of Jesus and heaven and I'll continue to do that. But he is not into that, he said. He was nice and all and said that he believes in an entity, that someone is in charge. Smile. But we have some good talks.

Two days ago I finally got to go to rec. Tiny was there and we was glad to see each other again. He said, Man, I read this book *Left Behind*. His lawyer sent it to him. We talked and Tiny said, Now, I'm not looking at this from no religious thing, but just the story. I said, yea, read the rest of them.

So I see God at work here. Step by step. So pray for Tiny.
—Donnie

March 31, 2000

Donnie wrote:

I love it when you share with me all that you do. And I'm glad that you read that book about heaven to Dale. It's good that you shared that with him. I always pray before our visits that God will be in our midst and He is too. God is awesome. I not only see Him change me, but others too. Smile.

I got Betty's letter out too. I wanted her to know I love her so much. She has a wonderful heart. She helps me so very much.

I just saw you and Dale and I already miss you. I love that guy so much. I loved it when he was telling me all about Steve and Cody's [Dale & Annie's son and grandson] racing. Proud papa and grandpa. These are things that I've missed in my life and always wanted.

I don't know, but lately God seems to be telling me to set and listen. I think I'm just to listen to you preach to me and talk about God more and more. I praise God that this family is God centered and believers in Christ. Smile.

Thanks for letting me hide behind you, Annie. When I get all out of whack I run to you. Can you just picture us standing before Jesus one day? We'll be laughing and talking about how he did this and that. Smile. I have so many thoughts.

You know, like the animals. If they're not there when I get there, as we are in spirit with Jesus, then they will be on the new earth after we come back to take this place back after the Seven Year Tribulation. I don't know, but for the lamb to be able to lie with the lion I think it's going to happen like Dale said. Cool. I'm so glad he said that to me. I hadn't thought of that in so long. But it was a piece to my puzzle and it made my day. Smile.

I keep thinking about that truck that I saw that morning. Heaven Bound! Neat, huh? I knew then that I was going home. Just a little time left and just a matter of time.

I still feel a need to write that judge. But I think God wanted me to get all that anger away from me that day and not mention any of the things about my trial. —Donnie

Donnie reminded me:

> Remember what you was telling me about this guy, Michael Card's book? It kind of goes with our yesterday and today's devotionals. —Donnie

I had written Donnie and told him about the book *A Violent Grace* by Christian author and singer, Michael Card. Card said that while he was researching for the book he gained a whole new appreciation for the crucifixion. He wrote that it was the worst kind of death anyone ever cooked up, and that the legacy of a crucifixion is still with us today in the word "excruciating," which means out of the Cross, to extend life, and thus the torment of the victim. Card wrote that the executioners took great care not to damage the victim's vital organs. If they performed everything properly, he could hang on the Cross up to nine days before death would finally come.

However, Card reminds us the violence of Jesus' death and that His grace for humankind began with a kiss. He said, "I think we all have experienced the Judas kiss, and unfortunately we have all been guilty of giving some as well."[2]

This is a humbling book. Although we know that God has promised to never leave us nor forsake us, there is an experience that a lot of Christians have in which they feel an absence from God. Card calls it, "a wilderness experience." The writer believes God calls us there to teach us how much we need Him.

Donnie replied:

> I can relate to all this, Annie. I just pray that I am becoming the person God wants me to be. I was looking at the picture I did of Christ years ago. I sat in the floor of the Parker County Jail and did that. I did it as if I was standing behind the cross looking up at Jesus. It was actually my first thoughts of what it would be like.
>
> Well, I went to rec and talked to Tiny the whole time. Came back and wrote my brother and Rachel a letter back. Got some

prayer slips from Calvary [church in Walters] and they don't have the address change. I need to write them and thank them so much for all the prayers all these years.

Also, I forgot to tell you about this guy I met at rec. He hollered at me in the dayroom. He was in the other side. He said he'd heard about me and that my time was short. Said he was going to do the same thing [waive appeals]. I told him it's not for everyone. He said, I ain't scared to die. I said, Well Bro. I'm not either since I know where I'm going. How about you?' He got quiet and just kinda looked at me. But we talked. Now here is a guy, Annie, that has feared me and I have tromped on before. Actually there was two of them. I jumped on both of them at once. They got on my nerves. But that was years ago. And now all that is gone. I holler at him when I see him and I felt a need to write him and tell him about Jesus.

And like today, Jack was suppose to go out. He was lazy. So I go out and just walk the wall and do my pushups. Guy they put beside me is a loud mouth. So as always, I'll not talk. But then he said, Ya gonna get a date? Yeah, I dropped my appeals and soon I'll be gone. Going home to be with Jesus. Well he was took back pretty hard on that statement. He doesn't believe in the Trinity. So I tell him all I can, but he believes there is a God. I tell him Satan believes in God. He has a junior view of it all really. Biased in a lot of it. Muslems [sic] and all that has him crowded. I see it all so I just pray that God let His Holy Spirit drop on us and give me the words to say. I don't shut up for thirty minutes. He's making faces and I hit him here and there on worldly things. And then it's time to go. I get on his level and let him know that I see this and that and explain the body, spirit and soul to him. But when they come to get me, it goes fast. Handcuffs and you're gone without hardly a goodbye. Smile! But he tells me, Stoney, I enjoyed it man. Smile.

I get to my cage and I hope that I have made a difference by doing and saying the right things to this guy. I was scared that I didn't say it the way it should be. I pray for the guy. It's all I can do, Annie. It's in God's hands now. I asked God to do this for me in these last days and He's keeping me busy.—Donnie

The Lord answered Donnie's prayer as he witnessed to many in his last days and as he took his last breath. In Donnie's death, he would give others a glimpse of his Jesus inside.

Chapter 22

Freedom rings around me

"This place is growing heavy on me."

April 1, 2000

Untitled Short Story
By Donnie Foster

I'm sailing on a clipper ship. All the sails are out, and it is so magnificent. It's the most beautiful ship I've ever seen, and made with the finest woods. I'm in the front of the ship on the little walkway and I'm leaning out over the rails. My arms are raised high and I'm just riding the waves as they rise, and they fall only to rise again. I have no fear because nothing can hurt me.

I can feel the wind on my body, and freedom rings around me. I can see for miles on the sea and all its beauty. After a bit I turn and say to the man at the wheel, My Lord Jesus, I thank you for the ride this day. And I ask Would you like to take a turn up here now?

April 2, 2000

Donnie wrote:

Answered prayer. I asked God to send me someone that I could share who I am with. Someone to see me for who I am inside, not just outside. And in you I know that has been done. I have not hid who I am from you or this family, and many times I have been so ashamed of who I am and what I was. But I had to face it and have been facing it for all this time that you and I have been together in this. Its not been easy, Annie. I've tried to do the right thing in all things. Whether I do or not, I try. I want to be right and please God most of all. I know that this life is over. I have to move on now. And with you and this family God has been preparing me to have somewhat a life of fulfillment and at the same time preparing me to come home.

I believe that one of the things that is your part in my life is to help me make the right decisions. We all know that I'm a bonehead. God has surely let you see that in me. Hey, before you came into my life I wasn't sure about who I was in Christ. Did I see things right or understand them right? Was I normal to feel a certain way? Things like that! We've talked about everything you can talk about too over the years and you have led me right. I'd run right into a wall before I'd do what I should do. Like pray and think about it. If I take time to think about it and pray I about always do the right thing. Smile. I wanted so much to explain to that judge what happened out there that day, yet it would in no way make a difference. I know that I am in God's hands and I'll go with that.

I've never sat in a church and prayed with real Christians actually living my life as one, ya know, church and all? I've wanted to though. But we have church here when you come. Smile. And I love having you and Betty to discuss things with that comes my way.

Man, I love that little book Heaven, Is It Real? Tell Ellen [Annie's sister] thank you so much for that. People come to me that need it bad and God lets me know that I got to tell them about Him. —Donnie

April 3, 2000

Hey Annie, I'm scared to memorize another Bible verse. I'm afraid I'll forget the one I just learned! Smile. —Donnie

Donnie would write Galatians 2:20 to me and sometimes I would include it in a letter back to him. "I have been crucified with Christ. It is not longer I who live, but Christ lives in me, and the life which I now live in the flesh, I live by faith in the Son of God who loved me and gave Himself for me."

April 4, 2000

Donnie wrote:

I'm so grateful that you have been getting things in order. But do you ever get that unorganized feeling? Like when I was sitting here looking at what stuff I had. I laughed, then I cried. Smile. I started laughing cause I was looking at this old ragged clock I got. To give it to someone is an insult really. Actually that goes for anything I own. I got nothing, Annie. I just got stuff that people would look at and throw away. It would mean nothing to them. Then it made me cry. My life is kind of nothingness, huh? But they say Jesus didn't have a place to lay His head. I just get lost in thought sometimes.

I'm so hungry. I got food, but I also know I got to lose this belly. I got put in the other side today [dayroom] and it has big windows and you can see yourself real well. Man, my gut is big. I'm healthy topside, but I got no business with this. If I was playing football that would be great. But I got to stop eating one meal a day here at least. And do something too. I don't even know why I should care either. But I've just never been this big before.

Everyone says if I'd lose this gut, I'd be in good shape. I said, No kiddin? Smile. —Donnie

April 6, 2000

After a visit from my daughter Bev and me, Donnie wrote:

I hope you're doing okay and got some rest from all the

traveling you've been doing. I know you had to be wore out. I prayed that God would fill your tank up again though. But I was so glad to meet Bev. It was a real pleasure too. She's a really neat lady. Thank you for getting her down here Annie. And today I wanted to talk to you, as we did some, about leaning on God's very Word for all things. I see those tears and they just run out of your eyes and I feel you're hurting. But I know that tears come in all ways, my friend. You and I know that talking about what we got to do is one thing. But doing it and going through it is something else.

I know that we are in this together and that God is with us. I know that somehow putting us together like this was for many reasons. I say it was for me, and you say it was for you. Smile. But it's for us all, huh? We have stayed close to God in all this and will all the way through it till I come to get you or we all meet in the air together. Smile. It's been a real adventure, huh Annie? But you got to see just how dumb I really am. I know you wonder or used to wonder, What's he gonna do next?

I've been screwed up way too long in some people's eyes. Some are family and friends, and it hinders me and makes me think I'm a loser, ya know. But I love them anyway and I will all the way to the table [gurney], and as I meet the Lord in a lot of my feelings. We got no time for that kind of thing anymore. Smile. I may not be going to die this month or next week but I am going to die. And at times I have to deal with that. I need my date so I can move on. This place is growing heavy on me.

I've lived here too long, Annie. I live in a different world and I carry myself as best I can as a man in here and try to please God also. But I don't live down the street from you. I'm different in ways. I want you to start praying with me that God kind of reveal Himself to me more. Something to help me walk right on through this. And you and I have seen some answered prayers, haven't we? Where would I be without you all holding me up to God all the time?

Stepping out on faith, Annie, just like Peter did from the boat that day he saw Jesus walking on the water. Smile. Today I saw you stepping out over the edge of that boat looking to Jesus. That's what I was saying about all this, we have to spend more time with God talking about His Word because that's what we have, and that is what will be holding you up and me up in all this. All we got to do, you especially, is don't look at the storm around us. Just keep on looking at Jesus. You won't sink an inch in the water, feet won't even get wet. Smile. And this family is going to be there for you too in that time. Somehow in it God is going to be doing some real fantastic works. And things will be happening that we may not see for a while, but I assure you that God will be there. I pray that you will have the same peace that I will have after I'm gone. And you will too, Annie.

I was thinking today as you and Bev was going that I may never see Bev again and it made me sad. But I got to meet her and I am blessed to have done that.

When I got in Big Jack always asks about you guys. He's a good guy and we talk a lot about things. We read all the same books. He's sad that I'll be leaving soon too. He's not a people person. He's the biggest guy on death row and he stays close to God in that radio and Bible. We've grown close and learned many things. He knows I'm an idiot too, or can be. I share things with him. He said to tell you thanks for sending those books.

You know Annie I'd like to have one hour in the pulpit in front of people that have come my way since I've been down here. I'd love to throw a sermon on them that they wouldn't forget. But oh how I love them all. Ain't no perfect people in this world. Smile.

Well, I'm going to stop here. I just showered but I don't feel any better. I know that this dungeon has made a difference in my body. No sun. My body will last just long enough to go home. I'm still working out too and I will till I die. But I feel weary at times through my body. —Donnie

Donnie had heard a sermon entitled "When Others Fail Us" on his radio, preached by a well-known pastor, Charles Stanley.[1] Donnie felt that if more people could hear that message then they could be helped that feel so all alone in this world. Stanley spoke about when the people deserted Paul; he related this to people, explaining how sometimes they step aside and allow a friend to go through a hardship alone. Stanley explains how insensitive some are to people's needs, but Stanley reminds us that we are all human and it's hard to be spiritual all the time.

I wrote to Donnie that Paul asked God to not hold it against his friends for leaving him, and I wished someone could be there every day to visit him. Although TDCJ did not allow visits but once a week, I reminded Donnie that God never leaves him.

April 13, 2000

A week before we got the news that Donnie's execution date had been set, Betty and I visited him at the Terrell Unit. Donnie kept us laughing with funny stories pertaining to humorous situations with inmate friends on Death Row.

After our visit, Donnie wrote:

> I didn't want to see you and Betty leave today. I was glad to see you laugh. And I loved the prayer too. I thank you for that and also for all the food I ate. Smile.
>
> I am glad that you guys had that revival. I wish I could have been there to hear all that.
>
> I love it when you guys get to talking about the ways of God, like once saved, always saved. Smile.
>
> I was thinking about something on that too. I guess if people are saved then it doesn't matter what they do or who they are.

> Like the people that are going to kill me that evening. I'm sure some are going to be Christians over there and yet they kill people. So it won't be held against them, huh? —Donnie

In his letter, Donnie wrote that it was just a thought, but I knew he was seriously wondering about the subject of those in charge of executions. So I took some notes and Donnie and I discussed it on our next visit. One of the scriptures I referred to was First Corinthians 10:31. "Therefore, whether you eat or drink, or whatever you do, do all to the glory of God." In the book *900 Bible Questions Answered*, William L. Pettingill wrote in reference to this scripture verse, "Let this test be applied to questionable things, and it will soon become evident whether or not they are expedient for a child of God."[2] Pettingill was a member of the editorial staff of the Scofield Reference Bible, as well as author of numerous books on handling difficult questions of the Bible.

I told Donnie that we don't know what God has in mind for those in charge of his execution because we don't know their hearts. I prayed if any weren't Christians, they would come to accept Christ as Savior and Lord before they die. Like Donnie said, "We all have a date to die." However, Donnie knew that God did not and does not zap people and make them want to trust Him as their Savior. God uses people and situations through their willingness to obey. Donnie asked to be used. People need to know, like any gift, that in order to receive the gift of salvation, they must reach out and accept it. Once we do, surrendering our lives to Christ, then eternal life is ours forever. Then I assured him that if the ones that executed him had ever accepted this gift of God then they would go to heaven.

I reminded Donnie in a letter that we live by faith in the One who is faithful, and He is in charge. Humans often tend to think that they are.

Donnie and I often reminded one another to keep our eyes on

Jesus and trust Him in all things. Many Christians are carrying around some heavy excess baggage that they don't have to carry. It is a tremendous burden to think that it is up to us to keep our eternal salvation secure, and that we could lose it. Christian author, Dr. Charles Stanley wrote in his book Eternal Security, "If you have placed your trust in Christ's death on the cross as payment for your sins, you are an eternal member of the family of God." Stanley included that, "Acting like God's child didn't get you in. Not acting like one won't get you tossed out. God's unconditional love is eternal."[3]

April 2000

This was a difficult time for all of us. After the competency hearing on March 9, my thoughts went back to something Donnie had told me about J. C. Cockrum. Donnie said, "JC will be executed because he confessed to the crime." I knew that Donnie would soon die because he admitted his crime. I knew that his execution date would be set any day and that his execution could take place within thirty days of the date it was set. Although Donnie and the family went through feelings of anxiety and sadness, we knew that we could not allow anger and bitterness to settle in our hearts. We would have to stay focused on the One that knew all that was happening. With God's help, we were able to concentrate on Donnie's destination more than his departure. Some of the family drove from Walters to visit him every week for a regular two-hour visit. Once a month an inmate was allowed "special visits" if visitors had to drive over 300 miles, so Betty and I would take the special four-hour visits.

April 18, 2000

Donnie wrote:

I visited Bobby and Sherry today. It was so hot out there today. My window fogged up so bad that I got up and wrote

'HELP' on the window. Then this lady who I knew came and saw it. They was laughing and she gave me some toilet paper to wipe the glass off. Then Bobby and Sherry and I got into talking about good stuff about God and prayed, and it actually got cool in there. Smile.

Sherry cried today too. I saw a need for God there and He was with us. We were talking about prayer being the key to all. But we must give what we pray about to God and stop handling it ourselves. Smile.

Two young bosses brought me in and I know one of the other bosses told them I was a vet. They asked me about it on the way in. I told them I was, and about being sentenced to death on Veterans Day. And then I told them I had dropped my appeals. One asked, You just got tired, huh? I smiled and said, Well, I believe in Jesus. I did the crime and admitted to it. The guys are just looking at me. Smile. But it must be that way Annie, from here on out, to keep God in front of all things. I get sidetracked and mad about just everyday life here. It's hard to stay in line at times.

I got a letter from a friend of mine [inmate]. Whitey cracks me up. I'm sending his letter on to you. Smile. —Donnie

Portion of Whitey's letter:

Hey, Stoney, what do you think of this place so far?

As you can see I've tried to write you before but I couldn't get your number. I thought maybe they would deliver it anyway.... From the time I wrote it, and it was postmarked in Houston, it finally got back to me three weeks later.

No wonder you didn't get my letter! I not only couldn't remember your number, but I thought your real last name was Armadillo! You might get a letter from one of the guys here telling you about it. It got some good laughs here. Smile. —Whitey

April 20, 2000

I had spent the night with Dale's mother at a local hospital. Before leaving the hospital, I got a call from my sister, Betty. She told me she had heard on the local news that Richard Donald Foster's execution date had been set for May 24. We agreed that she would call Donnie's dad, and I would call Donnie's lawyers. They had not been notified or heard that his date had been set by the District Court of Parker County, Texas, where his trial court was held in 1985.

Although Donnie was expecting an execution date to be set at any time, Alexa immediately made arrangements for a conference call to Donnie on Death Row, hoping to tell him herself before he heard it on his radio or from someone who had. Craig told Donnie that his date had been set for May 24, 2000. This meant that Donnie had 34 days to live.

April 20, 2000

> Sorry about the writing, Cous. My machine spun out. I'll try to get another. Hate to cause of so little time. I just can't write. My hands won't settle down. They came got me today and wouldn't tell me where I was going. Office.
>
> Craig and Alexa on the phone. No privacy and I'm in chains. So I got the news Annie. I thought of you that instant. Reckon you know, cause they said I'd see you Tuesday. I'll see them Friday.
>
> My heart skipped a beat today on the news. I came back and prayed, or tried, and cried some. I asked God to hold me and walk with me all the way, to give me strength and you too. So we're on our way, Cous.
>
> I'm sure I'll move tomorrow. I'll work on getting a machine. Pray about it. We're gonna make it. Please tell everyone hello and I love em.
>
> Give us strength, Father. —Donnie

I prayed daily for strength for Donnie to remain strong under the strain of each day on Death Row as his execution date grew near. The Lord did continue to give us strength, and we were going to need it to get though the rough time ahead of us. While God does not remove difficult times, He takes us through them. We all felt the Lord with us as we moved forward towards Donnie's execution.

"I have been crucified with Christ. It is no longer I who live, but Christ lives in me, and the life which I now live in the flesh, I live by faith in the Son of God who loved me and gave Himself for me."

(Galatians 2:20)

Chapter 23

Prayer

"God is all around me, in me, and over me"

April 23, 2000

*D*onnie wrote:

Easter Sunday. I had to ask God to settle me down. I've been thinking and praying for all you there. Lot of feelings and emotions going on. Smile. I have so much to say and so much to write. We have so much to do, my friend, things to take care of.

I'm praying I get my blue slip Friday so I can get my typewriter. My hands are clumsy when it comes to writing.

I haven't been moved yet; no room over there. A lot of people will die in May so a cell will come open.

How is Dale? Prayed up? How is his mom? What long, wonderful lives some have lived! But we don't live forever and thank God too. That cross gets so heavy at times. We need relief.

Annie, tell Dale I love him. —Donnie

April 23, 2000

Thank you for the books. I love Christian novels. I hope I get to read the new one on the Left Behind series before I go.

I must be an empty vessel for Jesus in these last days, for Him only, in all things. Oh how I praise Him for putting you in my life to go through this with me, to help keep me close to Him and His Word all this time. Yes, Jesus has us in His hands.

Annie, tell Bev hello for me and that I love her and Richard and the kids too. Bev is neat and a real together lady. I'm prayin for her.

Actually the closer I get to God the more I pray for everyone in this family. Sometimes it's so strange too. I feel so much and it's awesome. I can only say it is God's Holy Spirit in me.

I make commissary one more time and I stop shaving. Smile. I pray that I not get a case or get in trouble here for anything. I shaved last night, but no more. Trim maybe.

I slept late today. No rec. Just wrote you after dinner and I slept again. I read the book of John through. I did a puzzle, wrote you again and fell out again.

I know a guy here who I want to tell you and everyone in the family about. I've been talking to him. He loves the Lord. Smile.
—Donnie

I wrote Donnie about when and how I learned of his execution date, and how I had prayed that the Lord would keep his mind on his destination instead of the leaving.

Donnie had written that he had prayed or tried to pray when he heard about his execution date. I reminded him Romans 8:26-27 says in our weakest moments the Spirit Himself is interceding for us personally, not with mere words but with groans that words cannot express. How wonderful to know that on that day or any day before when we just cannot find the words to express our overwhelming feelings, we can cling to that divine promise that the Holy Spirit is praying on our behalf.

I called Cliff, Donnie's dad, to check on him and asked how he was doing after hearing the news. He told me he was expecting it and was prepared. Cliff already knew that Betty and I were going to be with Donnie during his execution and that Dale and I were bringing Donnie's body back to Walters for a memorial service and to bury him here.

"Are you sure you are going to be able to deal with this, Annie?" Cliff asked.

"Yes, I am," I replied. "I'm human, and I will grieve for Donnie as the rest of the family, but God is going to get us through this."

I had informed Ben Luna, a friend and former volunteer chaplain on Death Row, by e-mail that Donnie's execution date had been set for May 24, 2000.

Ben replied, "It's 3:30 a.m. I awoke and knew I had some unfinished business. When I read your email I wished I had never received it and I didn't know what to say. But knowing there is a heaven to gain and a hell to shun, and that Donnie has accepted Jesus Christ as his Lord and Savior brightened my day. And to know that he will be set free is a blessing."

Ben asked me if he was still on Donnie's visitor list?

I e-mailed a reply and thanked Ben for loving and caring for Donnie. I explained that if he visited him now, it would need to be a minister visit, which would not interfere with the inmate's one regular visit with family that he is allowed each week. I wrote Ben that some of the family would be visiting every week until his execution day was over. I reminded Ben that time was very short.

I explained to Ben that in the beginning I had tried to discourage Donnie from waiving his appeals, but he told me not to do that. I believed Donnie preferred to think of it as a happy ending to a sad story. And although I was sad and it would be the hardest thing I had ever had to deal with in life, I felt at peace. The family knew that the next 30 days were going to be difficult. But we trusted God to keep His promises of strength and comfort for us as well as Donnie.

I warned Ben that if he were allowed to visit Donnie, Donnie would be preaching to him.

"Funny you said that about being preached to," Ben e-mailed, "because one out of every two guys I visited on Death Row ministered to me and I loved it. Some chaplains didn't understand that, but I did because I knew their hearts."

April 24, 2000

Donnie wrote:

> I got a wonderful letter from Sandy. I really love that lady. She told me the story of their cat, Wheezer. How they were moving to a new home and she had prayed that he would accept his new home. They were waiting until the last load of furniture to take him to the new house cause they were nervous that he'd want to go back to their old place. In the meantime he miraculously showed up, on his own, at their new house meowing under Cassie's bedroom window wanting to come in. Smile. Look for God in everything! That story blessed me and needs to be in the Guideposts. God answered her prayer about Wheezer! Smile. —Donnie

April 25, 2000

Sandy and I arrived at the Terrell Unit to visit Donnie at 12:30 p.m. As we entered, I thought of the news article from The Dallas Morning News that Donnie had sent me saying that Charles Terrell Sr., a Dallas insurance executive and former chairman of the Texas Criminal Justice Task Force, said that he felt uneasy about having the unit named for him ever since TDCJ began moving death row there in June 1999. "I don't like my name being associated with death row," said Terrell after emphasizing he was still for crime victims and that he had spent his life working for the victims. The article stated that Terrell was not quite ready to proclaim himself an opponent of capital punishment. "For now he simply says, 'I have questions.'"[1]

Later in 2001, the unit was renamed for Allan B. Polunsky, a former TDCJ board chairman.

Many things went through my mind as Sandy and I prepared to visit Donnie for the first time since his execution date had been set. With his confession and dropping his appeals, I knew that Donnie was going to be executed in a matter of weeks.

Our visit seemed unsettled because of interruptions. People visiting others who knew Donnie and knew that his date had been set wanted to speak to him for a moment and get pictures. The two-hour visit went quickly, but Donnie loved that he was able to see his good friend, Blue, who was in another cage and also had a visitor.

April 25, 2000

> Hello Annie. 29 days. We never count the last day.
>
> Well, you and Sandy just left. That visit went too fast. This is not enough time.
>
> Things are going too fast. Going to take a lot to stay on track. Sometimes I relax in the Lord and sometimes I don't. I'm human, Annie. God held me together until I got back here. I never get to talk to Sandy in depth it seems.
>
> How did I miss so much? Why didn't I know? I would have loved knowing I could ride into Walters on my Harley, just off the road, and stay and visit you all. Just talk and share. When things bothered me I could have come over there and we'd have coffee and just talk. And I could have had someone to be there for, too. Will you tell Sandy, Bev, and Steve that I sure love them? Thank you.
>
> You are a wonderful mom and Dale is the greatest dad. And it pays, cause you can see it in all your kids. Kids? Smile.
>
> If people get anything at all from me in all this, it should be the cause of real friendship and unconditional love. What would I do without that from you?

Today I saw your notes and how you was getting things in order and it made me so sad. I thought, Lord, what am I doing to this woman?

I'm so powerless and useless here in this cage, but I know God is and will be with you.

In my last days it's not about me, but about these kids of yours, their kids, and all this family. I spend time in thoughts of them all and I pray for them. Some of my prayers you won't realize until after I'm gone.

We need that four-hour visit to get everything right and out of the way.

Annie, did you know that by your requesting that I be over on the other side today, that was an answer to my prayer in seeing Blue? Thank you for being in God's will. I love my brother, Blue. He was somebody out there (in the world), at least we thought we was. But God said different to me, and to Blue.

I got in and everyone was hollering at me and Tiny said he got some stories from you. Smile. And you did good in what you sent McFarland. Follow your heart here, Cous.

I forgot to tell you of this guy today. It's been bothering me and hopefully we can talk about it in person soon. But write this guy's name down. Joseph (Joey). Just a kid. Believes in God. But he don't have anything but a cup and a spoon. The guy told me, Hey Stoney, I know this lady we can write and she'll pray for us! I almost said, Hey man, I've have lots of family and I'm covered, but it was like that was what he had to offer. He never complains. I asked him, Man, don't you have a fan or radio or coffee pot or anything? He said, No, and every time I'd ask him if he is okay, he says, Just fine. I don't think he's been to the store [ordered from commissary] since he got here. Not once has he said anything to anyone, but in solitary and here, no one sees you. He said the people he knew said to write them and they'd help him but they never wrote back. All in all he has no one. He looks to his Bible studies and God, but he's alone here. From solitary at Ellis to here in this cell. Same thing, Annie. I feel God strong here about this guy. When I heard him say, I know this lady we can write and she'll pray for us. And me? I thought, I have all this family, and I'm the richest guy in the world and have everything. I just cried.

I'll have to tell you more about him on a visit, but I don't want to leave this world knowing he ain't got nothin. I know the Spirit is on me about this guy. He waits on me and Big Jack to shower so he can say hi and talk to someone. Too bad some churches don't have an Adopt a Guy Program. You know, like, Raise One Guy in Christ on Death Row! Annie just tell people about him and if they can spare a buck, fine. But don't try to do all this by yourself.

There are others I want us to pray for that I believe need Jesus in their hearts and not just on their minds. —Donnie

As Donnie wrote of Joey I could not help but consider my own grandsons, Cory and Cody, who were Joey's age, and how difficult it would be for them to be where Joey is.

I let Donnie know that I had contacted Chaplain Brazzil at the Walls Unit in Huntsville to confirm some things that he was concerned about. Chaplain Brazzil, who I found to be a very dedicated and compassionate man, would be Donnie's spiritual advisor on the day he was executed. He told me about the Hospitality House, a Texas Baptist Ministry that aids families of those incarcerated in prison, and they don't allow the press or picketers to bother the families while they are there. Brazzil said that the directors, Bob and Nelda Norris, would assist us in every way possible. Donnie would be allowed to call us at the Hospitality House in the afternoon before his was executed. Brazzil was not sure about visits at the Terrell Unit on days just prior to the execution. He said the Terrell Unit was new at this, and I should check with the warden there in Livingston.

Donnie had said he wanted to use this verse as his final statement on the day he was executed. I asked him if this was the version that he planned to use. He agreed.

"I have been crucified with Christ; it is no longer I who live, but Christ lives in me; and the life I now live in the flesh, I live by faith in the Son of God, who loved me and gave Himself for me" (Galatians 2:20).

April 25, 2000

> Late Tuesday night Donnie wrote:
>
> I got a nice card and letter from you. I got happy, so I get my coffee and get on my bed, opened my letter, and spent some time with you. I had some things on my heart I had to say, so here I am with pen in hand. Smile.
>
> Thank you for getting Tiny those stories. Also, thank you for writing George, for putting up with me in bringing these boys to you, and as you know now, this deal with Joey. I want to stop this, but at times God lays people on my heart and I can't stop the care and compassion.
>
> Now you and I have got to get things in order. You do, I mean. Smile. I'm sorry you're doing all this while I just sit here and do nothing. Just go one day at a time, Annie.
>
> And yes my friend, I know it is okay to shed tears. Out there I am strong for you cause it pains you, but I cried all day writing Sandy and you. God is all around me, in me, and over me.
> —Donnie

Donnie became focused on others more than himself; he also faced death like no one I had ever seen; he was getting ready to go home, and he looked forward to being free.

Chapter 24

For A Season

"27 days..."

April 26, 2000

Donnie wrote:

Well, I live at 12AF-80 now. 28 days. Moved a few hours ago. This pod went to the store on Monday; the old pod went on Friday, so I may have missed it and will have to wait till next Monday. Throws me all the way off too. Only four stamps left. But maybe by then I'll have my blue slip to get my typewriter. Not sure I should waste the money.

I hope you're okay. I miss you guys already. Wish we could visit everyday. —Donnie

April 27, 2000

27 days. I went out early and worked out some. What's the use? I'm a fat boy till I die. Smile.

Saw Red and talked to him and McBride for an hour. He will die on May 9 and McBride the 11th. The bottom three cells (75-77) are where we go as we get down to seven days. Red was in 84 cell, but they moved him to Gribble's [executed March 15] old cage. They have a desk out there, and within seven days, every 15-30 minutes they look at you. I don't like that.

So as soon as TJ [execution May 4] and Red and McBride go, I'll be moving down there. More dates set. So it's Richardson

May 23, me on 24th and Clayton's got one for the 25th. So it's three-in-a-row, T-W-Thursday.

I saw Edwin [volunteer minister] today in here. Smile. He didn't get to stop long. He was supposed to be on C-Pod. So God is answering prayers. I told him just to relax in the Lord. Smile.

I do need my machine. I'm in the mood to write and feel I need to. But I'm so ashamed of my writing. I use so much tension when I write that it hurts my hand. I can't relax and I guess it depends on my mood, too.

I'm worried about the last day visits. I think Bonnie and Todd [Annie's sister and her son] will come. I better be making a list to give to Helen [warden's secretary].

I miss Dale. Annie, after these four-hour visits, and then the next week of the eighth, that leaves me less than two weeks left. The week of the 15th we only get two hours, huh? I don't know. I know I want to see Dale. I pray he can make it. If not, he'll be here for the visit the day before I die. Smile.

A mess, huh? I'm gonna stop and pray about all this. I know that you know what to do and what has to be done. Smile.

I loved Bev's letter. She has such a caring heart. I'm very glad I met her. I've got to see and feel every ones heart in your family except Steve. But I know he's a great guy. I can truly say that God has come to me in Spirit about every one in this family. I've cried out to Him for them all at one time or another. —Donnie

April 30, 2000

Hi Dale and Annie! 24 days.
Grace, humbleness! How do you do that?
Submit is a military word. Smile.
We are Privates, but we act like Generals. We got to be privates and submit to God and say, Lord, here I am waiting

> your orders. He's the General. But I reckon you already know that. Smile.
>
> I'm listening to some sermons. I got up, went outside for an hour. Cloudy. And it seemed I was just blank until I got into this sermon.
>
> Hey Annie, you two sit and pray together for me, okay? Getting a lil lumpy here. I seem to just fall off into starin' at the wall and I've got too many thoughts where it jams me mentally. You know I'm brain dead anyway. I just get lonely and I miss ya'll.
>
> I'm sorry that you have to be the one to do all this Annie, but I know that God is with us and I am comfortable with you in everything.
>
> We have some good memories, Cous. Sometimes I laugh, sometimes I cry. With me being here and the times we've had. Even broke some rules. I guess I've about turned you into an outlaw in a way. Smile. But together we have come a long way in our walk with the Lord. We really have, ya know. —Donnie

After reading this portion of Donnie's letter, I was reminded of something I had once read, how some people may come into our lives for only a season. They're there to help us to learn, to grow, and to share. They may teach us something that we have never done before. They make us laugh and bring us unbelievable joy, and it is real...but only for a season.

Donnie's letter continued:

> And you all there have held me up to the Lord and never gave up on me. I think of that story you sent me, where the guy wanted God to reveal Himself to him. Smile. And then I remembered when I was telling you and Betty that I wanted that, and you said, He does, He sent us! Smile. You really woke me up that day.

Oh yes, through you all God has showed Himself to me. When I am with you all, I feel so loved. Even when you are there and I am here. God comes to me through you, my friend. It's the knowing that you're there and you'll be there till the end with me.

I still haven't anything on a blue slip for the typewriter. A guy who dies here, or gets killed on the 11th wants to leave me his. But I'm not sure about that. I'm not sure he can. I'm puttin off writing some letters cause of my handwriting. But I'm getting anxious about the machine.

You know, Cous, I feel bad that I have lived my whole life and it wasn't for God, maybe just the last bit. —Donnie

April 30, 2000

I was praying about Trey's leg being broke, for complete healing. We Christians go through life and all of a sudden something drastic happens. Why? Maybe God's trying to get our attention or teaching us to depend on Him or to even just call out to Him. I wrote Bev and was telling her about praying all the time, even in our thoughts. Then you were saying the same thing in your letter about that. Something, huh?

You know I got this second letter from Bev and I cried. God lets me feel their hearts and it's so nice and joyful. I prayed for them and put it in my Bible and you'll read it when I'm gone. Smile.

Annie, they say it is a true honor and a great privilege to be with a true friend when they die. Fortunate even!

Death is life's defining moment. It's the point where the final touch is put on each person's life's portrait. The masterpiece is signed and the paint dries, never to be changed again. It's finished. —Donnie

As we went into the last month of Donnie's life on earth, I called and spoke to the warden's secretary about Donnie getting his typewriter. She said she would check with the property's personnel on that and call me back. I also called the warden about the visits on the days before Donnie was to be executed.

I wrote Donnie that the warden told me we could have the regular, two-hour visit on Monday, May 22 (two days before his execution). Everyone on the list that Donnie had given them could visit all day on Tuesday (day before execution), visitors switching out two at a time. Then visitors would be allowed four hours on Wednesday morning (day of execution). I assured Donnie that Betty and I will get our special, two-day visit the week before his execution.

The secretary called backed confirming that Donnie's typewriter had been approved.

I wrote suggesting that Donnie have "promise" Bible verses where he could see them at all times, perhaps on the wall at the foot of his bed. It would be the first thing he saw when he awoke in the morning, and it would be the last thing he saw before going to sleep.

May 1, 2000

Donnie wrote:

23 days. New month already! Mad house here. TJ has 2 more days. They may move me in his cage, or maybe Richardson. I'll get Red's cell after he goes on the 9th. McBride dies on the 11th.

My coffeepot's gone (broke). I'm trying to get a new one. Probably won't. Not enough time.

Went to rec and talked to Edwin Smith [volunteer minister] awhile. He left, then a sergeant came by the day room. I said, How ya doin? Big black guy.

He said, Okay.

I said, Yeah, me too, with Jesus in my life! I asked him, Do you believe?

He answered, Yes.

We talked and I told him I'd be going home in 23 days. But I thanked him cause Jesus came to see me twice today. Confused him. I said, Yes, Jesus in you, came to see me. He just grinned. It was cool. I hope I can just keep goin. Use me Father. —Donnie

I knew Donnie had his machine when his handwritten letters were replaced with typed ones.

May 2, 2000

Donnie wrote:

Well, Guess what? Yep! I was laying here and the sarge came to the door.

He said, Hey, give me your card [commissary] and I'll get what all you need.

I said, Can I get a coffeepot too? Get anything you want, he said.

I had just prayed that I get this all done and as I fell asleep, there he was, the sarge. I didn't feel right spending the money, but I made commissary too. So I ain't wanting for anything. I want you to know that, Cous. I'm fine. Don't send me anymore money at all.

The keyboard on this thing is small. So is my brain, but my hands won't float around on it like the other one.

But I was just wondering if you called and talked to someone to get all this done? Smile.

I have so much going on in my head that I'm starting to worry about all I'm leaving behind. I'm worrying about the cost of my burial for you all. It would almost be better to be buried here and not have to pay all that to put some old worthless, wore out body in the ground. Anyway, you know what I mean. This body is just a shell that house's my spirit, and my spirit will be in heaven.

Smile!

    I had told George that after I'm gone you may back off some to grieve. But after a time, I see God using you in his life more. I got the nicest letter from him and a picture of his family. Smile. George is really trying. He is growing, Annie. And to turn your back now would be wrong and maybe even devastating for some here. God is going to tell you what to do my friend.

    As for Lisa [Donnie's sister], I'm going to send her one more letter and a picture she once drew for me on her envelope years ago, a little pink elephant that says, I miss you. It was so cute. I saved it all this time.

    I ate. I had barbecued beef with chili beans, jalapenos and a half pickle and Fritos, all in a flour tortilla. Smile. Shared with my fat neighbor. We have a crack in our doors that I didn't have in the last cell. So we talk a lot.

    I'm trying to get a boss to carry *Within Heaven's Gates* over to Red for me. I want him to read this and his neighbor, McBride, too.

    Annie, I had to ask God to forgive me of any bad feelings I had about my mom, my real mom. I read a story today in the Guideposts, and it kind of brought something out that I saw in myself. I guess as long as I'm alive I'm always going to hurt about all that, but it's funny how things come out at you.
—Donnie

I replied to Donnie that God wanted to mend his broken heart, like the guy in the story "My Bitter Heart."[1] Reminding him how God works, I told him that God let him know about his bad feelings so he could give those feelings to Him to heal. Donnie was so much like that hurt little boy.

    I didn't go out today, but Red went out and I got up and talked to him. I got that book to him too.

It's hard to think in here cause of this one guy who never shuts up. I get my hands on him I'll shut him up. Stuff a Bible in his mouth. You know one of those little ones? Smile. —Donnie

May 3, 2000

20 days. I want to start getting some things together for you to pick up on visits and get a little lighter here on stuff. All I have is pure d old junk. Smile. You can do what you want to with it, Annie. But some things are for certain people. I'll tag them and make you a copy of all that I have and who gets what. And the rest is yours, so just get out the trashcan and throw it all away. Except for my pictures. Smile.

I am so pleased to hear what Phillip Hart [funeral director] is doing in helping us all out. He must be one heck of a guy. I'll never get to meet him here on earth, but I'll look forward to meeting him one day in heaven.

Ya know, I've been worried that I'm getting all my blessings down here, and I'm not going to have any where I'm going! Smile. Know what I mean, Annie? You all have laid the world out for me and took such good care of me that I am overwhelmed at times. And I can only praise God for you. You may never know how you guys made this old boy's life worth living and brought me all the things I have longed for all my life. You made me a part of something and loved me and I loved you all back. You took me just as I am. I'm going to miss you, and I already know that in time, in heaven that the angels and other friends will come to me at my place and tell me, Annie is coming soon. Let's prepare for her. And I'll run to my Lord and ask to be the one to come and get you, or meet you within heaven's gates. Smile. It just might be that while I'm in heaven, I'll still be praying for you! Ever think of that, Annie? Oh yes, it could very well be!

I was glad that you and Betty got to pray with me today about my friends Blue and George and Joey and Tiny and the others, and yes Trey. Just things that I have on my heart and I believe the Lord put them there. Smile. Annie tell Trey I love him.

Are you okay, my friend? Annie, God isn't going to just let you sit around and do nothing after I'm gone. He's going to have plenty for you to be doing. Just be sure that you see it when it comes to you. Remember we do all things for God, and we have stayed God centered at all times.

Annie, as you know, Dad is a good man. I have memories by the hundreds growing up about him and all that he had done for me. He was there Annie. We just couldn't seem to connect. Maybe it's more my fault than his. All I know is he's a good man. Those young days then were okay. They got worse. But I hung onto those early days. Always have.

The spirit sways within me at times, struggling with this worldly stuff. But it's time for God to shine in our lives and to be the center as I said. It's not about me anymore.

You know I wished that I could remember everything that comes out of my mouth when God is using it. I could learn something too, that way. Smile. Couldn't be just common sense cause we all know I ain't got any. That's how I got here, cause I didn't have any sense. —Donnie

May 4, 2000

19 days. I wasn't going to write tonight, but I felt the need to. I need you to pray for my friend, Tiny. He's the one that you have been sending stuff to.

Annie, I know I said I didn't need anything else, but send Tiny one of those lil books on heaven and pray for him. I got a letter from him tonight. I cried and I sat down and wrote him back but I don't know if I got all the bases covered. I had been reading that Eternal Security book and all that he needed to know was right there for me to share. I just want Tiny to take that step and ask Jesus into his heart. I know that God is calling him so I wanted to get some prayer power going for him.

They killed TJ tonight so I'll be moving soon. —Donnie

Approximately one week after Donnie was executed, Tiny shared this letter with me.

Portion of Donnie's reply to Tiny:

Hello My Brother,

Got your kite [letter] tonight and was so glad to hear from you. I miss ya and old Murph too. Holler up there at Big Jack and Joey and tell them hey for me.

I'm on the wrong side, man! I can see where they took TJ out today about 12:30 and threw him in a van. Looked like 50 cops around him. Weird. But they killed him tonight. My old Bon Jo-Jo Kitchens goes on the 9th, then McBride on the 11th. Yo Yo on the 23rd, me on the 24th, and Clayton on the 25th. Regular old killing machine here, huh?

Tiny, listen to me. Do you remember the thief on the cross? See how simple it was that day for him to be with Jesus in paradise?

And as for all of this man made stuff you got in your head, set that aside. The Bible proves itself over and over, man. Oh, how I wished I had the time to school you. Smile. Bring it to you where you can see it and know it. Tiny, there is no such thing as coincidence or luck in life. Everything is manifested by God for a reason.

Do you know what keeps you out of heaven Brother? It's not your sins. It's not accepting what Jesus did for you and all your sins. Brother, there was not one sin that was not covered that day Jesus did that for us. We are saved by grace. Do you know what grace is? Grace is an undeserved series of events enacted for our benefit. In other words, he died for us because he loved us. He did it to secure us an eternal relationship with Him forever.

Tiny when you accept Christ into your heart, you don't have to be perfect. Matter of fact you have to realize that you are human and you're going to be a goof up till the day that you leave this body. You're going to fall and fall and desire this and that and fail. But when you accept Christ in your heart and believe that Jesus died for you, you are covered.

Are you scared what others will think of you? Pride? Well, you're human. Tiny, you have to pray and ask God to do things as in showing Himself to you in all ways. Look at me, I was just like Thomas. I even told the Lord that I could not believe in something that I could not see, and that He had to show Himself to me. And He did Tiny. It's not all going to come to you at once. But you make that first step. Tiny we are all sinners. He came for people just like you and me. All you have to say is, God, I do not understand your ways and I have a problem believing and my faith is low. But I come to you and say:

God, I know I am a sinner.

I know my sins has earned for me eternal separation from you.

I believe Christ died in my place when He died at Calvary.

I accept His death as the full payment for my sins.

I accept Him as my Savior.

Thank you for saving me.

In Jesus Name I pray.

Amen

Tiny, you said you read the Bible. Get an understanding of your body, soul and spirit. Human spirit. We all have a human spirit and God communes with us through His Holy Spirit. Satan can commune with us the same way, in spirit. Tiny, you have a conscience. You know when you do something wrong or if something is wrong. Tiny, only a fool can say there is no God!

I see God working on you. Brother, no matter if you understand it or not, just say the prayer and believe all you can. Read and study when you can and pray and ask God to show Himself to you. I know as I sit here that I am going to see you again in heaven, my brother. And I am as happy as I can be about it too.

Do you think if I had doubts or didn't believe that I would be doing what I am? No way! I know what lies ahead, my brother. And Tiny, no one here is going to stand with you on that final day. You know it is just a matter of time before you will be with me in heaven, if you accept Jesus into your heart. Don't worry about what anyone thinks of you. This is your life Tiny.

I'll be out on a visit Thursday and Friday of the week of the 15th and I'll be out there the following Monday, Tuesday and Wednesday morning till they take me away at about 12:30. So I pray that we will see each other again. If not, know that what we talked about is the most important thing that you will ever talk about in your life.

I'll be waiting on you, Lee Andrew Taylor. I enjoyed meeting you.

I asked that He bring me home and He is. See Brother, I got tired and I want to go where I'll be free. Be looking in the mail for a little booklet about heaven, I'll get Annie to send you. Nothing happens for no reason my friend. Stop believing in yourself, and know that you cannot save yourself. Make that step and believe all you can and your name goes in the Book of Life. And it does not get erased.

God does not give us something and then take it back. By grace we are saved. It's a gift, man! There's not one perfect person in this world. But it's not our sins that keep us out of heaven, but not accepting that Jesus died on the cross for us to save us.

   Wake up Tiny, Please wake up!

   I love you Brother,

   Respect and loyalty always.

   Heaven Bound, Stoney A.

   Donnie Foster

After receiving Donnie's request for prayer for Tiny, I replied to him that his desire and willingness got all the bases covered. The Holy Spirit does the interpreting and convicting.

As I read Donnie's words about God's Grace, I was reminded of an article in *Focus on the Family Magazine*, entitled, "Lessons on Perfection and Grace," by Andrea Vinley.[2] Vinley wrote about gospel singer, Russ Taff's conversation with his dad, who had become an alcoholic while in the ministry. Though the circumstances were very different, the message was the same. "God's amazing grace is never beyond reach." While in rehabilitation for his alcoholism, the elder Taff, concerned about his ministry, asked his son, Russ, "Son, who is going to listen to me now?" Assured of God's grace, Russ replied to his father, "Give me someone whose been to hell and back, someone who has been forgiven a tremendous debt…when he stands in the pulpit, he has a whole lot to say about the grace of God."

Texas Death Row had become Donnie's pulpit.

"I see God working on you. Brother, no matter if you understand it or not, just say the prayer and believe all you can. Read and study when you can and pray and ask God to show Himself to you. I know as I sit here that I am going to see you again in heaven, my brother. And I am as happy as I can be about it too."

Chapter 25

No Fences

"…14 days…"

I can see the gates from here. Wow! They're opening! Who are those guys standing there? One has a clipboard.

Foster? Yes sir, that's me. Number 459000000. No wait. Number 267247. No wait. I'm all goofed up. It's 815. Smile!

Wow! Where are we going now? And hey, what is my number here? Do we have to wear white? And will my hair grow back now?

Wow! Whose house is that? Huh? Mine? You mean this is my house? I'm going to live here? Can I go anywhere I want? I mean, you know like, step out of the yard here? Man that sure is a big yard! Are you sure it's okay for me to just walk around?

I see you got no fences here at all. No walls either. And wow, is that a river? Look at that water! It's so clear and it's like, well, like sparkling and so beautiful. I feel so strange.

Oh, I almost forgot with all this beauty around me. I'm in heaven and I need to see Jesus right away. I have to know so many things. And are you sure I belong here? Can you help me find some people? Oh, I just need to sit down a bit.

What? Set in the water? Okay, I don't mind that at all. I love to swim. When will I see Jesus?

And as I stepped in the water I realized it was Jesus that I had been talking to. And as the water flowed through me, all my *questions were answered and all my hurts, pains and worries were washed away. And as I cried Jesus held me, and He told me why, and He told me all.*

Short story by Donnie Foster

May 5, 2000

Donnie wrote:

Annie, I'm worried about a few things that I'm not sure that you or anyone else has thought about. And that is the media and the people that seem to love it when people get killed here.

I don't know who all will be out there that evening. May be a few that are against the death penalty and a bunch who are for it, and they may say things to you. You just never know.

I had not thought about this till the other night and it came to me and I was a little upset about it. Not everyone loves us here on Death Row. And they don't even have to know who we are. They just come and get on TV with all that hate. I'm hoping it's like it usually is. Maybe just a few out there or not even any at all. So let's pray about that. Sometimes I am so sorry that I ever got you in this.

I visited with Red some today, and Yo Yo. We'll all be down there soon. I may not get moved until Red is gone. They moved Gary Graham in here today. He's already got a date and they're going to kill him on June 22nd. So after I'm gone look into that. He's got all those movie stars behind him, and all these black organizations behind him that are so full of hate for the white man.

I went outside and worked out some today. Pushups. Then came in and ate and then talked some and stared at the window. We always watch people coming in and out of the wing. Rank [officers] comes in and out all day checking on this and that, with the people that are going to be killed. I know this, I'll be one tired dude by the time they get me to the Walls Unit on the 24th. No kidding on that.

I love my book Eternal Security too. That is a great book and I've learned so much in it, and it has helped me too. That is a class A book for people also who have not yet come to the Lord. Smile.

I'm going to get this in the mail to you. Stay in the Word and God will give you all that you need my friend. —Donnie

May 8, 2000

With only 16 days left to live on this earth, Donnie wrote a letter to Joey, the young man on death row that he was concerned about not having anything.

Donnie wrote:

Brother Joe, I wanted to get a letter in the mail to you today and let you know there is money in your account. I want you to get a radio and headphones and a fan. Don't hesitate to do this. You might wait on the coffeepot cause I think I'm going to be able to leave you mine. So we'll see. If not then get one. But dude, get all that stuff that you need, bowls and buy soup by the case. Only $6 a case man.

Also, when I die I'm leaving my money to my cousin, Annie, and she is going to send that to you. Just get that radio and tune in to some sermons and preaching and some of that good music. Gospel!

I know that we didn't get a chance to know one another well, but I'm praying for you and I have my family praying for you too. Hang in there and stay close to Big Jack and Duncan, and Tiny.

Anyway, I'll be gone soon, on home to be with the Lord, and until then I'll be thinking about you and praying for you all.

Stay close to God, man. You get tired, don't do anything dumb. Pray about it. Me, I prayed that God would bring me

home and He worked it out for me.
Your Brother in Christ,
Donnie Foster

May 8, 2000

Cliff, Dale, and I visited Donnie. Since only two were allowed to visit, Dale and I changed out so that Cliff could spend the maximum amount of time with his son.

After our visit, Donnie wrote:

Annie I have sat here and just had the hardest time of things in my thoughts and all. But I couldn't share that with you today cause I had to hold up for dad. But I want to thank you and Dale for bringing him down. I was cuffed and it was like everything just got in slow motion. I saw dad and it made me sad to see him standing there with those dark glasses on, and a cane. I saw how old he had gotten and I wanted to hug him. I tried to holler at him to look at me and he didn't hear me and you were talking to George. But I was pleased to see you talking to Red and George. I had to smile and I felt good about it. I saw Jesus in you.

Annie let me hug you for sending Joey something. I have been so worried about that guy. I just wanted him to have something before I go. Do you realize how you have touched lives here? I saw it today when you were over talking to George and his wife. You've got to meet quite a few men before they die, either on that day or the day before, haven't you? You've sent them something and God touched them through it and God used you that way. People that know me and have heard me talking about you all this time know you when they see you. Even Irene and Kathy [ministers] have told me the same thing.

I know that after a while the Lord is going to have you doing something bigger and even greater again. —Donnie

Thinking on Donnie's remarks, I remembered from *The World: Playground or Battlefield*. The great Christian, Macarius of Optino, when told that his spiritual counsel had been helpful, he replied, "Only the mistakes are mine. All good advice is the advice of the Spirit of God; His advice that I happen to have heard rightly and have passed on without distorting it."[1]

Realizing what I soon must face, I believed like David in Psalm 27:13, "I would have lost heart, unless I had believed that I would see the goodness of the Lord in the land of the living."

I reminded Donnie when he started to feel those dreadful human emotions of loneliness and fear, to remember that he has been insulated in prayer and he belongs to God. I told Donnie that Gloria Gaither wrote in *365 Meditations for Grandmothers* that life doesn't give in easily that is why he was feeling these human emotions. Gaither wrote that though the process of death may look threatening and have its ugly moment death itself will die. Our Lord's resurrection is proof of that.[2]

Betty's friend, Patty, told her to remind Donnie that the definition of fear is false evidence appearing real.

Donnie continued:

> Annie, I'm going to call it a night, so I can get up early and holler at Red before he leaves. When he goes out the door it will be the last time I see him. He dies tomorrow. I'll look out the window and watch him get into the van.
>
> It made me so sad to see Dale go today. He saw me crying. Not often do I let anyone see me cry. And yes, I know I have that right. I cry a lot in here alone with Jesus. Dying this way isn't an easy thing. —Donnie

May 9, 2000

> 14 days. I had dad on my mind, so I wrote him and reminded him of a time we once had together and told him I loved him.

Today was a weird day for me. I saw Father Walsh. We talked and he was telling me that I can't sin no more and that this here in this prison before death is like payback time. I got to treat everyone right and love them, and not sin. Smile.

Then I get another chaplain. She comes to tell me that tomorrow is my execution summary and to have all my addresses ready and all. I had them in my hand and I said, Oh, you mean these? She just smiled.

I ask her, you see Red? She said she had just talked to him. I told her that I believe in Jesus. Praise God, She said. Then I just said, Let me ask you something, do you believe once saved always saved? She said No. I told her, I do. Smile. Then she got to preaching about Timothy being circumcised and Paul had him do that and about Paul being off-track and beat and thrown into prison and when he got it together God let him out, freed the chains off him. I was just listening. It was so off to me, but she was really in to it. Smile.

I've been thinking about Red today. Got to see him this morning and then again when they put him in the van right below me. I banged on the window and was waving and hollering at him. He got to see me doing that as he rode off and he was grinning from ear to ear. So he's at peace with the Lord as I am typing this and you are reading it. Smile. —Donnie

After reading Donnie's letter, I wrote to remind him that Romans 8:38-39 says, "Neither death nor life, neither angels nor demons, neither the present nor the future, nor any powers, neither height nor depth, nor anything else in all creation, will be able to separate us from the love of God that is in Christ Jesus our Lord."

Gaither wrote that perfect life will win, even over the love of human life.

Before he was executed, Donnie was receiving letters from many differing beliefs and faiths. As he shared them with me, some sent chills down my spine. It caused me great concern because many Death Row inmates do not have the faith and knowledge of God's Word that Donnie has, and I know they must all receive this mail. But the great deceiver, Satan, uses these means of confusion to keep souls from accepting Jesus Christ as their Savior and Lord. We Christians must remember that someone is going to tell them something, and if it's not about Jesus, then it is a fearful thing.

This is often where Christians fail. Perhaps A. W. Tozer was referring to such when writing about sinning with silence in *God Tells the Man Who Cares*, "At this hour in world history the state of religion is such that the church is in grave danger of losing the priceless treasure [wisdom]. Her gold is being turned to copper and her diamonds to glass."[3]

Donnie wrote:

> I really have been searching my heart, Annie. I believe the best I can and my faith may not be the most but I think I do have some. Then at times I can't stop the fear. Dumb I know. But you know in that book about heaven the angels were always carrying around notes and papers and filing stuff? Could be the notes they're going to use against us, and for us! Smile! I'll have a little box of good stuff maybe and a big file cabinet of bad stuff. I mean how can I ever catch up? It's not about works I know. But the Judgement Seat of Christ is a real thing, and it makes sense to me too. We will be judged by our deeds. Our rank in His future kingdom is decided then. So looks like we won't be living in the same neighborhood, Cous. —Donnie

I knew Donnie would be casting his crowns at Jesus' feet and overjoyed by his heavenly neighborhood. I knew this because of his prayers and concern for others, the sick and the elderly, and the less fortunate like the young man on Death Row to which his heart went out. His love of children far outweighed some in the free world, but this is not to downplay others. I choose to believe that God is far more interested in giving rewards than withholding them. We must not be so fearful of the punishment we think He is anxiously waiting to give out.

My own human nature is to be like Martha, in John 11 in the New Testament. A personality thing that says, I must do or finish this first. Her sister, Mary, chose to impress Jesus. I realize this world needs some Martha personalities. But like Mary, we Christians would do well to care more about impressing Jesus than others. All too often, I am afraid we go around a dire need directly in front of us in order to get something done to impress someone else. Spending more time with Jesus would cause us to be more aware and concerned about the needs around us. The last words of a song "Broken Cisterns Walled in Stone" sent to Donnie by Father Walsh:

Loose the waters of your word,
Let their leaping joy be heard.
   Fill the love forever fresh
Hearts once stone, but now are flesh.[4]

Whatever time we have left on earth, whether it is an hour, a day, a week, a year, or twenty years, we Christians must be about God's business of bringing people to Jesus. God wanted Donnie to make use of the two weeks he had left.

Chapter 26

Nearing the Execution

"...13 days"

May 10, 2000

Donnie wrote:

13 days. They said my lawyers would have to be on my list [to witness execution].

So the five witnesses are Annie, Betty, Bobby Nance, Craig Budner and Alexa Parnell. But they need Craig and Alexa's address as it appears on their driver's license. Tell them they must call and give that to the people here at the Terrell Unit. I just want to make sure that all goes right. The paperwork must be in order.

Annie, you are to start picking up my property on Monday [May 22]. Then on Tuesday you will get everything except my coffeepot, coffee, eats, and lil stuff. Then you'll get the rest that Wednesday [execution day]. The only thing I'm taking to the Walls Unit is my Bible and some pictures. Chaplain Brazzil will get those to you after I'm gone. The black Bible that has your's and Dale's picture in the front is yours. The green one is for dad.

Also, you'll get my trust fund money to send to Joey's account. You and Dale are on the paperwork to pick up my body. So everything is done as in paperwork. I'm sorry these are things that have to be taken care of Cous.

Long day here. I moved today so I'm in Red's old cell. I asked them to move me and not wait. I wanted to get away from some people that talk all night. I felt bad about the feelings of anger towards my neighbor but prayed about it and I'm cool now.

I picked all dark blue for the execution. 2XX shirt and 42 pants. For my last meal, I told them white meat on the chicken, fried, and jalapenos, rolls and butter and a beef fajita, and a salad with blue cheese dressing, a blooming onion, and vanilla ice cream. A pot of coffee too and a coke. Smile.

As for a minister or spiritual advisor I asked for Chaplain Brazzil. He would be there anyway, but everyone speaks highly of that dude.

This morning the lieutenant was real nice to me and everyone was cool. No one has said anything more about me shaving my goatee. McBride shaved. I think he did it for his mom.

Anyway they said if I need anything to get with them and say so.

That lieutenant got a phone call and I could hear his conversation. Someone was asking him if Red went yesterday and if he was the one who took him? He said he was and that there was no problems. And then I knew that whoever it was on the phone was asking if I was going to be a problem? Smile. The lieutenant said he didn't think so. I just played stupid. But some more rank [officers] was in here and was asking me how I do all those pushups and if I am really 47. I don't want them to be scared of me, so I cut it up with em some and had them laughing. I told the lieutenant that I believe in Jesus. Smile. They treat us okay. I'm glad too cause the last thing I want is problems. —Donnie

May 12, 2000

Thank you Annie, for your prayers. I need it more than you know, my friend. I let things bug me when I thought I had gotten over them. Then here it is back at me again. "Be good to your fellow man and love them no matter what." I've heard that twice in the last two days.

Like my neighbor here? He hollers all night long and has no respect for anyone, not even himself and it shows. But he hollered last night and I got him. I got down on his level so he could understand me. I feel bad about it too. But he has no respect for the ones here that have dates to die the next day, like Red for one and for TJ. He kept them up all night. It made me mad, Annie. Then he told another guy, I can't stand to just sit around and be quiet. I like a little drama in my life. I told him if we were in group rec he'd have plenty of drama right now.

So you see Annie, I'm not doing too good right now, huh? But today after I prayed, I asked that sarge to move me on to here and he got it done. They'll have YoYo and Clayton in here beside me in a few days. I'll be okay. But that guy is blessed that I couldn't get to him. I can't stand to be around people who have no respect.

I read about Red's crime in the paper. Tomorrow there will be all that he did and said and all that stuff. Can't we just go out without all that? I'm just a rotten fellow. And it robs me I know. I'm sure glad Jesus forgives rotten fellows.

That workout I had was awesome. I'll be sore tomorrow. It was fun though. It's built into the wall in a case like. You can't get it loose. But it's heavy and no one uses it. But I did shoulder rolls front and back and traps. Then I lay down, slide under it and lift up. I used it as a bench press. Wore myself out too. Smile.

I wanted to write a few more letters tonight, but I'm too tired after the workout. I bought me some more Ensure too, so I could put on some extra weight. Smile. No, the food here is just bad.

> I'll live. I'm not starving to death that's for sure. I'm a real live fat boy. Smile.
>
> Anyway, after I got through working out in the yard I just started talking out loud to God, as I do when we're alone. But I told Him I was sorry for acting like I did. And asked Him to forgive me and forgive me for doubting and unbelief and having so little trust at times. I told Him I was human, and how you ever get over that, I just don't get it? We talked. I cried and walked more and talked more, and I asked that He put seven of His strongest angels around me and hold me up, and help me through this and help me to act right, and say the right things, and do the right things and all. —Donnie

As I read Donnie's letter, I thought of I Chronicles 28:9, "The Lord searches all hearts, and understands all the imaginations of the thoughts; if thou seek Him, He will be found of thee."

Referring to this verse, A.W. Tozer wrote in *Christ the Eternal Son*, "Now if you have one of those mousetrap minds, open and shut...you will dismiss it and leave it, or tuck it away in your memory among the unused items in the attic of your soul."[1] Tozer says to pay attention and realize what this verse is saying. God is God! This is His nature.

Continuing, Donnie wrote:

> Father Walsh came by and told me he was leaving and wouldn't be back until the day after my execution, but told me he loved me and wanted to bless me one more time. Nothing wrong with that, but I am not Catholic so I don't call him Father. I call him Brother or Mr. Walsh. He notices that too. I love the guy, and it was good to see him again.
>
> Today, they took Graham out to visit. They have to use the camera on him coming and going. Well, he goes out, but they carry him back in on a stretcher and had peppered him good.

And he had the sort team all dressed out for war and they threw him in the cell. Man, that guy's going to go out hard!

Annie, as you know, I'm leaving my watch to Betty and my fan to Cory. I'll clean it up best I can and oil it. The green Bible goes to dad. The rest is yours. Oh, I've got this old alarm clock that I've had for a long time. Pop Holland [executed in 1993] had it and then JC [executed 1997] had it, then me. It's old and all broke up too. I've been in it and worked on it a hundred times. It's got an old ice cream stick in the bottom of it to help it stand up. Smile. But I wrote Dale's name on it. It keeps time. One day it may be a little slow and then next a little fast, but it'll keep you on time. Smile. Tell him to get a speaker for the radio which will be easy. I'll have it all hooked up for you. You will just need to plug it in. Then, if it don't work, wiggle the FM and AM switch, and it'll come on. Annie actually you could just throw the rest of this stuff away. My pictures, you'll always have for the kids to go through and look at when they got nothing to do. Love my pictures. Smile.

Annie, I read more in the book Eternal Security. Looks like I'll be nothing in heaven too. I was sad about something that came to me.

We'll be judged by our deeds. We'll give an account of our lives, good or bad. But how can I be poor in the Kingdom of Heaven? —Donnie

My Response to Donnie:

Heaven is going to be wonderful! I did finish Eternal Security, and of course I know that I won't have the rewards that some will have, but I don't deserve to. I believe that I will be happy with what I have because there will be no sorrow in heaven. We can't possibly expect to have the same eternal rewards as a Christian who left everything to go to a far land and eventually gave their lives that a pagan nation can hear about the love of God.

I know one great thing, after May 24, we'll never have to say good-bye again. It won't seem like any time at all that you'll be greeting Dale and me in heaven.

Sandy said the First Baptist Church sent you prayer-grams. They sent them to Dale and me also. I appreciated that and cried again. I cry easily these days, but I wouldn't be human if I didn't. You either my friend. Like you, I go through stages. Sometimes even angry, wondering how such a thing can happen…to being so sad that my whole body hurts…to being happy that you will be free and with Jesus. I'm going to miss you, Donnie. I cried during church services today, you know those silent tears that just keep coming. I started once to get up and leave but I knew it would just draw attention to myself. I felt I was going to burst as I sat there in silence blotting the tears as they rolled down my face. I keep thinking that this really can't be happening, yet I know it is. We love ya Donnie.

Dale wants to write you a letter, so I will close and try to get some sleep. Betty and I will leave at 4 a.m. and be there by noon tomorrow to visit you. Smile. —Annie

Portion of Dale's letter to Donnie:

Donnie, I just wanted to say some things to you and since I have such a hard time with words I thought I should write them down. I wanted to talk about Eternal Security, the book you and I are reading, and what I got from it.

When I began to read about how we can't lose our salvation once we accept Jesus into our heart it gave me a lot of security. I think I have asked myself all of those questions at one time or another, about have I committed the unpardonable sin, or if I was ever a Christian or not, and if I was a Christian would I have done the things I did after becoming a Christian? Some days I would feel all right, like I was saved. Then the next day I may have doubts again.

The book helped me to understand about God's love and grace. I believe God spoke to me through this book in a real way.

When I got into the rest of the book it was something else. It made me kind of sad but the more I read the better I understood. It makes sense. God wouldn't be fair if I received the same rewards as missionaries who gave up every thing. Some even gave their lives to go tell others in foreign lands about the plan of salvation and how Jesus died for them. Men such as Billy Graham and others who have given their whole life to preach the Word of God would surely deserve more rewards than I do. After reading this book I know that I need to do more. Like you asked Annie, "How will I ever catch up?"

Donnie, when I think of what it will be like in heaven when heaven comes down to earth and we will have a new earth and we will live here. In the book it says that it will be like the original Garden of Eden before man sinned. Donnie I think you will have many rewards in heaven, because God looks at the heart. He knows the concern you have for others there and for their salvation. Remember Malachi 3:16, 18? "Then those who feared the Lord spoke to one another, and the Lord listened and heard them; so a book of remembrance was written before Him for those who feared the Lord...and who meditate on His name. Then you shall again discern between the righteous and the wicked, between the one who serves God and the one who does not serve Him."

I thought of you as I did my devotional this morning, the scripture was Mark 9:41. Jesus said, "Anyone who gives you a cup of water in my name because you belong to Christ will certainly not lose his reward." You have shared what you have with others there. You witness to them about the Lord, and even if they don't come to Christ now you have planted the seed and that is what Christ says to do. We are to tell them and the Spirit does the convicting. God's Word does not come back void, so that tells me some, perhaps all of those you tell the story of Jesus will be saved in time.

Think about how it will be to be free and live in heaven. I know it won't be long until we will be there too.

I love you, Dale.

May 14, 2000

Donnie wrote:

9 days. I went out today and witnessed to YoYo who will die before me. And he hasn't taken that step yet in asking Jesus into his heart. He said he was going to do that before his time.

I said, Man, you been telling people that all this time and it's like it's a game to you. So I explained what is going to happen to him. I believe God was with me too. I told the guy, Now is the accepted time! I told him I would help guide him if he wanted me to, but he said, before Monday he was going to do that. I talked and explained what he had to know and I got on my knees in front of him and said, I am not ashamed of my God and I love Him. I wanted him to say, Hey, lets pray right now. I wanted him to do it, and I told him I couldn't do it for him. Sincereness is what I told him, and God knows if you're sincere.

Well, when I got in from rec I cried for the guy. I cry about a lot of things lately, especially the kids in this family. I have something to say to them and I hope they listen too.

Witnessing scares me at times. But so many need to know that we are human and we are going to be certain ways. Like Tiny was saying that so many think you have to be so right and you can't fall down. I tell them that they will fall. But I think you have to get on a certain level with them so they can see and know what you are saying.

You tell them your faults and fears so they will know they are not alone.

I just hope YoYo will get his heart right before his time. He will be moving down here beside me soon so I will not give up.

I went through my photos a while ago. I cried again. The look and the faces and the times. I love you all so dearly. Those photos have meant so much to me, Annie. All the stuff that you shared with me over the years. I wish I could have been with you all.

I'm down here all by myself. Gets kinda lonely at times.

YoYo is growing a goatee too. The lieutenant was getting on him about it. Got nine days to live and they're concerned about that? No one has said anything to me except that one guy and he's a nobody as for rank. One lieutenant told YoYo, You can't have phone calls until you shave. But not me. I haven't asked them for anything. I've just been settin here and they just look at me.

You next? No, I tell em, YoYo dies, then me, then Clay, then someone else and on and on and on. It never stops.

I'm just overcome with emotions today, Annie. I can't get away from them. I think of every member in this family and I just break down and cry. Like I'm praying for them or something. I just care about them and love them so much.

Dying is not easy, Annie. Smile. —Donnie

I thought back to the time when Donnie was dreading his friend, JC Cockrum being executed. I reminded Donnie of how Elisha hated to lose Elijah (II Kings 2), but there came a time when Elijah had to go and he had to face life without him. I sometimes thought of Donnie as my Elijah because he kept me on my toes, kept me searching God's Word and praying. Prayer was so vital to this Death Row experience.

"The Lord searches all hearts, and understands all the imaginations of the thoughts; if thou seek Him, He will be found of thee." (I Chronicles 28:9)

Chapter 27

A Final Visit

"Six days."

May 15, 2000

*N*ine days before he was executed on Texas Death Row, Betty and I had a special two-day visit with Donnie.

"I can't imagine that I would or could be any help to anyone," Donnie said, when I told him that he had made a good impression on the kids. I told him I was glad he loved my family and assured him that they loved him too.

Donnie had written that he would try to bring his Bible out on our next visit so I wrote some scripture down for us to read. Rules prohibited inmates from carrying anything from their cages to the visiting area. Rules also prohibited visitors from carrying Bibles in to visit inmates (only ministers). But seated next to Betty and me was a little old *minister*. We thought he was waiting to visit another death row inmate. We now believe he may have been an angel. He had a very used Bible held together with silver duct tape. When the old minister realized our problem, he offered to look up our Scriptures for us. Betty held his Bible up to the glass so Donnie could read about our final victory in 1 Corinthians 15:54-55. "So when this corruptible shall have put on incorruption, and this mortal has put on immortality, then shall be brought to pass the saying that is written, 'Death is swallowed up in victory. O death, where is thy sting? O grave, where is thy victory?'" (KJV).

In I Thessalonians 4:13-14 Donnie read, "But I would not have you to be ignorant brethren, concerning them which are asleep, that ye sorrow not, even as others which have no hope.

"For if we believe that Jesus died and rose again, even so them which sleep in Jesus will God bring with Him"(KJV).

Then Donnie read Isaiah 25:8, "He will swallow up death in victory; and the Lord God will wipe away tears from all faces; and the rebuke of His people shall He take away from off the face of the earth: for the Lord has spoken it"(KJV).

The old man's inmate visit never came. Shortly after we returned his Bible, he was gone. We never realized when he left.

May 17, 2000

Donnie wrote:

Six days. I loved my visit with you and Betty. I was glad we got to talk about things of God and the kids and values and all. It meant so much to me.

Betty almost got me when she was telling me all that she did. I love Betty so much. I can't imagine that I could be anything to anyone, but I know that God does work in mysterious ways. We've seen plenty of that, huh? Smile.

I didn't want to see you go Tuesday. I walked out the door and all I could think about was you and if you were all right. But I could actually see my prayers working through you. I have been praying for much strength to come to you and for God to keep you busy. You're very important to Him, Annie. So don't get caught up in sadness or things like that. He needs you to carry on my friend. God loves the way that you love Him.

I came from our visit and I had two letters from you, one from Cory and Bobby and prayergrams from First Baptist there in Walters. I came in and a Bible was in the bean hole on my door. I knew that someone had been here. So when I got in, here came Tom Nixon. This is the guy I told you about that I preach to and he comes to hear me too! But he is down about all this. But you're going to meet him. I told him to come out there and meet some of my family. So on the 23rd [day before execution] he will be around. But we had a good visit back here. We prayed about others here that he is witnessing to.

I got to go out in the yard last night too. Some of the bosses watched me work out. One said, Well man, I hope you go to the right place? I said, Brother, Jesus came for people just like me.

I got up and praised God and went to the yard and met with Carter. He dies on the 31st. We talked and prayed that God would send someone to talk to YoYo, and that he would listen. When I came in someone was at his door. Smile. And that someone came to my door, and I let it go and we praised God about being saved. Page was his name. Boy can he pray! And I had to get in there too, of course.

Monday you'll be back and I'll try again to bring my Bible out.

I was glad that day you were talking to Buck. I had to smile when you said something to me about that kid. Annie, Buck is not a kid. He just looks that way. Smile. But he has heard me talk of you many a time. Everyone has. They know you Cous, and have read most of the stuff you send down here and know about the letters you write to this system. That's why he asked for you. They know that you care. You touched their lives and let them know that there are some real caring people left in this world.

Well, my neighbor YoYo is on 30-minute watch now. I go on it tomorrow. Death watch.

I got prayergrams from Calvary Baptist [Walters church]. I want to get a letter out to them, as well as First Baptist there, thanking them for their prayers. —Donnie

May 17, 2000

After returning home from our visit, I wrote to remind Donnie of an unsourced story that my daughter, Sandy, had received in an e-mail and passed on to Donnie some time before. My summarized reminder told of a lady with terminal cancer that had only a short time to live. She contacted her pastor to discuss the arrangements for her funeral. She told him the scriptures she wanted, the songs, and in what outfit she wanted to be buried. When her pastor started to leave, she told him there was one other thing that was very important to her. She said she wanted to be buried with a fork in her hand, which puzzled the man.

She told him in all her years of going to church and potluck suppers that when the dishes were being done, someone would always lean over and say, "Keep your fork." She said that was her favorite part of potluck suppers because she knew something better was coming…like chocolate cake or a wonderful dessert.

She said she just wanted people to see her there in her casket with a fork in her hand. She wanted them to wonder what the fork was for. She told her pastor, then I want you to tell them, "keep your fork…the best is yet to come." Her pastor knew that this lady had a better grasp on heaven than even he did because she knew that something better was coming.

May 18, 2000

Donnie wrote:

> Five days. Annie, you remember that one guy that said something to me about shaving? I told him today that I wasn't going to shave that I'm going out this way. I did apologize later for being contrary. But the guy said, It's okay I already knew you wasn't going to shave. A few guys on the farm [prison unit] that have known me for years told him, Yep that's the Armadillo. Plus he read some articles about how I come to be here and

then how I dropped my appeals. So now when I see him I holler at him and kid him some. He came by at mail time and I asked him, You got family? He shook his head. He came back later and I witnessed to him some and let him know where I was going. It affected him.

I've learned one thing lately. These people over here are new at this and a lot of them don't believe in the death penalty. It's bothering them. Not all, but some. But I got to tell two of them today about Jesus.

One of them, a lady, came over to me today and asked if she could ask me something. I said Yeah. She asked, Are you scared? I said, No. I have Jesus in my heart and angels all around. It was hard for her to understand I guess, but I want them to know that I believe in Jesus. —Donnie

May 19, 2000

Donnie wrote:

I've been writing some of the guys here, Big Jack, George, Harris, Murph, Blue and others, to say goodbye and hope to see them in heaven and I will if they know Jesus. They say they do. Smile.

I got letters from you, Dale, Sandy, Linda Rae and Jerry [all cousins]. Sandy sent me pictures of Wheezer [her cat] and Luca [her dog]. Cool! I've got to put these in my albums. I've packed up three bags of stuff for you to try and get Monday after you leave. Then I'll get the rest together for Tuesday. I just need to get it on out of here. To set in an empty cell for a while won't kill me. Smile.

I have so much to be thankful for and things happening to me that baffles me. You and Dale stole my heart. And I've loved every second of it too. Smile

Anyway, I'm getting ready to go, Annie. I've got less than a hundred hours, huh? I'll be gone by the time you read this, my friend.

I tried to call you, but no one was home. But I got into an argument with the lady and yelled at her cause she was acting so hateful. It was bad. I said, Just dial the number and let the lieutenant run the show. She said, You got to shave before I can give you a call. I said, No! Then she said I'll write you up [report him]. I asked her, You need a pen? One of the old bosses told her, Just dial the number! Smile.

I woke up this morning and said, Lord, let me go out last to lift weights today. The guy came by and I asked and he said okay. Some got upset and the guy made them stay in cause of their mouths. So only I got to go out. It was nice too cause I worked out hard and got tired. I'm at 256 now.

This lil guy I call Hobo that wanted me to send him some commissary got moved upstairs, but I'll send him some.

—Donnie

I recalled an earlier letter from Donnie saying he would be poor in heaven as well as here on earth, because he felt he had done nothing for the Lord.

Donnie wrote:

Annie, it won't matter where we live in heaven. All I'll have to do, like you said, is wish and I'll be there with you guys. Like in the book Within Heaven's Gates, remember how they were coming and going? It'll be like that I'm sure.

I'll just be glad to see you Monday. I'm restless. I have been on my knees praying to God. I'm staying as close as I can, Annie. That gal got me off track there for a bit, but they have been treating me good here.

I'm worried about YoYo. He's not ready to die. He's scared to death. He makes calls and has an investigator working on his case. Another guy said that he did it and YoYo was just there. He's hoping for a stay. I told him that man is going to let you down, to get his eyes on God. I hate to be the one to rain on his parade, but he needs to wake up. He'll be out there Monday and Tuesday. I'll get you to say hi to him.

This hasn't been too easy on Blue. I had to write him and make sure he has trusted Jesus. I put his letter in my stuff, so when you feel like it you can go through them one day.

I got a help sign in my window. People come by on the outside and see it and crack up. I'm right by the front here on the ground floor. They know this is the death watch cells. I can get up on my mattress and watch people coming and going. The van they take me in parks right outside my window. I watch them get things ready. Smile.

I'm going to lay down and read some and try to fall asleep. I'm so tired of them coming by every 30 minutes. When I get down to 72 hours they will come by every 15 minutes and check on me. —Donnie

May 20, 2000

In my final letter to Donnie, I wrote that after Wednesday we would never have to say goodbye again, and I was sure we would live forever as neighbors and friends for all eternity. And of course we will meet and know one another. Matthew 17:1-4 says that Peter, James and John knew Moses and Elijah!

Charles Stanley wrote that the Bible does not say absent from the body, buried in the ground. The Scripture, II Corinthians 5:8 says, "We are confident, yes, well pleased rather to be absent from the body and to be present with the Lord."

I wrote Donnie about a portion in the book *Facing Death*, by Billy Graham that tells about his wife Ruth's experience with Velma Barfield, a woman executed on death row in North Carolina. They became very close. I told Donnie that Ruth Graham had told Velma after comparing the dreariness, the isolation, and difficulty of her cell to the glory that lay ahead of her as a Christian, she could wish for Velma's sake that God would say to her, "Come on *home*."[1]

May 20, 2000

In a letter I received after his execution, Donnie wrote:

I am so mad at myself that I forgot Mom's Day. I feel rotten that I let it pass right by me. How stupid and thoughtless can you get?

I wrote Bev and gave her my last sermon, bless her heart. I wanted to send Trey some tracts [spiritual] that I had for him. I am so glad I got to meet Bev. She wrote me and I was full of joy about that. I never say goodbye, so that will be my last letter to her, I think. Smile.

I love music. Always have and I love to sing. Just don't have anyone to sing to anymore. Smile. I do sing to Jesus. I make stuff up as I go. Smile.

I'm about to give up on my neighbor (YoYo) being saved. He sleeps all the time, like a drug addict. I can't get him to read anything. He starts out and falls asleep. They have to come and get him all the time and they have to wake him up. I started that book Within Heaven's Gates again last night and decided to get him to read it. Well, I gave it to him and he's over there sleeping.
—Donnie

After sending and receiving cards the Christmas after Donnie was executed, I received a letter from Mark, a friend of Donnie's on death row:

Dear Annie,

As soon as I saw your name on the envelope I remembered who you were. Yes, I got to know Stoney at Ellis and knew him for about the last year and a half of his life. He lived directly above me. We had a love-hate relationship. We got along like a couple of youthful brothers, but we did like each other. I tried to talk him out of dropping his final appeals but he grew tired of the struggle. It's hard too Annie. After being on death row for so long. Ten years for me here but locked up since 1989. And then the state just keeps taking everything away.

The good thing to know is that Stoney gave his life to Christ Jesus and so he was rescued from his faults, and yes I'm a Christian too. Towards the final days at Ellis, Stoney even yelled it out "Jesus is my Savior!" Hearing it from him was highly unexpected from the fellows because they didn't know him. And therefore, it was a blessing.

I didn't become a Christian until I came to death row, and then it took a few years. I always fought against the tenderness of Christ because I thought it was weak. But sure enough as the years went by, I began to realize that what I thought was weak on earth, well, it was actually strong in heaven and likewise, what appears to be strong on earth is actually weak in heaven. When I finally accepted Jesus Christ and was baptized I was changed forever. I was able to accept what I had done and forgive myself. I might be executed but I am not distraught about it. I've got right with God, so I know he will take care of the rest of my problems.

Friend, Mark

Earlier in our correspondence, Donnie commented often on being of self, but in the last weeks of his life, his heart was set on Jesus and others, like a man driven to accomplish in days God's purpose for his entire life.

Donnie wrote:

Annie, all these letters are not going to be there before I leave and I forget about that. But there are things I want to say and I'm afraid I won't have time or the opportunity. I have to spend some time with you and this is how I do it. I want to get Dale's letter going too.

Annie, I love dad. He was there for me. We just didn't handle it the way it was supposed to be. We all mess up somewhere down the line, huh? Look at me. I've been doing it all my life. I know all that now and that's what I want to pass on to the kids in this family. You all share so much.

I wrote something down for the kids. Smile. I want Cody & Traci, Cory & Cass, Lauren & Trey [Annie's grandchildren] and Nick [Betty's grandson] to know all this. Felt I had to do this for them and the parents too. So important this is.

To the kids in our family:

I know that we don't know each other that well. But for years I have thought about you, listened to all that you do and go through. I have prayed for you and cried for you. I have been happy for you and sad for you. I have looked at pictures of all of you kids all these years now, and I have read articles on you. Things you have done and achieved. It's been such a blessing to me to have been able to share in all that. Oh the days that you have helped me through here while living in this cage. I've enjoyed life through all that you do. I thank you so much for that too.

I know that you know of me and where I am. I thought, well I'm here as a screw up and those kids aren't going to listen to me or anything I've got to say. But if they knew that I really cared for them they might.

Well, if you could see these tears on my face and see inside my heart, then you would know. Yes I once was lost, but now I'm found. Smile. I'm stable. I would think at this point in my life, getting ready to be killed and go be with Jesus, a man would have to be somewhat stable. Smile. My feet are on the ground.

How can I love you when I don't know you? Well, I know Jesus, and when you know Jesus you can do those kinds of things. Smile. Yes, I love you all. Each one of you has a special place in my heart and I wanted to pass along something that I learned in this life. And believe me I'm paying dearly to learn this. You might say that I paid the highest price one can pay for it. Death. If I would have only listened. I've learned so many things about life now. But I learned too late. But at least I learned, and now I can tell you and share with you some things. Something that is to me the most important thing there can be in life and that is family.

Now I've looked in these families. I've met the moms, Sandy and Bev. I've met Sherry and Bobby. I've yet to meet Wade, Richard, Steve and Sherry [Wampler]. But still I know these families. I know a blessed family when I see one. Fine Christian homes and people. I see moms and dads that love their kids and that have been there for them in all their years. Raising them right and instilling in them godly values.

Now, all that is wonderful and so very important. But I want to share this with you.

One day you're going to leave home. No telling what life is going to bring your way. I assure you life is not bump free, and the trials are going to come to you, especially if you are a believer in God.

I don't know what roads you will go down, what situations you'll face, or problems you will run into. I know I didn't have this, or know this, or do this. If I had I wouldn't be here today and going to die in a few days by the hand of the state. I was so bad that my society had to kick me off the planet. Well, if you can learn anything from my life, then please do. From what I can see you'll never get in this shape with the loving families that you have. But it's a very rough world out there.

What I am saying is this, listen to your mom and dad. You have a problem? Talk it out. What you kids are learning and going through, your mom and dad went through that very thing. Trust me on this. I can tell you things are going to happen. There will be times when you think, what should I do? Who should I talk to?

Well look back. Who is it that raised you? Who is it that loves you and was there for you and gave you all that you needed? Someone with balance. Well, in this family that would be your mom and dad. You see, that is what moms and dads are for.

No matter how dumb, stupid, or ignorant or bad you can be, no matter what, when you take it to your mom or dad and just lay it out and say, Hey, I screwed up. That pulls a family together and makes life worth living. It's this way with God too.

And parents, kids aren't the only ones who screw up, but families can hold up through anything when they stick together. Unconditional love.

Just listen to them when they talk to you. I'm talking to parents and kids alike. But kids, there are rules now, and we have to live by the laws of our moms and dads and as you grow up you must live by the laws of God always, and we got man's laws too. It's called life.

If your mom or dad is in the house or wherever walk up to them and say, maybe its just I love you. Maybe you want to say, hey Mom, I want to talk to you about this problem I'm having, or Dad, can we go for a ride?

Sometime after I'm gone I want you to test this out for me. It's not magic, but it's a spiritual thing. And we can have that with Jesus in our lives.

And you kids have each other that you can talk to. You're family. Stick together, and stand together. Hold each other up. That's part of the joy of living.

And for goodness sake don't go down the roads that I have. I just praise God that He made a way for a person like me. It's not hard to wind up in prison or on probation. It's so easy. I'm not going to get political on you now, but believe me this system we got they call the judicial system it's not working too good, and they don't care a lot about you when they get you here. It don't matter who you are either.

To learn all the little secrets of life about families I had to pay a price to know it. I learned the hard way, but I learned. I'm sorry if this cousin of yours was an embarrassment to you. I just screwed up. Never been worth five cents. But I learned at last. Stay close to home and listen to what is being taught to you by your moms and dads. Don't get caught up in the trends and fads and let pressures of school and life as a teen or college student get to you, or peer pressure from trying to fit in with the crowds.

Please be who you are. No matter what, be who you are! And when you are that, then you are a role model for someone else. Not all kids are as blessed as these families that I am speaking to. My kin! Smile.

I could go on and on, but as teens I know you've got somewhere to go. Smile. And so do I. I love you. In this cage I am on my knees for you and I ask God to protect each and every one of you. I'll see you all when I see you. Smile.

They call it communication! Smile.

Your Friend and Cousin, Donnie

As Donnie requested, I copied the letter and added a personal salutation on each one for the children in our family; they were humbled that he would take the time to write and encourage them on in their lives ahead, especially when he was only a week away from dying.

Loose the waters of your word,
  Let their leaping joy be heard.
Fill the love forever fresh
  Hearts once stone,
    but now are flesh.

— Broken Cisterns Walled In Stone

Chapter 28

Going *Home*

"Annie, you were a vessel from God"

May 20, 2000

Bill Shipman, one of the staff at Hart-Wyatt Funeral Home, measured my truck for the container that we were to use for bringing Donnie's body to Walters. "Folded, it will fit," Shipman said, "but not unfolded with Donnie in it."

On Sunday May 21, 2000, before my daughter, Sandy, and I began our final trip to Texas Death Row to visit Donnie, we made plans for Dale, the grandchildren, Cory and Cassie, to bring Sandy's Tahoe to Livingston, Texas, on Monday. I had measured the back of the Tahoe and believed it would serve the purpose for bringing Donnie back to Walters. So that was all set.

Donnie had previously written:

> Annie, if you will bring a speaker phone, I will be able to have a last conversation with all of you and not be limited to talking to only one at a time. —Donnie

Chaplain Norris and the staff at the Hospitality House in Huntsville were very helpful and agreed to help us set up the phone and commented that it was the first time anyone had requested to use a speaker phone. I took inventory to be certain I had everything: The phone, the recorder, and blank tapes for recording our final conversation with Donnie as well as his final prayer.

Before Sandy and I set out on our trip to Livingston, a small town forty miles east of Huntsville where Texas Death Row was now located, we prayed for strength and guidance in the coming days with Donnie.

I later wondered why we are so amazed when God answers our prayers, when we ask in His Will, depending completely on Him in such a humbling situation? "Humble yourselves before the Lord and He will lift you up" (James 4:10). A more humbling circumstance I had never experienced.

It was difficult saying goodbye to Donnie after visits in those final days, but God kept us strong for one another. I constantly prayed for direction in all that I said and did concerning Donnie. I found through the most vulnerable times in my life that God's love and concern for us, His children, is sufficient beyond all understanding. Over and over again, our God came through in all His glory. Some might say, "But Donnie died, he was executed by the State of Texas!" But I would say, "They finally set him free."

On our way to Livingston, Sandy and I stopped at the Huntsville Funeral Home to drop off the container and Donnie's jeans and tee shirt to be used after his execution.

It seemed Donnie needed to know that every detail had been taken care of. On Monday when Sandy and I visited him, he had lots of questions and was satisfied that everything was in order. He was a little disappointed that the container would not fit my truck with him in it, but we assured him he would not be riding home in a hearse.

I told him the music for his service was chosen. He had previously told Cory and me of songs that he had heard on a gospel station on his radio. I had purchased the tapes and sent the words down for him to read. Shortly before the execution, he had narrowed the list of songs to four.

Donnie had asked Betty to be in charge of a schedule for the visits on the Tuesday and Wednesday before his execution. All those on his visitor list would be allowed to go to the visiting area, but only two at a time could visit with Donnie. We knew if we didn't have some type of system to see that the visits were scheduled, at least to some extent, it would be more difficult for everyone to get his/her share of time with Donnie.

May 22, 2000

On Monday after Sandy and I had visited Donnie, He wrote:

Time? Very near. I can hardly see the keyboard for the tears, but I just had to set down and tell you how much I love you, Cous. Are you okay, Annie?

Today was rough, huh? It went too fast and I wanted to tell you thank you so much for everything.

I hate to leave you down here, but I know that God is not near through with you and that goes for Dale too. I know God is going to use Dale in ways that he won't even know he is being used.

But I can't help but worry about you in all this. I can't say yet, Well, I know she will be okay. I just need to know it I guess. And I think, Man, I hope in no way does she think I cut out on her and was selfish in it all. Please don't think that. God has been and is among us. We are one in spirit and what we have in Christ is real. Kind of like that poem that you read to me today about the heart. —Donnie

During our visit, through my tears, I had read to Donnie a fictional, yet true in a sense, non-source story someone had e-mailed to me. I felt the story would help me to tell Donnie what he meant to this family.

This was a summarized story of a lady with a heart that appeared to have pieces removed, because she had given away parts of it to others. And often times others would give her a piece of their heart which didn't always quite fit the deep gouges of her heart, therefore leaving rough edges. But she cherished the rough edges because they reminded her of love they had shared.

"Giving love is taking a chance," the lady said. "Although these gouges are painful, they stay open to remind me of the love I have shared with these people."

Donnie wrote in a letter I received after his execution:

> Yes, we all in this family have a piece of each other's heart. You know Annie, you were a vessel for God, and when the time came you did all that He wanted you to do. That is, when I wasn't having you do everything else in the world. Smile. But what God did here is bigger than all of us. No way could you or I ever do that in a lifetime among these families. I just pray that they hold on to all God has shown them in this, and when the battles come they won't sag and get weary. I hope that all this will teach others what family is about, and how we should conduct ourselves as we pass at our time. Here, we have to stay tough taking everything to God in prayer and look forward to the good life in heaven. Smile. And my friend I can't wait to see you everyday up there and set and talk and enjoy the presence of our Lord, Jesus.
>
> I know that I have to be strong for this family cause I love you all so much. But you got guts my friend, and boldness, and you step right on out there and get it done. So I'm asking you this, Annie when you get settled get another copy or two of that Eternal Security. Then ask one at a time in this family to read it. But have it to pass around to all the family and friends. Always ask them to sign it in the back and return it for someone else. I am leaving my copy to Glenda. —Donnie

May 23, 2000

As the family arrived at the death row unit on the day before Donnie's Execution, he was already locked in his little cage in the visiting area. Dale and I were first to go back to visit. Donnie had the cartoon character, Snoopy, taped to his window. Snoopy was hugging a heart and Donnie had drawn a tear falling from Snoopy's eye. (Chaplain Brazzil gave it to me along with his Bible and his calendar of pictures of the family after his execution.)

We were allowed to visit for eight hours through a glass, using phones. Relatives and close friends had phoned that they would be praying for Donnie and the family during those final two days and God was truly in our midst. Donnie never ceased to be a witness. He had to have been exhausted when the day was done. But Donnie was concerned about getting a message to the kids. He spent much time with Cory, Cassie and Nick as well as Todd and Dawn Stone (my sister, Bonnie's son and his young wife). God had their total attention the day before Donnie was executed as he witnessed and prayed with them. He never let any two leave without prayer. He told the kids how easy it is to be in the wrong place at the wrong time and with the wrong people and how easy it is to get off-track. He knew that this would be his last opportunity to make a difference in their young lives. And God used Donnie mightily the last two days of his life and none who witnessed the experience will ever be the same.

May 23, 2000

Donnie wrote in a letter that I received after returning home from the execution:

> 9:40 p.m. I got in from the visit and went to the yard and worked out some. Then came in and fixed all my property up for you to pick up tomorrow. And the lieutenant is going to get my machine and hotpot to Joey. He thanked me for not giving them a hard time. But we all ate together and I sent that commissary up to Hobo. Smile.
>
> I wrote Betty a few lines and told her how much I love her and

> thanked her for being there for us both.
>
> Sherry was so beautiful today, and it was like God was saying, I healed her as you asked. —Donnie

In early 1999, Sherry Nance had a Bilateral Mastectomy for breast cancer. She is still cancer free in 2006.

Donnie continued in his letter:

> Long day, huh? I love you Annie Wampler. You and Dale mean the world to me and I'll be waiting on you both. Thank you so much for taking me just as I am my friend. It won't be long and we'll all be together again. Meantime, get over the hill and be a good soldier and say, Lord, what next? Smile. —Donnie

Execution Day, May 24, 2000

It was an exceptionally warm and sultry day as we arrived at the Terrell Unit just as it opened. It seemed to take the personnel forever to get all of us identified. Again, as we entered the visiting area, Donnie was locked in his little cage waiting anxiously for us to arrive. Dale and I were so anxious to see Donnie again; we went straight back to where they had him caged. Donnie was excited to see us and said that before everything got going, he wanted to remind us again how much he appreciated all that we had done to make his last years as comfortable as possible.

So much to say, yet Dale and I knew we had said it all so many times before in our letters to Donnie. But again we told him how much we loved him, how he had blessed our lives, and how much he would be missed. We knew the morning would pass quickly, then they would come to take Donnie away at 12 noon. We shared our time with him as best we could with the rest of the family.

Many things went through my mind as I thought about this being Donnie's last day on earth. I even thought about Sister Helen Prejean, spiritual advisor to Patrick Sonnier, whom the book *Dead Man Walking*[1] is about. I wondered if I could be as strong as Sister

Prejean as she witnessed the execution of Sonnier.

"By the grace of God I can."

Donnie's dad, Cliff, and his wife, Diane, came on Donnie's final day to spend some time alone with him.

Edwin Smith, a volunteer chaplain at the time, came to say goodbye to Donnie and encourage the family.

Donnie's attorney, Craig Budner, and his legal assistant, Alexa Parnell, came to say goodbye and spend time with him. They remained with the family while we waited for the dreaded execution hour to come.

As we went back two at a time for our visits, Donnie talked to get all that he had to say out. He had special things he wanted to say to each one, and he didn't want to miss anything. But like the day before, he never failed to pray before each two walked away.

My sister, Bonnie, shared with me the final moments of her visit with Donnie:

> After spending time going over memories of our past troubled lives, Donnie looked at me and said, "Bonnie, stay in prayer. Pray about everything." It took my breath away. How did Donnie know I was having problems praying, because of guilt of past sins? I looked into Donnie's eyes and knew he knew better than anyone that we were forgiven. Donnie spoke to me about the feelings of guilt and shame of our lives that Satan uses to hold us prisoner. I had been letting the guilt of my past keep me from calling out to God for forgiveness. I knew it was true; God had been there all along.
>
> So I began to pray. Donnie and I had been restored through Jesus Christ and the restoration continues. —Bonnie

I thought back to the time when Donnie would say, "God doesn't hear my prayers, Annie!" Well, he found that God was hearing his prayers. God knew what was to come, what he was going to allow.

As Donnie surrendered his will to God, he began to recognize God's hand at work in his life. He began to look forward to God allowing him to come on home.

In those last months before Donnie was executed, prayer became foremost in his heart. Each time Donnie would write, he would ask prayer for certain inmates on death row. He became focused on others more than himself. He would write or say, "Joey is just a kid, he doesn't have anything Annie, just a cup and a spoon, and he's having a hard time and he's never had a visit since he came here except for his lawyers. Annie pray for Joey.... Blue needs our prayers, Annie. I am going to write him. He's not doing too well in all this. I want to make sure he's all right with the Lord.... Annie I need you to write and witness to Tiny. He's on the verge of accepting Jesus.... Annie I want you to keep in touch with George. He loves the Lord and I trust him with your friendship."

Betty and Donnie had scheduled me last to have private time alone with him. Although my heart was breaking, he joked and made me laugh to help me relax. Then we talked seriously about the kids, the family, and his dad, Cliff. Then we talked about the best friends we ever had in this world, which were each other. But God's supply of strength was without measure. Donnie prayed with me, and Donnie prayed for those helping him to go home.

As our time slipped away, the family began to gather with me in front of Donnie's cage and he actually got to see us all before him at one time. He smiled through his tears as he saw all the love before him. He began to say his last words to each one giving us instructions.

Donnie insisted, "I have to be the most blessed man in the world."

As the guards began to gather behind his cage door, we knew our time was short. Although the sorrowful tears were kept at bay for the time, the silent ones slipped down our faces as most of the family knew this would be their last time to see Donnie this side of heaven. The witnesses, Craig, Alexa, Betty, Bobby and myself, the ones he had asked to be with him during his execution, would see him one other time.

Things moved fast after the guards removed Donnie. In a recent letter Donnie had told me:

> Annie, get to the Hospitality House as soon as we are finished with our last visit, cause they will take me immediately to the Walls Unit. I want to call you as soon as they get me settled in.
> —Donnie

After they took Donnie away, Dale and I left the Terrell Unit immediately to go to Huntsville, where Donnie would be executed at the Walls Unit in a matter of a few hours. As the rest of the family left Texas Death Row, they were able to see the van that Donnie had talked about in his letters being parked outside his deathwatch cell that transports the guys to be executed as their days comes to die.

Donnie later told us as they were leaving for the Walls Unit in Huntsville, where the death chamber is located that he told the guards transporting him, "That's my family! I'm riding home to Oklahoma in that Tahoe!"

"Oh yeah?" one replied. "Man that's a nice truck!"

"You guys got Jesus in your hearts, right?" Donnie asked those transporting him. They kind of nodded and said "Yeah." I told em, "That's good, but you know you can be poor in heaven too." Donnie thought they should have been a little more excited about having Jesus in their hearts. But I thought, maybe they just hate their job.

As Dale and I drove to Huntsville, the sadness became overwhelming. I was no longer able to control the sorrowful tears. If I may borrow from Christian writer, Mary Jane Worden *Early Widow*, "I wish I was a screamer."[2] I knew that Donnie was going to be fine, safe at home with Jesus in a matter of hours, but as Worden said,

"The evil behind death peers through and it seems such a horror." My human nature was taking control and the sadness and void I was already experiencing caused me to fear that this pain might be permanent. I wondered if I would be able to keep eye contact with Donnie as we quoted Galatians 2:20 as I had promised, or if I would cry out in anguish from all that was happening. But then the Spirit of God began to bring to my remembrance, "Weeping may endure for the night, but joy comes in the morning" (Psalm 30:5). And Blessed be the God and Father of our Lord Jesus Christ, the Father of mercies, and God of all comfort" (2 Corinthians 1:3). I realized the pain would not last forever.

The weather was extremely warm and sultry on May 24, 2000 in that south Texas town of Huntsville, known for its lethal-injected executions.

As we arrived at the Hospitality House in Huntsville, Chaplain Bob Norris and his staff immediately took charge to make us as comfortable as possible and informed us of the procedures that were to follow. They helped Bobby to get the speakerphone set up for Donnie's call. I thought of how over and over again these people have dealt with the trauma of death by execution with so many families before us and how some folks may not always be considerate to those helping families of death row offenders. Then there are the protest groups, some for, some against the death penalty. Borrowing again from Luci Swindoll's devotional *Moses' Choice-Your Choice*, "Faith willfully chooses even disgrace or mistreatment because it sees, through an act of trust, the eventual reward that comes from Him who is invisible."[3]

The Hospitality House staff not only helped us to cope, some cried with us as they listened to Donnie's last conversation with his family.

Chapter 29

No More Chains

"I'm finally free of my chains!"

May 24, 2000

*C*haplain Jim Brazzil, later described as the "The Last Human Touch" by *The Ft. Worth Star-Telegram*[1], called us at Hospitality House around 2 p.m. to set up our telephone conversation with Donnie.

"Is that you Annie?" Donnie asked, sounding anxious.

I replied, "Yes! We have the speakerphone hooked up here, and we're recording you. Is that going to make you nervous?"

"It's not gonna make me nervous at all," Donnie answered. "I wish I could see you though. Seems odd talking to someone and not being able to see them."

Donnie had been used to looking through glass while talking to us on the phone during visits.

"Are ya'll doing okay?" Donnie asked.

"We're fine," I replied.

"Chaplain Brazzil assured me that all over here are believers," Donnie said. "I'm not being mistreated in any way. I'm sitting here on the cool floor drinking ice tea."

"Do you have your cuffs or chains on?" I asked.

Donnie quickly answered, "Oh no! And they just told me I would not be chained again! I'm finally free of my chains! After a while we're going to get back here and pray together and get everything took care of in that way. I just told these men here with me that I'm the most blessed man in the world."

In our phone conversation, we talked about our grandson Cody's 66 Corvette dragster that Donnie loved so much that he framed a large poster of it for the transmission shop, before the piddling program for death row was discontinued. We talked about the blooming onion and ice cream that he had requested for his last meal. Donnie jokingly said, "You gotta give up a whole lot to get treated like this!"

Everyone, including Donnie, tried to keep a sense of humor and hold one another up under the dire circumstances. But after a time, the conversation turned more serious.

Donnie said, "I'm so glad this family has come to me and help hold me up in these last days. I don't know what I would have done without you. And I have to tell you this thing about prayer," Donnie continued. "God has done some mighty works here in this family. I told Sandy in a letter last night concerning Wade's (Sandy's husband) dad (who had lung cancer), when we don't understand why difficult things happen in this life, we just have to remember if we are praying for God's Will…this is God's Will. God has a way of breaking us down some times, one way or another. He takes us and refines us like gold. You know gold has a lot of trash in it and has to be refined. We get bumped for one reason or another. He (God) has to put "may knots" on our head occasionally. They may go down, and they may knot. But we take what we get and we ride with it."

"Are you all going to stay here (Huntsville) tonight?" Donnie asked.

"Yeah," Bobby answered, "we'll have a wagon train taking you back to Oklahoma tomorrow. Head em up, move em out!"

"All right! That's what I wanted to hear!" Donnie said.

Time passed in our conversation and as he began to talk about the kids; obviously saddened, Donnie took a deep breath and become silent for a moment.

After a bit of silence, I quietly assured him, "We love you, Donnie."

"I know you do. There's not a doubt in my mind about that," he replied.

My sister, Bonnie, reminded Donnie of a conversation they had had earlier, that Satan may come to discourage him in these last moments and try to take away his peace. In Hebrews 13, the same chapter that says, "Remember the prisoners as if chained to them…" God's Word also says God has promised that He would never leave nor forsake him.

"I'm pretty sure Satan will be glad to get rid of me," Donnie stated. "But I hope I'm leaving behind some things that will hinder him from now on."

"Yes, you are," Bonnie said, confirming his hope.

Reminding Donnie again, I said, "You asked me to keep reminding you that when you take that final breath here on earth, you will take your next one in heaven. And Donnie, the Bible says, "No eye hath seen, nor ear heard; neither have entered in the heart of man, the glory which God has prepared for them that love Him"(I Corinthians 2:9 KJV). That is you, Donnie!"

"Yes, I will be okay," Donnie assured us, "but I'm concerned about you all."

I replied, "Yes Donnie, it's as you say, a little lumpy right now, and we will be crying our hearts out after you are gone because we will miss you so much, but we will know you are safe in the Father's care. You will never be isolated, lonely or have to hurt again."

Donnie admitted, "You know it may sound weird, but I'm glad to know that some will be crying their hearts out for me. I don't mean to put you through anything, but it's good to know you care that much. You all are etched in my memory. It's kind of like the raggedy heart with the jagged edges and deep gouges. Each one of you has a piece of my heart and I have a piece of yours. And I just can't believe I won't miss you. But I'm going to get back here with Chaplain Brazzil and the others and say that prayer and take care of anything that might be jumbling me up right now. It's kind of like going into the big game, ya know, you gotta get ready for it."

Dale reminded him, "We're going to be lifting you up, Donnie."

"Alright. Thank you," Donnie said. "I want you all to know that I love each and every one of you. I'll see you when you get there, okay? Love ya'll."

As we heard the final click of the phone, our hearts gave way to sorrow and grief for what was about to happen.

At 5 p.m., one hour before Donnie was scheduled to be executed, Chaplain Brewster, a very gentle and caring lady, came to Hospitality House to get the five witnesses to drive us three blocks to where the Walls Unit and death chamber was located. The personnel in charge met us at the entrance and directed us to an area where one at a time we were identified and asked routine questions as to our relationship to the offender, Richard Donald Foster.

We were then seated in a waiting area where Chaplain Brewster kept a conversation going in an effort to keep down the dread of such an occasion. Within fifteen minutes we were escorted to another waiting area close to where the execution would be taking place. It seemed only a few short moments before we were taken on to the witness room where we could clearly see the death chamber ahead. As we approached the death chamber, we saw the curtains were already drawn and Donnie's arms were outstretched and strapped to the extensions of the gurney. Both hands were wrap completely and the I-Vs already in place.

"Are they here yet?" I heard Donnie ask as we entered the witness area. Almost at the same time he looked over at us and smiled and asked, "Are ya'll okay?" We nodded silently as we stood holding hands.

Donnie called each one's name. "Craig...Alexa...Bobby...Betty...Annie. I love ya'll."

Bobby put his arm around my shoulder to support me.

Still smiling and looking directly at me, Donnie asked, "Are you ready, Annie?" He was unable to hear us in the witness room, but could see us plainly. I nodded affirming I was ready. I looked directly into Donnie's eyes, as if holding his hand and Betty and I joined him in quoting the Scripture, Galatians 2:20. "I have been crucified with Christ; it is no longer I who live, but Christ lives in me; and the life which I now live in the flesh I live by faith in the Son of God, who loves me and gave Himself for me."

"I love you, Annie," Donnie said. "You have been the best friend I have ever had in the world. I'll see you when you get there, okay? I'm ready warden."

I continued to hold eye contact with Donnie as the lethal injection began to flow into his arms, until he had breathed his final breath on earth...then I knew he had breathed his first in heaven.

Richard "Donnie" Foster was executed May 24, 2000 on the birthday of his best friend, Michael David Bonds, the one he had accidentally killed in Vietnam. He wrote this remembrance to Michael on May 28, 1999:

In Memory of Michael David Bonds
To The Vietnam Veterans Memorial

"I'm Standing on the Hard Line"
Hey Bro.
 Been a long time. I wanted to leave you a message.
I still miss ya. Not a day goes by,
I haven't thought about ya.
I guess I ruined everything we was gonna do.
 It should have been me, Mike.
My life has been so messed up.
I guess I deserve it, and maybe I'm where I belong.
I'm not sure at times about so many things.
Only thing I got is God, and I'm believing He makes
Everything right.
And that you're with Him.

Bros. Forever Mike. I'll see you soon.
Your Brother in Arms, Donnie Foster[2]

On May 13, 2001, almost a year after Donnie was executed; after retiring as Senior Warden of the Walls Unit of Texas Death Row, Jim Willett wrote in *The Washington Post*, "I oversaw the execution of 89 inmates at the busiest death house in the nation."

Willett said, "In most cases, I don't think the inmates I talked to were anything like the people who had committed the crime."

Referring to Donnie, Willett wrote, "Richard Foster I remember, because he was so lively. He was what we called a "volunteer," meaning he waived his rights to further appeals. As much as a warden could, I enjoyed my conversation with Foster. He admitted in a moment that he had committed the crime and said he had had time to set things right with God. If you can imagine it, he was cheerful when he was strapped down."

"I think and believe that no matter what, I'm going home."

Chapter 30

Home

"Do not stand at my grave and cry;
I am not there; I did not die"

May 25, 2000

As I read the news article from *The Huntsville (TX) Item*[1] the day following Donnie's execution, I thought back to August 1999 to a comment Donnie had written, "I think and believe that no matter what, I'm going home. He'll [God] make it clear to us what He wants, surely. And we'll be able to live and be comfortable with it."

The reason Donnie was comfortable to the point of being almost cheerful was because he had learned to pray for God's will for his life. He had said in our phone conversation just a few hours before he was executed, "If we are praying for God's will…this is God's will."

As we drove home to Walters following Donnie's execution, the family went from emotions of extreme sadness because of the void in our lives, to anger about how such a thing could happen, then to the complete opposite feelings of peace in knowing that Donnie was at last free in heaven.

As we continued our trip, I opened Donnie's Bible that Chaplain Brazzil had given me just before the execution. Just inside the cover, Donnie had placed the picture that I had sent him a few years before of Dale and me together.

I cried silently as I read the words, "To my family" written in the margin beside the highlighted Scriptures of Matthew 25:34-40. "Then the King will say to those on His right hand, 'Come, you blessed of my Father, inherit the kingdom prepared for you from the foundation of the world, for I was hungry and you gave Me food; I was thirsty and you gave Me drink; I was a stranger and you took Me in; I was naked and you clothed Me; I was sick and you visited Me; I was in prison and you came to Me.'

Then the righteous will answer Him saying, 'Lord, when did we see You hungry and feed You, or thirsty and give You drink? When did we see You a stranger and take You in or naked and clothe You? Or when did we see You in prison, and come to You?' And the King will answer and say to them, 'Assuredly, I say to you, Inasmuch as you did it to one of the least of these My brethren, you did it to Me.'"

Throughout his Bible, Donnie had neatly placed notes, pictures, and cards that different ones had sent him by appropriate verses. He had listed the family's first names on the page opposite Dale's and my picture. He had highlighted Galatians 2:20 with a smilie face in the margin.

Although I felt at times I could cry forever on the days following Donnie's execution, I could never fully describe the peace that I felt the day I had to say good-bye to my dear friend. The only explanation was that God answered Donnie's prayers that he had prayed for us as his family and for himself on that very morning he would die of a court-ordered lethal injection on Texas Death Row. What kind of peace is this? And from where does it come? It is the peace of God that passes all understanding.

"Be anxious for nothing, but in everything by prayer and supplication; with thanksgiving; let your requests be made known to God; and the peace of God, which passes all understanding, will guard your hearts and minds through Christ Jesus" (Philippians 4:6-7).

Donnie kept a prayer journal of some of his latter days. I found this prayer dated Monday, May 15, 2000. Donnie wrote this prayer eight days before he died:

Donnie's prayer:

Father in heaven, thank You for this family that is seeing me through all this and holding me up.

I'm a little scared, Father, but I've got to leave here. Please give me the strength to go through this.

Father, I need You to also give Annie and Dale the strength to go through this with me and to take care of things and help me to close my book out right here on earth.

Father please be with Annie, Betty, Bobby, Craig and Alexa. I know You will fill them with the strength like no other, Your strength to handle this. Let Your Holy Spirit fall on them all. Be with my Daddy and tell him what to do.

Father use me till I go and even after. I am so grateful for everything. In Jesus Name.

Amen.

We arrived at the funeral home in Walters with Donnie's body at approximately 4:30 p.m. May 25, 2000. Phillip Hart, the funeral director, told us he would have Donnie ready at 8 p.m.

Later as we drove back to the funeral home, I noticed that dark clouds had begun to gather in the western skies. I hoped that it would hold off raining until after the service the following day.

But as we went into the chapel, we quickly forgot about the clouds.

The family worked through some of our grief as we shared experiences that we'd had in our relationship with Donnie. At one point I thought about the conversations Donnie and I'd had about tears, and that it was okay to grieve because God had given us this way of expressing our sorrow and pain, but the real comfort came in knowing that Donnie was free, and the freedom that he now possessed, no one could take away. He had been rescued.

I took great comfort from knowing Donnie already claimed the promise of II Corinthians 5:8, "We are confident, yes, well pleased rather to be absent from the body and to be present with the Lord."

On the day we returned home from Huntsville, I smiled as I read the words "Heaven Bound" written on the envelope of Donnie's final letter that I had taken from the same mailbox I had taken his first letter almost five years before.

In his final letter, Donnie wrote:

> T. R. Nixon, a fine man that came by and prayed with me and listened to my preaching several times wanted to meet you all, but they said No. —He stayed until 5 o'clock and waited on me and we prayed together. Would you send him some of my stories please? Thank you. See, I'm gone and still buggin you. Smile. —Donnie

Donnie mentioned in his last four letters that he would be gone by the time I received them. And for some time I continued to find little notes that he had scribbled while he packed his property and hid away in his things for me to find later:

I found a tiny little note tucked underneath a small stapler that read, "Annie, I'll be doing all I can to come get you friend. Surely God listens to things like that. But for now, stay busy and doing God's work. I'm doing fine! Donnie. Smile."

May 26, 2000

On the day of Donnie's funeral service, I arose early. By the time I made coffee, the wind outside had begun to blow quite hard. It was 5 a.m., and I hoped that it would settle down before the service.

The wind did settle down, but it was after a tornado had struck the western portion of Walters causing considerable damage and knocking out electrical power for the entire area. That left the whole town, as well as the funeral home, without lights and no air-conditioning on a very warm and sultry day, so warm that some folks were driving around in their vehicles with the air-conditioners on in order to stay cool.

The ladies of the First Baptist Church had coped with electrical outages and many other difficulties through the years. They succeeded in preparing a wonderful meal for the family to share before the service. Phillip Hart and the staff at the funeral home lit candles and passed out hand fans and the memorial service went as scheduled.

Those attending the service found it humorous when Phillip Hart, before reading Donnie's obituary said, "I started to apologize for the air and electricity being off, then I had to wonder if Donnie could have had something to do with this?"

Knowing Donnie so well, I thought to myself that Donnie would have loved the funeral director's comment.

In a very short time, I began to receive condolences from Donnie's friends on Texas Death Row, most of whom I had met at one time or another in the visiting area of the prison. Some I still have not personally met. But while corresponding with some, I told them of the circumstances of the storm. One inmate wrote that Donnie had jokingly remarked to him, "I'll finally get to go home to Walters and a tornado will probably come through there and blow me away!"

Another letter came from Tiny (the young man that Donnie had written about) saying, "Annie I need you to write to Tiny. He's on the verge of accepting Jesus." After Donnie was executed, Tiny wrote that he accepted Jesus into his life the day after Donnie was executed. Tiny later wrote, "Donnie had a light I wanted."

As Phillip Hart continued in the service, he read Scripture that Donnie had chosen himself for his service to now comfort us, his family. Scripture that he, Betty, and I had shared from the little old minister's duct taped Bible.

"So when this corruptible shall have put on incorruption, and this mortal has put on immortality, then shall be brought to pass the saying that is written: Death is swallowed up in victory.

"O death, where is thy sting?

"O grave, where is thy victory?" (I Corinthians 15:54-55 KJV).

Another, "But I would not have you to be ignorant brethren, concerning them who have fallen asleep, that ye sorrow not, even as others which have no hope.

"For if we believe that Jesus died and rose again, even so them which sleep in Jesus will God bring with Him" (I Thessalonians 4:13-14 KJV).

Lastly, "He will swallow up death in victory; and the Lord God will wipe away tears from all faces, and the rebuke of His people shall He take away from off the face of the earth; for the Lord God has spoken it" (Isaiah 25:8 KJV).

Some family members and friends who had visited Donnie in his last years requested to speak at his service in memory of him.

Cliff, Donnie's adopted dad, shared a humorous ordeal he'd had helping Donnie get home from Fort Lewis Army Base in Washington many years before in his rattle trap of a car.

My sister, Betty, told of her experiences in visiting Donnie on death row and how blessed she was to have been a part of his life. My daughter, Sandy, tearfully spoke of how she, Cory, and Cassie, had come to love Donnie and how blessed they were for having known him and been a part of his last days on earth. Bobby spoke of his family's love for Donnie and how they would go to death row hoping to encourage him, but he would turn it around and lift them up.

Bobby told how Chaplain Brazzil of the Walls Unit had shared with us how Donnie, on his way to the death chamber to be executed, had told them he had a bad taste in his mouth and asked if one of them might have a piece of candy. One of the guards pulled a Lifesaver from his pocket and said, "This is all I have."

Donnie replied, "I'll take it, but I don't think it's gonna work."

Donnie's lawyer and friend, Craig Budner was unable to attend the service because of another death but had sent a letter for his assistant, Alexa Parnell, to read at Donnie's service.

Craig wrote of how he and Alexa had been given the honor and privilege of defending Donnie during the last ten years:

> As a baby lawyer, I visited Death Row with a great deal of fear and concern of who I would meet. After all, what kind of monster would reside on Death Row? What I quickly found out was Donnie Foster was no monster, but a person, still filled with a great deal of anger at the world for what had become of his life. But over the next ten years, Donnie and I built a genuine trust and respect for one another. We were not the same. Donnie was a man from a small town who had experienced combat and much suffering. I was a city boy who had been shielded from the horrors of the world.
>
> Despite those differences a mutual respect developed that transcended a lawyer-client relationship. As Donnie allowed me to be a part of his life, I discovered a man with a deep sense of honor and dignity, a man more concerned with comforting others than him self. After meeting this family, I now know why. I cannot express in words how meaningful it has been for me, for you have treated Alexa and me as members of your own family.
>
> Donnie was freed Wednesday, and I know we all wish we could pass into the next world with Donnie's courage, peace and calm.
>
> Donnie, I will miss you with all my heart. I love you, Craig.

Donnie wrote as a part of his own memorial service:

> I want to thank a very special brother. I call him Lil Brother.

His name is Cory Anderson.

Son, I thank you for being there for me and sharing all that we have together, for taking time for me. I look at all these pictures of you, Cody, Nick, Patrick and Trey playing football and I can't wait till we can do that in heaven. The Big Grid Iron! Smile. God's going to tell you just what to do. Just go slow and pray about every move.

Donnie had written his own testimony and asked that Cory read it at his service for his family and friends:

First, I want to say, praise God for all things! I have so much to be thankful for. Most of the time these last few years I have been looking back over my life and this here cage that I live in. Been here for so long. I've lived in a cage for almost twenty-three years now in all. And I say, Something has to give.

I think, Well, I believe in Jesus and heaven and that's the final frontier anyway.

So, I say to myself, Son, why be here when I can finally be free? I mean, free of all my chains and cuffs and leg irons they have had me in all these years. The cement, and the steel, and the fences and gates. No more razor wire, no more looking through glass at my loved ones, and no more pain and heartache.

I say, This is the right thing to do, huh, Lord?

I have Jesus that saved me and made a way for me. I may be here in this cage separated from every person and everything I love about life, but how blessed Jesus has made me!

Let me say now, that no one screwed this life up here on earth, but me. Yeah, I've had some bad breaks, but I've had some good ones too. I just messed everything up. I just got lost in the world. No excuses.

I should have been able to make it. And I'm sorry I've let

you down. If I have been an embarrassment to this family I apologize. I apologize, most of all to my daddy, Cliff Foster. I wish I could have been the son you wanted me to. I'm sorry Daddy, but as I sit here today, I will say that you did not know me in my last days or years. But you still are my hero. I leave you my favorite picture of us together.

From what I know of this family that I have come to love and feel, I don't think an apology is needed, cause I know as I sit here that this family truly loves me. Never have I known a love like this before.

I have hid nothing from you, about me. I've lived a strange life. It's been a hard one too. I admit that I have been a lover of riding Harley Davidsons, and wearing leathers and carrying guns. I've been a fighter and a brawler and a lover of music that don't quite fit everyone's ears.

I've rode with clubs which you call gangs in the scooter world. I was a 1%er, an outlaw motorcyclist. I have been in gangs inside this prison for years, and was once the El Presidente of the Brazos River Bandeleros. All, with which my growth in Jesus Christ, I have laid down and gave it all up. A man must choose one or the other. I chose Christ, or rather He chose me.

I can't blame anyone or anything for all this. I used to say Nam did it to me. I came home and I had the disease called, excitement or adrenaline highs. They said I had survivor's guilt syndrome too. They said I had a lot of things. All I can tell you now is that if I would have had Jesus Christ in my life, all these things would have been solved and taken care of. He was there all the time, but I chose to go the other way. So no one screwed this life up but me.

Anyway, I guess if there ever was an outlaw in this family that would be me. But yet, in all that I was still Donnie, and yet they called me Stoney Armadillo or Stone cold. Those names followed me through many a year out there and in here. This was just my life and I realized that trying to be a man of survival in here and to be what God intended for me to be was not an easy thing. Yes, I did some things wrong, but I really tried to walk and be a good man in my morals, even in here in this world behind the walls.

I'm just so glad I finally got someone to talk to about it all and about how my life has been. Cause before Annie came into my life, I wasn't sure I was right or not, especially in the ways of God. My early teachers were Glenda, and Sonny Buckingham. God used these people in a way that brought me to my knees one night sixteen years ago and I still remember my prayer that night. I cried and cried and I never hurt like that before. But I told God that He was going to have to show me that He was real and that I was just like Thomas, I had to see Him, that I couldn't believe in someone I couldn't see. And that I was different than most folks, cause I can never seem to do anything right. Please show me You are real. And He has over and over in all these years. No matter what they say I did, or was, I was a changed man. God took my heart of stone and gave me a heart of flesh. He let me see this world for what it really was. He gave me a picture like He does us all and He filled in the pieces one by one.

As you hear this, I am not dead. What you see in front of you is just an old worn out shell that housed my spirit and soul. I'm still alive and in heaven with Jesus and waiting on you to catch up. Man, I want this family experience again and we will do it again, I assure you. This time we'll get it right.

In the families of the family, and other families that I have come to know and love so much, it's been awesome. I still remember the prayer I said to God one night. I said, Lord, please send someone to me, Donnie Foster. Someone in this family that I can share my life with, and tell them everything about me, nothing hid at all. And God sent me Annie Wampler. And as our friendship grew God used both of us in each other's life. I could never begin to tell you how awesome it has all been to me. And as time passed she brought her family to me one by one and then other family members. She told me all about them and shared everything with me. And as I met them one by one, God let me see their hearts and He loved me through them all.

There have been times that God has had me on my knees for each and every one of these people and even the town of Walters. And through Annie I had the honor to watch her kids and grandkids grow and have been able to keep up with you all. It's been such a blessing too. You all have helped me more than you know to make it down the many roads I've been down here.

Annie, the one who led me to other friends in this family, the one who taught me what a real friend was. The one that God put in my life for a reason. With all that, she opened up the doors to her family and home and made me feel more human than I ever felt in this life. She made me realize that I am not alone in this life. That I was loved and cared for, and so much more too. How can I ever say thank you my friend? Little did you know that you were fulfilling the dream of this man's life. I've just wanted a family that could love me for who I was, accept me for who I was, and what I was. Someone to stand beside me and you did, Annie. You took and accepted me, just as I am.

Thank you for never giving up on me. Thank you for constantly bringing the Word of God to me over and over. Thank you for hurting with me when I hurt. Thank you for holding me up to God day after day in prayer.

And Phillip Hart, thank you for everything. Everyone spoke very highly of you and I got to thinking, Man I wish I had met this guy! May God bless you over and over my friend, and I praise

Him for your giving heart.

Now, one last thing. Smile. I want to share something I learned that will help you all on your journey in life. I said it was prayer and it is. But I want to tell you something about prayer.

It's all in how you approach God. How you approach the throne of God. How your heart is, the sincereness of it.

You know that feeling you get sometimes about a person, or something that a person is going through? Heavy heart. Sometimes you may get that and not know what you're feeling or who it is for. But that is God praying through you. And that feeling let's you know that the Spirit is there and the doors of heaven are open and you pray and cry out to God. That is when prayer gets answered. Those prayers don't just hit the ceiling and bounce off. Caring, compassion, and so full of love that you cannot contain yourself. That is God my friend. And that is when you are real in what you are praying about.

In those prayers always, I say always, plead the blood of Jesus over everything and every person and problem that comes your way. The bloodline. Without it, how can you stop the enemy? I am sorry to preach but right now, my compassionate and aching heart is crying out for all of you. I raise my hands to heaven here in this cage and I say, Jesus, Jesus, Jesus, thank you for them all. They loved me just as you love me, just as I am.

A poem left in Donnie's Bible ended in these lines:

> **Do not stand at my grave and cry.**
> **I am not there; I did not die.**[2]

"Jesus has borne the death penalty on our behalf. Behold the wonder!"

C. H. Spurgeon

ANNIE WAMPLER is founder/director of LifeBoat Ministries, a ministry "redeeming the time...." (Ephesians 5:16) to helping people in need. She has worked in a family-owned business since 1976. She and her husband, Dale, celebrate their Golden Wedding Anniversary in 2006. They have three grown children, six grandchildren, and six great-grandchildren.

Notes on Sources

Chapter 1
1. Oswald Chambers, *My Utmost for His Highest* (Grand Rapids, MI: Dodd Mead and Co., 1935). Renewed in 1963 by the Oswald Chambers Publications Assn. Ltd., and is used by permission of Discovery House Publishers, Box 3566, Grand Rapids MI 49501. All rights reserved. 11/5.
2. Omartian, Stormie, *Just Enough Light for the Step I'm On* (Eugene, Or.: Harvest House 1999). 7.

Chapter 2
* Donnie's uncle, Ted Foster, was not in Thailand at the time—he was actually in Viet Nam serving in the military

Chapter 4
1. Oswald Chambers, *My Utmost for His Highest* (Grand Rapids, MI: Dodd Mead and Co., 1935). Renewed in 1963 by the Oswald Chambers Publications Assn. Ltd., and is used by permission of Discovery House Publishers, Box 3566, Grand Rapids MI 49501. All rights reserved. 10/28, 10-29.
2. Charles Stanley, *Eternal Security* © by Charles Stanley (Nashville, TN: Oliver-Nelson, A division of Thomas Nelson, Inc.), 80
3. Luci Swindoll, devotional "Moses Choice-Your Choice", *Women's Devotional Bible* Copyright © 1990 by The Zondervan Corporation, Guidepost edition),1364.
4. Spurgeon, *All of Grace*, 44

Chapter 5
1. Spurgeon, *All of Grace*, 19.

Chapter 7
1. Charles Colson, "Exchanging Lies for the Truth: The Johnny Cockrum Story". (Breakpoint with Charles Colson, May 10, 1995. Article No. 50510). Used with permission.
2. Spurgeon, *All of Grace*, 15.

Chapter 8
1. Spurgeon, *All of Grace*, 9.

Chapter 9
1. Hannah Whitall Smith, *A Christian's Secret to a Happy Life* (New York: Fleming H. Revell Company, 1942) 82.

Chapter 10
1. The Nelson Study Bible, "Citation from Romans 8:28, NKJV. (Thomas Nelson Publishers, 1997) 1893. Used with permission.

Chapter 11
1. Oswald Chambers, *My Utmost for His Highest* (Grand Rapids, MI: Dodd Mead and Co., 1935). Renewed in 1963 by the Oswald Chambers Publications Assn. Ltd.,

and is used by permission of Discovery House Publishers, Box 3566, Grand Rapids MI 49501. All rights reserved. 6/4, 6/5.

Chapter 13

1. Pamela Binnings Ewen, *Faith on Trial* (Nashville: Broadman & Holman 1999), dust cover.

2. Joe Brown. Article "North Texas Terror" Wichita Falls *Times and Record News*. July 10, 1999, 4B

Chapter 17

1. Charles Stanley, Article "Away to Arabia" © 1999 by Charles Stanley In Touch Ministries Magazine. Atlanta, GA. www.intouch.org

Chapter 18

1. Spurgeon, *All of Grace*, 15, 16.

Chapter 19

1. Corrie ten Boom and John and Elizabeth Sherrill, *The Hiding Place* (Chappaqua, New York: Chosen Books LLC. 1971, 1984), 181. Used with permission. All rights reserved.

Chapter 20

1. Graham, Billy, *Facing Death and the Life After* (Minneapolis MN: Grason, 1987), 238.

2. Springer, Rebecca Ruter, *My Dream of Heaven* (Forest Grove, Ore.: Book Searchers), 60.

3. Graham, *Facing Death and the Life After*, 248.

4. Amy Carmichael, Citation on prayer. "Of one thing we are sure." Unable to locate source of small clipping sent to me.

Chapter 21

1. Oswald Chambers, *My Utmost for His Highest* (Grand Rapids, MI: Dodd Mead and Co., 1935). Renewed in 1963 by the Oswald Chambers Publications Assn. Ltd., and is used by permission of Discovery House Publishers, Box 3566, Grand Rapids MI 49501. All rights reserved. 3/8.

2. Michael Card, *A Violent Grace* (Sister, Ore.: Multnomah Publishers, Inc. 2000), 98.

Chapter 22

1. Charles Stanley, Sermon "When Others Fail Us". In Touch Ministries.

2. William L. Pettingill, *900 Bible Questions Answered* (Grand Rapids, MI: Kregel Publications), 207.

3. Stanley, Charles, *Eternal Security* (Nashville, TN: Oliver-Nelson, 1990, A division of Thomas Nelson, Inc.), 54.

Chapter 23

1. Steve Blow, Article "Death Row Doubts Follow Crime Fighter" Dallas Morning News. April 2, 2000. 25A.

Chapter 24

1. Rita Roskam, Article "My Bitter Heart" reprinted with permission from Guideposts. Copyright ©2002 by Guideposts, Carmel, New York 10512. All rights reserved.

2. Andrea Vinley, Article "Lessons on Perfection and Grace". *Focus on the Family Magazine*, 10/2000. 10-11. Used with permission. All rights reserved.

Chapter 25
1. A.W. Tozer, Reprinted from *The World: Playground or Battlefield*, compiled and edited by Harry Verploegh, copyright ©1989, pg. 63, by Christian Publications, Inc. Used by permission of Christian Publications, Inc. 800.223.4443.
2. Gloria Gaither, *365 Meditations for Grandmother*, 1994. Used by Permission. All rights reserved. 38
3. A.W. Tozer, A. W., Reprinted from *God Tells the Man Who Cares*, compiled by Anita M. Bailey, copyright © 1992, pg. 179, by Christian Publications, Inc. Used by permission of Christian Publications, Inc. 800.223.4443
4. Genevieve Glen, OSB; "Broken Cisterns Walled in Stone" © 1999, Benedictine Nuns, Abbey of St. Walburga, Virginia Dale, CO. Published by OCP Publications, 5536 NE Hassalo, Porland , OR 97213. All rights reserved. Used with permission.

Chapter 26
1. Tozer, A. W., Reprinted from *Christ the Eternal Son*, compiled and edited by Gerald B. Smith, copyright ©1991, pg. 51, by Christian Publications, Inc. Used by permission of Christian Publications, Inc. 800.223.4443.

Chapter 27
1. Graham, *Facing Death and the Life After*, 14.

Chapter 28
1. Helen Prejean, C.S.J. *Dead Man Walking* (New York: Vintage Books, a Division of Random House, Inc.)
2. Mary Jane Worden, *Early Widow* (Downers Grove, IL: InterVarsity Press), 105, 107. Used by permission of Harry Clark. All rights reserved
3. Luci Swindoll, devotional "Moses Choice-Your Choice", *Women's Devotional Bible* (Zondervan Corporation. Guideposts edit), 1364

Chapter 29
1. Michael Graczyk, Article "Last Human Touch". Ft. Worth (TX) *Star-Telegram*, Oct. 14, 2000. 3/F, 6F
2. Donnie Foster, "Your Brother in Arms". Veterans Memorial. Posted May 28, 1999.
3. Jim Willett, "89 Executions", *The Washington Post*, May 13, 2001. B01. Used with permission.

Chapter 30
1. Michelle C. Lyons, article "Man Executed for Killing Store Owner", *Huntsville (TX) Item*, May 25, 2000. 3A
2. Author unknown, poem "Do Not Stand at My Grave and Cry".

www.ingramcontent.com/pod-product-compliance
Lightning Source LLC
Chambersburg PA
CBHW022059150426
43195CB00008B/197